Study Your Way to Your Perfect Career

Sara Miller McCune founded SAGE Publishing in 1965 to support the dissemination of usable knowledge and educate a global community. SAGE publishes more than 1000 journals and over 800 new books each year, spanning a wide range of subject areas. Our growing selection of library products includes archives, data, case studies and video. SAGE remains majority owned by our founder and after her lifetime will become owned by a charitable trust that secures the company's continued independence.

Los Angeles | London | New Delhi | Singapore | Washington DC | Melbourne

STUDENT
SUCCESS

Study Your Way to Your Perfect Career

How to Become a Successful Student, Fast, and Then Make It Count

Lucinda Becker

Los Angeles | London | New Delhi
Singapore | Washington DC | Melbourne

Los Angeles | London | New Delhi
Singapore | Washington DC | Melbourne

SAGE Publications Ltd
1 Oliver's Yard
55 City Road
London EC1Y 1SP

SAGE Publications Inc.
2455 Teller Road
Thousand Oaks, California 91320

SAGE Publications India Pvt Ltd
B 1/I 1 Mohan Cooperative Industrial Area
Mathura Road

New Delhi 110 044
SAGE Publications Asia-Pacific Pte Ltd
3 Church Street
#10-04 Samsung Hub
Singapore 049483

© Lucinda Becker 2019

First published 2019

Editor: Jai Seaman
Assistant editor: Charlotte Bush
Production editor: Victoria Nicholas
Marketing manager: Catherine Slinn
Cover design: Shaun Mercier
Typeset by: C&M Digitals (P) Ltd, Chennai, India
Printed in the UK

Library of Congress Control Number: 2019934298

British Library Cataloguing in Publication data

A catalogue record for this book is available from the British Library

ISBN 978-1-5264-3500-2
ISBN 978-1-5264-3501-9 (pbk)

At SAGE we take sustainability seriously. Most of our products are printed in the UK using responsibly sourced papers and boards. When we print overseas we ensure sustainable papers are used as measured by the PREPS grading system. We undertake an annual audit to monitor our sustainability

This book is dedicated to Etty and Elphi

Contents

About the author   xiii

Introduction   1
   How to use this book   2

Part One   Getting started   5

1 Your first week   7

   When should I arrive?   7
   What might be on offer?   8
   Who might I meet?   9
   Where can I get help?   10
   How can I fill my time?   11
   What about registering?   12
   What about socialising?   13
   Should I be studying in this week?   13
   Should I go home at the end of the first week?   14

2 Your first course/module choices   15

   How much choice will I have?   15
   How much time will I have to decide between modules?   16
   What should I look for in choosing a module?   16

3 Getting involved in university life   21

   How many clubs and societies are there likely to be?   21
   How can I find out about clubs and societies?   21
   How much do clubs and societies cost?   22
   Should I try a new activity?   22
   How many university organisations should I join?   22
   What other options do I have?   23

4 Your first personal tutorial   **27**

What is a personal tutor?   27
What is a personal tutor meeting?   28
Is this the only time I will see my personal tutor?   29
How should I talk with my tutor?   30
How can I make the most of each tutorial?   31
How do I make this a sustainably productive relationship?   33

5 Your first lectures   **35**

What are lectures all about?   35
Where should I sit in a lecture?   36
What if I miss a lecture?   36
Do I have to attend the whole lecture?   37
What should I take with me to the lecture?   38
What will be covered in the lecture?   38
The general lecture   38
The structural lecture   39
The informational lecture   40
The inspirational lecture   40
Making the most of lectures   41
How do I develop my lecture skills over time?   44

6 Your first seminars   **47**

What is a seminar?   47
Seminars – will the practicalities suit me?   50
What will it feel like to be in a seminar?   50
What is the purpose of a seminar?   51
What should I do to prepare for a seminar?   53
How much should I speak out in a seminar?   55

7 Extending your reach   **57**

Your family and home friends – are they in the loop?   57
Refreshers Week – does this exist for you?   58
Reading lists – how useful might they be?   59
Your Students' Union – what could it offer you?   60
Study advice and support – are there online courses?   61
Student/campus cards – what more can they do?   61
Clubs and societies – where did they go?   62
Social study spaces – when should you use them?   63
Socialising – is it helping or hindering your efforts?   64

Modules – what next? 65
Slowing down – will you get the chance? 67
Free training – what is out there? 69

8 What graduate attributes have you now acquired? 71

Looking back – what have you achieved? 71
Transferable skills 72
Graduate attributes 72
Turning skills and attributes into benefits 72
Recognising your value 77
Finding your graduate attributes and skills 77
Being selective 79
Looking forward – what next? 82

Part Two Effective studying 87
Learning styles 87

9 Reading lists 95

How do I find my reading list? 95
Might there be multiple reading lists for my modules? 97
Am I expected to read all of the texts on my
reading list? 102
Primary vs secondary sources 103
How do I make the most of a reading list? 104
Can technology help? 105
Where is the best place to study? 105

10 Your first sets of notes 109

Do I need to make any notes at all? 109
How reliable is this source/situation? 113
What is the best design for these notes? 117
How can I sharpen my notes? 117

11 Your first presentation 121

Where and when might I give a presentation? 122
Who will be watching? 125
How long might a presentation last? 126
Will I be presenting alone? 126
Will I be using technology? 129
What about making presentation aids? 133

What is the best way to rehearse? 134
What if I get nervous? 136

12 Study groups **139**

The lecturer appointed study group 139
The peer learning group 141
The student-led study group 142
The revision study group 143
Virtual study groups 144

13 Your first doubts **147**

What doubts might I have? 147
How might these doubts feel? 149
Problems that are deceptive 151
How can I make my doubts go away? 153
How do I move forward from my doubts? 154

14 Managing your time **155**

How do I know if I need to work on my time management? 156
How can I make more time? 156
How can I save time? 159
How can I best use my time? 164

15 Shaping your professional development **167**

Where do I start? 168
Can I use the experience I have already gained? 171
How much experience do I need? 172
What type of experience do I need? 173

Part Three   Successful assessment **175**

16 Your first assessed essay/report **177**

When might my first assignment be set? 177
How long would an assignment usually be? 178
Will I have a choice of questions? 178
What about making up my own title? 178
Can I use images or my own format? 179
How much time will I get to prepare and write my assignment? 180
Should I plan or jump straight in? 181

How can I avoid plagiarism?   182
What if I go over the word count?   182
What is the best way to check my assignment before submission?   183
If the submission goes wrong, what do I do?   184

17 Your first marks/grades   187

When and how will I receive my marks?   188
What if I am disappointed with my mark?   190
How can I understand my mark?   191

18 Your first marking tutorial   195

What is a tutorial?   195
How do I talk to the lecturer?   196
How can I take some control of a tutorial?   196
Moving forward from your first marking tutorials   197

19 Your first research project   199

How do I decide on a topic?   199
How do I find my research questions?   200
What is the right format to present my findings?   202
How should I organise my research project time?   203

20 Group projects   207

How do I get started on a group project?   208
What role should I take in the group?   208
Keeping in touch   210
Making the time count   211
What if someone is not contributing?   212
The future of the group   213

21 Your first placement   215

What are placements?   215
Why would I be interested in a placement?   216
Preparing for the experience   217
Reporting on a placement   219
Some placement adventures   222
Making the most of the opportunity   223
Would a placement suit the type of
person I am?   224

22 Your first exams — **225**

What type of exams might I face? — 226
When should I begin to prepare for exams? — 227
How can I revise most effectively? — 227
How do I keep going with my revision? — 229
What about the practicalities of exams? — 230
What revision methods should I use? — 232
Should I do mock/practice exams? — 234
How can I calm my nerves? — 234
What should I do when I get into the exam room? — 236
What should I do in the last few minutes of an exam? — 239
What should I do when I leave the exam room? — 241

Part Four   Making it count — **243**

23 If you have not chosen a career by your final term — **245**

Have I done something wrong? — 245
Will I be behind in my career? — 246
How do I move forward? — 246

24 If you have chosen a career by your final term — **249**

How can I make the best move now? — 249
Where do I go first? — 249
Do I need a long-term plan? — 250

25 Things to do before you graduate — **251**

26 Graduation day — **253**

Glossary of terms used in higher education — 255
Index — 261

About the author

Lucinda Becker is Professor of Pedagogy in English Literature and award-winning lecturer and tutor at the University of Reading. She has dedicated her professional life to creating independent learners who are confident in themselves intellectually, professionally and personally.

Lucinda has written numerous study guides for students and works with undergraduates and postgraduates across the university. She is also a professional trainer and consultant, helping new graduates in engineering, science and law to become successful communicators and leaders.

As a Director for Teaching and Learning at her university, Lucinda has the chance to introduce innovation in teaching. In her most recent project, she has launched a Student Impact Network to support students who want to work in partnership with academics to facilitate excellent learning opportunities.

Her experience, both in higher education and the professional world, has convinced her that students at university who master some key skills, both in life and study, are better equipped to enjoy their study lives and make the most of their career options. Learning to be an effective and successful student leads to graduates who are more likely to face their careers with confidence and a clear sense of what they have to offer and what they plan to achieve. That, she believes, is the secret to success.

Introduction

Many of us are familiar with the phrase 'practice makes perfect' and, in many areas of our lives, this is true. Very few people can sit down at the piano and play a beautiful melody by ear, just as only a small percentage of us can speak in front of an audience with confidence the first time we try. Waiting to be good at something can be one of life's pleasures, but when you are at university it makes sense to hit the ground running. You will not want to wait too long until you begin to succeed; your aim is to become as good as you can be, as fast as you can get there.

There is little point in wasting the first half term being reluctant to speak out in a seminar because you have not quite worked out what the purpose of a seminar is, nor, more importantly, is it worth your while to spend hours in lecture theatres only to realise, as you face your first exams, that you have gained little of value from the experience. You will want to make the most of the opportunities you have and to achieve your very best with the least possible wasted effort or stress.

That is what this book is all about – helping you to make the most of every situation you are likely to face at university. But why does this matter? The answer is complicated. We know that there is a complex transition to be made from how you worked at school or college to what is expected of you at university. I know, from many years' experience as a university lecturer, that it is the students who can master that transition quickly who tend to succeed most easily.

Of course, you can achieve an excellent academic result after three years of anxiety and very hard work, but you can gain the same result in a much less stressful and more streamlined way. Getting things right from the outset can make a huge difference to your confidence and your determination to succeed; it will also help you to recognise that university is a crucial stage in your journey into professional success.

Your time as a student can offer you so much more than a degree – it is the point in your development when you are becoming the person you will be for much of the rest of your life. You need to know how to maximise your chances so as to secure the right result for you and also to find out who you could become. That is precisely what this guide is all about – making it count.

The skills and attitudes you need in order to be a successful student are also those most likely to help you to succeed as a professional. It is why you will hear the term 'graduate attributes' used within your university. Graduate attributes are those skills, personal qualities, knowledge and attitudes that employers are looking for in the graduates they employ. The problem for many students is that they find it difficult to recognise their own graduate attributes, and also struggle to take a strategic approach to the development of those attributes. At each stage in this book I will be offering you help on how to overcome both of these challenges.

How to use this book

Although the focus throughout most of this book is on your first experiences at university, you can, of course, use it at any time. If you are having trouble making connections between lectures and essays, you will find the answer here, even if you are in your final year, because the chances are that you missed a point of connection early on. The guidance offered will help you in your first few weeks at university, and these will be crucial, but it is also a guide you will look back to from time to time to remind yourself of how you work best.

In the first term you will be facing your first lectures, seminars, essays and so on, but it might not be until your second or third year that you undertake an extended research placement, or prepare for giving an assessed presentation. You might read this book right through in the first instance and then go back to sections as you need them, or you might choose only to read sections as you face each new challenge: either way will work well.

Knowing that you might return to the guide again and again has determined its structure. Each chapter will help you to understand why you are being asked to do something, what is expected of you and how you can succeed. There will be checklists to keep you on track, some insider knowledge to give you the edge and some top tips to help you move forward fast. Although much of the advice is designed to help you in your first year, I have taken you right through to graduation, and beyond. These will seem like points in the distance for many first year students, but thinking about the end of your journey at the outset will help you focus, keep you motivated and give you the best chance to make the most of each new opportunity.

Although the learning events in the book are in the order in which you are likely to encounter them, there is no timeline that would fit every student. Some students will take their first exams within a few weeks of starting university; others will not sit an exam until many months after they enrol. Some students will see their personal or academic tutor in the first week of term; others may not be allocated a tutor until much later in their first year. This need not concern you. Being aware of these differences I have ensured that each chapter stands alone as a unit of advice: you can jump around in the book as much as you like, reading chapters when the need arises, and returning to them whenever you need a reminder or as your study life develops and becomes more demanding.

You have a whole career ahead of you, so I will focus from time to time on the skills, knowledge and attitudes you are acquiring, so as to help you see your university career as an effective start to a perfect career. The word 'a' is important here: you will have several careers that could be wonderful for you, so the aim will be to help you recognise what is on offer and then choose between several great options. Although I will be referring to employers from time to time, I recognise that a career as a freelance worker or starting your own business might be the perfect goal for you. In that case, you could happily replace 'employers' with 'clients' or 'investors' and the points would still stand.

Throughout the book, you will find 'career moments', where I will be drawing your attention to a specific aspect of university life and how it could translate well into your future life. That way, you can make everything you achieve count in more ways than you could ever expect.

I have worked with thousands of students, so I know that they come in all types, from the confident achievers who nevertheless sometimes struggle to move from school to university, to the quiet members of seminar groups who suddenly shine in an essay, to the students who enjoy the social life of university so much that they sometimes cannot quite remember why they came in the first place. There is room for them all, and I know that I enjoy working with them all, but I also know that success is often rooted in that first time you encounter something new. The ability to take the challenge and run with it is a fundamental life skill and one that will make university, and your professional life, a success for you, however you decide to define that. Now that you have this book beside you, nothing at university will ever seem insurmountable again, because nothing will ever be entirely new – I will have taken you there first and guided you onto the path to success.

GETTING STARTED

Because this is the first part of the guide, I want to focus with you on some of the first challenges you face at university. We will return to some of these in more detail later, but to begin with I want to help you make the most of your early opportunities. In my experience, students who can pick up university life speedily and who make good decisions in the first few weeks usually find the whole first year far easier.

However, there is no need to feel anxious if you are picking this book up for the first time and you are already half way through your first year at university – there is plenty of help here for every point in the year.

1

Your first week

The names given to aspects of university life differ in a rather confusing way. 'Seminars' in one university are called 'tutorials' in another; a 'personal tutor' in one university might be doing the same job as an 'academic tutor' in another; a 'module' might, or might not, be the same thing as a 'course', depending on where you are studying. As we go through this book together I will point out as often as possible how some terms differ from place to place, but there are always new ways to designate people and activities, so go by the description I am offering rather than just the term(s) I am using.

When should I arrive?

In the excitement of going to university, making decisions about when to arrive and what to do once you get there might seem minor, but making the most of university life really does start here. It is about knowing who you are, deciding what you want to get out of this and then making it happen. These are the key principles of this guide, and we will return to them, in various forms, again and again. At this point the most important of these is the first – knowing who you are. It sounds simple, I know, but many students decide to be a whole new person at university, and it can trip them up.

It is natural to want to make some changes with this, perhaps the biggest change in your life that you have ever made happen, and this can be to the good.

Source: Imag

Some students decide to open entirely new social media accounts just for their university life, or even give up social media altogether for a time. Others decide that this is their chance to become vegetarian, or to give up (or take up) socialising in a new way. For some, changes might seem minor but are profound in terms of impact (I will dye my hair blue to reflect the person I am) and sometimes the changes are to do with studying (I will take up planning all of my essays well in advance).

Whatever changes you make might *reflect* the person you already know you are, but they are unlikely to *affect* your core self, at least in the early stages of university, so it makes sense to recognise this and to make small, manageable changes (that could nevertheless be significant in their long-term impact) and to avoid huge personality shifts that you might struggle to maintain. So, if you are very close to your family and are excited about university but also dreading leaving them, make sure that they all know this. Some of my students spend their first few days at university with their families nearby so that the break is gradual; others prefer to make a clean break, but do it at the very last minute they can, so that there is no going back.

Top tip

The first week of university for new students (sometimes called Welcome Week, Freshers' Week or Enrolment Week) usually takes place the week before other students arrive back at university for their second, third or fourth year. This means that the university campus (and perhaps also the university town or city) should be quieter than usual. This makes it the perfect time to explore quietly, knowing that next week the queues for student cards will be huge, and the nights out in town will be crowded.

What might be on offer?

Learning what to expect is going to help you decide when to arrive and how to fill your time. Any material you are sent will only give you some of the information you need – make sure that you keep on checking online (through any online student portal you have been offered) for any up to date material. Student groups and clubs, for example, are likely to be advertised on the Students' Union website, so you will want to go there as you begin to think about what might appeal to you. Reading lists are often online, so you can browse them; even if you have been offered reading lists (or links to them online) for any compulsory modules for your course, it would be a good use of your time to see what material is being covered in any optional modules open to you.

Top tip

> Online reading lists can be confusing if you do not know that older versions might stay online for many years, so make sure that you are looking at the most up to date version. Also check to see if there is a 'key reading' or 'advanced reading' list for your modules – these can be more helpful at this point than a fuller (and perhaps a bit daunting) list of all the texts you might encounter on a module.

Who might I meet?

You will meet dozens of people this week, so you need to decide who is most likely to be able to support you right now, and in the future.

Checklist – people to find

✓ **Your personal tutor/pastoral tutor/academic tutor**: the name varies, but the role is similar: this is a member of academic staff whose role includes making sure that you are succeeding at university. Throughout this guide I will refer to a personal tutor, as this is the person who is designated specifically to support you, even though you may know that role by a different name.

✓ **A member of staff who knows what happens at university**: this might be a student supporter, or a department administrator, or a member of staff whose job is to welcome you.

✓ **An organiser**: the first week at university is sometimes organised by one member of staff from your department, who can advise you on what to do and where to go. This person is going to be very busy, so make your query clear and quick if you can.

(Continued)

(Continued)

✓ **A wellbeing guide/counsellor**: if this is what you were used to in school or college you will be reassured to find this person and you may already have arranged for this support in advance. If not, now is a good time to set this up for yourself, with the help of a study supporter or your personal tutor.

✓ **A study advisor**: even if you do not need significant help with your studies, getting to know where the study advice centre is makes sense. There will be a physical space – sometimes several – where you can go for advice and support, and there will also be a wide range of help online. Look at the library and Students' Union website first – often study advice is flagged up there.

✓ **A librarian**: this can sound overly keen, given that you have not started your studying yet, but librarians are the unsung heroes of student life, and they are always keen to help students get ahead. You may well have a librarian dedicated to your course or your modules, so it is worth tapping into that expertise early.

✓ **Your hall warden/hall counsellor/hall manager**: again, the names may vary but the role is similar. This is the person who will make sure that you are happy in your hall of residence and will be the 'go to' person if anything worries you.

✓ **You housemates**: depending on the style of your hall of residence, you might be living very closely with other students, or you might have little need to see them at all. In this first week, try to buddy up with two people in particular: a housemate who is on the same course as you, and a housemate who has something in common with you. This latter might be someone from a similar town, or a student who, like you, is the first in their family to go to university. This person might not become a good friend, but will be able to empathise with how you are feeling. If you are not in a hall of residence, a similar strategy still applies. Student houses are often large, with eight to twelve occupants, so finding the best people to support you is a good plan.

✓ **Familiar people**: keeping a connection to the way you live your life at home will help to ward off homesickness. So, if you are used to worship, or cycling, or meditation, or a reading group, you can be confident that these will all exist at university, and finding them in your first week will help you to make a streamlined start to your studying.

Students new to university often find it daunting to approach members of staff. This is quite understandable, and it need not hamper you. If you are more comfortable talking to other students first, head for the Students' Union, or talk to one of the student helpers that you might notice around campus. They will be happy to point you in the right direction and advise you on how to approach staff.

Where can I get help?

There will be a central point for help – either a permanent student help desk that you will see all year, or a help point set up just for this week. Even if you have made all of the contacts I have suggested above, the central help point would be the first place to go, so that you can be pointed in the right direction.

As central help points are sometimes temporary, and will often send students off to other places for advice, it is a good idea to walk around and get your bearings, aiming to find some key locations, such as the Students' Union building, the Student Finance Centre, the Library (which might be called your Resource Centre). Make sure you also take a stroll around the building that houses your department, looking for useful noticeboards, department libraries or additional resource rooms, the offices of your personal/academic tutor, and/or your course or module leaders, the toilets and a place to eat and drink between lectures and seminars. Listen out as you explore: how are other students addressing or referring to their lecturers? By their first names or their full names with their titles? Where are they arranging to meet each other? All of this will help you to feel more at home, more quickly, and this will make the rest of your term easier.

INSIDER HINT

Lecturers often use this time to make last minute plans for the term, so you might well find them in the photocopying room for your department if they are not in their offices. However, they might also be at home working on their lectures and seminars before the rush of term starts. There will be talks by your department during the week, so the safest option is to try to ask your questions during those events, or ask them of an individual lecturer straight after the event.

How can I fill my time?

Universities vary in the number of events they offer students during their first week, so make sure that you have a failsafe plan in place. It can be lonely and surprisingly tiring to find yourself with not much to do except meet new people, try to work out where everything is and think about the choices you are making. If you have a plan to fill some of these hours in another way, your experience will remain positive.

You will know by now which areas of your subject you are going to be covering in the first term, so prepare some reading material in advance of arriving at university. Take with you some files and paper, and some general supporting material (this book is a good start!). That way, you can plan to do some studying this week, but only if you find it necessary. If you enjoy meeting new people, or attending a meeting of the club you have just joined, or exploring the local town, all of these things will happily take up your time. Whether you end the week with some work done, or with a new life opening up in another way, you can judge the week a success.

What about registering?

Register for everything you possibly can this week, because next week the queues will be long, as everyone returns to university. There will be some registering that you will be told you have to do: obtaining a student or campus card, and/or a library card, and perhaps a parking permit. There are other options to consider: library and/or resource centre tours, registering early for any job vacancies service offered on campus, offering yourself as a student rep for the Students' Union, if that appeals to you.

Top tip

In your frenzy of registering, avoid joining up to too many university clubs and societies. This is the most important recruitment time for these organisations, and it is too easy to become carried away and pay out to join a whole bunch of them, only to find that you never seem to have the time to become involved. The societies will still be there, and keen to recruit, in a few weeks' time, so there is no great rush.

It will be vital that you register for an email account. One will be created for you automatically through your university enrolment system, but you may have to ask for help in finding out what your new email address is. It will not necessarily be registered to the private email address you have used to communicate with the university up until this point, so ask as early as you can (perhaps when you pick up a student ID card, for example). All official university communication (and much else besides) is sent through that formal, university email address, so make sure you check it regularly and/or have it forwarded to your private email address if this facility exists for you.

Top tip

A word of caution: some students like the idea of forwarding their university emails direct to their private address, but then find that they work better with a 'study' and a 'private' account that are separate, so that they are in the right frame of mind when they look at one or the other. Take time to consider before you set up a forwarding service.

What about socialising?

You already know yourself well enough to predict whether you will spend much of this week socialising, or whether you would rather spend most of your time alone. It makes sense to strike up a friendly relationship with a few people on your course (if nothing else, it might mean that you can ask them to give you their notes from lectures if needs be, or let you compare the notes you took with theirs, to make sure that you all have everything you need). Beyond that, there is no pressure to do anything more, and it is likely that the formal events organised by your department (such as sessions advising you on choosing your modules/courses) will give you plenty of chance to meet other students finding their way.

INSIDER
HINT

Students act in unpredictable ways in this week, and it is perfectly understandable. On what, for many, is a first major move away from home, students who were the centre of the social life in their schools or colleges can find themselves unexpectedly shy and lost in this new setting. Conversely, students who were never very keen on clubbing throw themselves into that social life with great gusto, and find themselves exhilarated but exhausted by the end of the week. Neither of these responses will matter in the long term; you will get into the swim of things within a few weeks and revert to your more usual pattern of socialising.

Should I be studying in this week?

Although this will depend on where you are, the answer is probably 'not much'. You might be given some reading to do in preparation for the start of classes next week, and you might already have brought with you some materials for taking notes in case you have the time and inclination to do it, but beyond that, there is no need to worry.

There is just one exception. Very often students believe they should only seek out the study advisors if they are facing difficulties. This is not true. You will find all sorts of useful information that is designed to help *every* student, both in leaflets and online, through your study advice centre (which may be housed in your library/resource centre).

Your study life is about to become more demanding, so working through some guides on planning, or time management, or good writing practices, would be a sensible move at this point, and would help you to feel positive and in control as you face your first classes next week.

Should I go home at the end of the first week?

Probably not. For most students, immersing themselves completely in their new lives is the best way to move forward positively. However, if you decide *in advance* that you will need to have a weekend at home to take a break after your first week, then make sure that your family and friends know that this is a provisional arrangement. If you find that you have no need to leave university, and are settling in well, then you can postpone the visit.

If, at any point in this first week, you decide that you need to go home, right now, because it is all getting on top of you, you might be right in your judgement, but make sure that you talk first to your personal tutor and your family. It can sometimes help if you give permission for your personal tutor to talk to a member of your family in order to help you decide.

Top tip

> If your home is fairly near your university and you plan to go home regularly, you might still want to think about delaying going home until you feel properly settled into university life.

Sometimes it is pressure from a family that makes a student feel obliged to go home on that first weekend. Having clear conversations and making firm decisions with your family before you go to university will help avoid this potential problem.

CAREER MOMENT

Your future career might seem a long way off at the moment, and this can be a very good thing. You are at university to develop as a person, to study a subject you find interesting and to enjoy your life.

However, even if you are studying what is considered to be a highly vocational subject, that does not mean that you will necessarily end up in a career that rests directly on that subject matter. As a result, you will have to highlight your skills and attributes away from the direct topics you studied. If you have an idea of a career – even a very long-held career goal – the time you spend at university might turn that on its head.

All of this means that it makes sense to just take a peek at your career at this very early stage. If you have a choice over some of your modules/courses, think, for example, about how they are taught and/or assessed. If you can choose options that give you the chance to work on team-based projects or to give a presentation, that will look great on your CV. If you undertake these types of courses in your first year and find that you do not very much enjoy team-based learning or presentations, that might inform the choices you make in your second year, when your marks could matter far more, but you will still have those skills on your CV.

2

Your first course/module choices

You may find that your study units are referred to as 'units', or 'modules' or 'courses'. Whatever the term that is being used, they are the building blocks of your degree programme and for the purposes of this guide I will call them modules, so as not to confuse them with your 'degree course' – that is, your entire degree.

How much choice will I have?

This will depend entirely on the degree and the university you have chosen, and it may have played a part in why you made that choice. However, you chose your university on a whole host of features and there was probably no need to pay much attention to any optional modules.

Whatever the balance between compulsory and optional modules, think about not just how much choice you have in terms of the number of optional modules, but also how wide that choice is. Your first year at university can be a valuable opportunity to try out something new, so be alert to module choices that are slightly unexpected – they can be great fun and might open up whole new areas of interest for you, as well as a wider friendship group.

Universities base their planning and structures on the assumption that most students will only take the standard options open to them, and will not range much beyond that – and they are right. However, there could well be other options: learning a language for free, or being able to attend lectures on modules other than your own so that you can pick up some interesting material from a live event rather than a book or online. Be curious and a bit pushy about what you might be entitled to do – you are paying to be at university, so you have the right to make the most of it.

How much time will I have to decide between modules?

Not very long – a few days at the most would be the norm. So, you need to focus and think it through carefully. You may have decided in advance on your compulsory modules, because they will form part of the degree programme you chose, but your optional modules can be a bit bewildering. The best way to approach it is to take in all of the information that you are offered during any events open to students as they choose their modules, but then take time away from the chaos to consider what would suit you best.

Top tip

You will not have to rely only on the module information you are offered. For each module you are considering, type the module code into a search engine, perhaps with the university name as well. This may give you access to online key readings, or short videoclips or screencasts about the module, or even student reviews and blogs. You might also want to type in some keywords within the topic more generally to get a sense of whether a module would suit you.

What should I look for in choosing a module?

You might find that a module instantly appeals to you, without you really having to think about why. It is exciting when this happens, because you know that you are going to have an enjoyable time studying it. Beyond that, you will be able to make the most productive choices by viewing each module option you are offered in the light of this checklist:

Checklist – choosing modules

✓ **Subject matter**: this seems obvious, I know, but try not to be swayed too much by an exciting module title. Look at the detail of what you would actually cover each week. Does it appeal to you? Will it, perhaps, fill a gap in your knowledge that has been bothering you? Can you see yourself happily studying on the module for several months?

✓ **Shape of your degree**: look at your modules in combination. Canny students will often choose modules that work well together, the material from one complementing the subject matter in another, so that they are not coming to each module completely anew each week, with no backup from other modules.

✓ **Module links**: this will not be made explicit in the information you receive, but material and concepts on an optional module you could choose now might help to prepare you for some optional modules that you plan to take next year.

✓ **Methods of teaching**: although the majority of your modules are likely to be taught in a similar way there may be modules that give you the chance to work differently. This might include a module that relies heavily on workshop activities, or virtual teaching sessions online, or group activities away from the classroom. If you are intrigued by these possibilities (or absolutely put off by the idea of them), that will sway your decision.

✓ **Modes of assessment**: this is likely to affect your judgement, but be cautious … you might not enjoy exams, but if you love a subject area, it would be a shame to miss the chance to study it just because the assessment (or one part of it) is not ideal for you. It is usually more productive to choose the module you want to study and then get the support you need to tackle the assessment effectively.

✓ **Timetabling**: in your first year most of the teaching sessions will be set up during the first week, so you will not necessarily be able to base your decision on trying to balance your lecture load across the week, for example, but there is sometimes flexibility (to change seminar or lab groups, for example), so bear this in mind.

✓ **Workload**: consider how much time is being asked of you in terms both of learning activities and assessment tasks. Being required to create an extensive learning journal as part of your assessment in one module would not be a problem, but if it were a necessary part of every optional module you have chosen, you would need to be ready for that workload. Similarly, assessment by group presentation might take you longer than preparing for a multiple choice exam, so aiming for some variation in learning and assessment (without being too bound by it) can be a good idea.

✓ **Group sizes**: you might not be able to find out about this during your first week, but if there is an indication that a module will be taught either in small groups or in very large groups, and one of these options appeals to you, it will feature in your decision making.

(Continued)

(Continued)

- ✓ **Cost**: you should already have been given a good idea of how much your degree, and each compulsory module, is going to cost you in terms of requirements, such as books, equipment, field trips and so on. In choosing your optional modules you will not want to make cost the only deciding factor, but you might need to take it into account. If a module seems expensive in terms of these additional costs, check whether there is a way for you to reduce these costs (second hand books on sale through subject societies run by students or your library, additional funding on offer through your department or Students' Union for those students who need it, for example).

- ✓ **Recommendation**: there will be students around in your first few days who are there to help you find your way around and get used to university. If you ask if they would recommend a module you might not get an unbiased opinion, but it will be honest and from someone who has actually experienced the module.

The checklist above might leave you with the impression that you will have plenty of time to pore over the descriptions of your modules, but this may not be the case. Some material might be sent to you in advance, and there might be module outlines offered in booklets, but very often students only see a full description of a module when they are on the online system, about to make a choice. Be ready for this and use the checklist to help you make an informed decision even under time pressure.

Top tip

> Your family and friends would probably find it quite easy to choose the modules that they think you should do, that would suit the person they think you are. Try to avoid letting anyone else make this choice for you in the first instance – they will always be tempted to choose a module that they would like to do themselves!

A checklist such as this can help in your decision making, but do still take a moment once you have made your provisional choice. Leave it overnight if you can, so that you come to it fresh the next morning and confirm (or not) that it still feels right to you. Once you feel really happy with your choice, you have reached the stage to talk it through with family and friends, if you would like them to share in the process. Sometimes an outside eye can pick up an obvious glitch in your plan that you have overlooked completely. Personal tutors, too, will be expecting some tutees to turn up at their doors to talk through their choices, so take advantage of this if you would like a second opinion from someone who probably teaches on some of the modules.

INSIDER
HINT

You might well be told, repeatedly and firmly, that you are making a final, irrevocable module choice in your first week at university. However, for many students there is the chance to change your mind on your optional modules in the first two or three weeks of term. Knowing how disruptive such a move can be is why universities tend to dissuade students from making such a move; they also know that students sometime struggle to settle in and blame a module that would actually work well for them if they felt better about their circumstances. If you know that you have mistakenly made a choice that is not going to work for you at all, and that is making you dread each lecture and seminar on a module, whilst you are enjoying your other modules, then ask whether it is possible to change, whatever you have been told officially.

You will have noticed by now that, even if your university-scheduled activity is fairly light in this first week, you have plenty to do in order to set up the best path for you for the rest of the year. By the end of the week you will probably be tired, but you will also feel set and ready to go, eager to get on with your studies. This is not necessarily because you are the most avid student; it is as likely to be a natural anxiety to know what it is like to study at university, and to be reassured that you will succeed.

Even though you are making many decisions this week, and trying to establish a new life for yourself in your university, there is still time to think for a moment about the impact that all of this could have on your career…

CAREER
MOMENT

Much of the advice I have offered you in this chapter will benefit your future career. Successful young professionals can talk persuasively about the range of modules they chose, and the overall shape of their degree. They have achieved well because they managed their study time and kept an eye on the forms of assessment being used. They chose to shine in areas that are relevant to their future career (maybe group activities, or presentations, or extensive lab work) and they recognised how to craft a degree programme well through the choices they were given.

There is one other move you can make at this stage … stop, and look around you. Are IT courses on offer as a standard part of your library or resource centre provision? Does your department, or your university, offer an employability scheme for which you could enrol, and would you do this now or do you judge it better to wait for a while? Are you allowed to sit in on some lectures outside your chosen modules, so that you can get a little more backup information in an area? In essence, university is full of free options, so make the most of them, knowing that you are developing lifelong skills.

It would be unfair to end this chapter without reassuring you. Your choices in this first year will not make or break your university experience. Indeed, it may be that your results at the end of the year do not even count towards your over-all degree outcome. Your first year at university is about making the best choices you can, but there will be no need to despair if you make some choices that turn out not to be perfect for you – it is all part of your development as a student.

3

Getting involved in university life

How many clubs and societies are there likely to be?

Too many – always, too many! You will have to be selective and that means resisting the sales pitches you will be offered in your first week. Take your time, never sign up on the spur of the moment, and think about what you want to get out of the experience of joining a club or society.

How can I find out about clubs and societies?

There are likely to be stalls set up somewhere (usually in a Students' Union building or in your department) during the first week, and you might also receive emails. Your course or programme handbook will give information on how to find out about clubs and societies, and a look through your online student portal or Students' Union webpages will take you to them easily.

Top tip

> Avoid the assumption that every club and society is run from the Students' Union. There might also be reading groups in your own department, and your lecturers might also encourage (and help in the setting up of) study groups or film viewing groups.

How much do clubs and societies cost?

The costs vary from university to university. Some universities do not charge for membership of clubs and societies, but in many cases a club or society needs to recruit enough members to remain viable year on year. Although there may be a cost involved, they are usually incredibly good value, so it is money well spent as long as you have the time and enthusiasm to be involved fully in the activities on offer.

Should I try a new activity?

University is the perfect place to try out a new activity – it is probably a bit less perfect for trying out six new activities, all at once, in your first term. Strike a balance here: join a society that you know will help to make university feel familiar (doing something that you enjoy already) and also try out a new activity as part of your new life.

INSIDER HINT

Students often tell me that they would enjoy being a student rep (a course or department representative, able to take students' concerns to academics, but also contributing to the development of courses, policies and initiatives) but did not realise in time that this was open to them.

Be ready for this: students are often asked to volunteer for this within a couple of weeks of being at university.

How many university organisations should I join?

Top tip

You might choose not to join any clubs or societies at all in your first few weeks at university, if you cannot make up your mind between them or you are not sure how you will find the time to be involved. There will be invites to social events open to potential new members later on in the year, and you can sometimes join for free on a trial basis once the first term is over.

For most students two would be enough at this point, perhaps three if you find a society with activities that relate to your studies and which is not too time

22

consuming (such as a debating society, for example, if you know that you are going to have to give assessed presentations throughout your course). The mention here of time is an important one: clubs and societies can be hugely rewarding, but also very time consuming, so make sure that the clubs you join, and the role you volunteer to play in them, allow you to achieve the vital balance between studying and the rest of your life.

Source: Clem Onojeghuo/StockSnap.io   Source: Quino Al/StockSnap.io

What other options do I have?

There are options beyond standard clubs and societies that you might want to consider. Working as a student ambassador, for example, will bring you in some money and could offer some excellent training opportunities. From your second year onwards you might be offered the chance to become a peer mentor to new students, or to help run independent study groups for the students in the years below you.

There are also national and international opportunities for students, in travelling, voluntary work and career development such as working in schools. Your personal tutor should be able to point you in the right direction, so it might be a good idea to make a note to yourself to explore these more extensive options once you have settled in.

INSIDER HINT

As well as all of the other options outlined here, there are also less well publicised opportunities. Lecturers are increasingly working in partnership with students in all sorts of ways, from designing a curriculum that suits everyone's needs, to creating new learning material on a

(Continued)

(Continued)

module, to being imaginative in how learning is assessed. This might involve completing a survey, or joining a focus group, or running an entire project. This can sometimes lead to giving a presentation on your project at a conference on teaching and learning: you can decide how far you want to take it, but it can be a great way to get involved in something that makes a real difference. Your personal tutor should know if there are any projects like this running in your department, and you might receive emails about them.

One of the key reasons why some students are hesitant about joining a club or society is that they need to dedicate some of their time to earning money. This can leave you feeling that you are not making the most of your chances at university, but this is not necessarily the case. A club or society might be enjoyable, and it might help you develop your skills and experience, but so does part-time work, so you need not feel that you are inevitably missing out if you cannot join a club or society at this stage.

CAREER
MOMENT

Getting prepared for a successful career is much easier if you think about it every now and again from the outset of your time at university, rather than having a panic in your final term. Clubs and societies, and a part-time job if you have one, are a good example of this. You are probably not going to join a club just for the sake of your career, and you have a job because you need the money, but being just a little bit selective now will pay dividends. If you know that nothing in your experience will demonstrate your public speaking skills, then aiming to become a committee member of your chosen club or society makes sense: that way you can talk in future about the presentations you gave at committee meetings. If you know that attention to detail is not your strength, then you might choose part-time work in a library or call centre, where detail will be important, rather than in a shop or restaurant where it might be less so.

Thinking about your career will not require you to change your plans radically, if at all – it is more about being able to analyse what you are gaining with each new experience so that you can be explicit about it in future. It is also a good way to save yourself time. I have seen students undertake arduous and time consuming (and sometimes expensive) extra-curricular courses in social media campaigning, when they could just as effectively (and far more easily) have run the social media campaigns of their clubs or societies. I have also been told by students that they have no job skills at all, despite having worked part-time throughout university. Early career success often relies on the ability to analyse and advertise your graduate attributes, and that is where this guide will help.

If you do not enjoy being part of a formal group such as a club or society, then do not join. If you do, it will make you feel bad when you realise that you have wasted your money on something that you do not enjoy and in which you are never going to be fully involved. Plenty of students have a wonderful time at university without ever joining a club or society, so you need never feel anxious on that count.

4

Your first personal tutorial

What is a personal tutor?

Whatever the person is called (personal tutor, academic tutor, pastoral tutor, mentor) you are likely to be allocated one member of staff whose role includes supporting you individually. You might expect this to be an academic, but it might as easily be a member of the study support team, and the role varies from university to university. Despite all these variables, the purpose of a personal tutor is to help make sure that your time at university works well for you.

However, your personal tutor's place in your studying is not quite the same as a teacher or tutor in your study life before university. A personal tutor will expect students to be proactive and take control to some extent. It will be up to you to accept invites to meetings (your tutor is unlikely to chase you very much on this) and you are in a position to decide what is discussed (beyond anything that your tutor has been asked to raise with all tutees). Taking notes in meetings is fine, and keeping regular contact by email is also acceptable.

One point is worth noting here: if you are not offered a personal tutor at your university, this does *not* mean that you are attending an inferior university, or that they do not care enough for your wellbeing and development. It simply means that your university has taken a different approach to supporting its students. The guidance offered in this chapter will still be relevant, even if your university's support structure is a little different – it might mean that you will be talking to staff with slightly different titles, or you will be interacting with a range of support staff, each taking on one aspect of the role of personal tutor.

Your personal tutor will have been given a wide brief, which might include talking to you about your academic progress, helping to support you as you face new challenges in your learning and assessment, directing you to the right people to help with finance and housing, as well as talking to you more generally about how you are doing and how you feel about your course.

You would usually be expected to ask your personal tutor to be your referee when you apply for jobs, so it makes sense to build up some sort of relationship. If your personal tutor has never seen you, it means that the only reference you can be given is a confirmation of your marks and final grade, and you will want a far fuller reference than that.

You will probably be assigned a personal tutor who will stay with you for your whole time at university, which means that you can build up a productive relationship over time and so make the most of the support on offer. Your personal tutor might never actually teach you, although in some universities efforts are made to ensure that you are taught at least for one module by your personal tutor so that you get to know each other a little better in that formal academic setting. Actually, not being taught by your personal tutor can be an equally valid approach to take, as this leaves you clear to talk about all aspects of your course without any preconceived ideas on either side.

Top tip

This has the potential to be a fruitful relationship whilst you are at university, and beyond, but do not feel that you have to see your personal tutor for every single problem you have. If you are able to identify the right place to go for help with some of the issues you face or the queries you have (the checklist in Chapter 1 will help with this) then you can reserve the meetings with your personal tutor for areas of university life that are best suited to that situation.

What is a personal tutor meeting?

It is a regular opportunity to meet with your personal tutor to make sure that you are on the right lines and to talk through any concerns you have. It is also a chance to talk about how you can do better. These meetings are usually scheduled once or twice a term, and might be group or individual meetings.

Top tip

> As with so much at university, the same names crop up for different things. A tutorial might be a personal tutor meeting, but it might also be a one-to-one or group session with the person who has marked your essay. In this guide, tutorials are taken to be this latter type of meeting.

Group meetings are often held to talk about general areas of relevance to all students, so you would generally expect to see your personal tutor in a group meeting to talk about how the whole group is settling in to university, and then to be offered an individual meeting later to make sure that everything is meeting your expectations.

For group meetings your tutor will usually have in mind a topic for discussion and may have prepared some activities for you to do as a group (preparing for seminars in the first meeting, for example; much later on, talking in a group about your dissertation ideas, perhaps).

Individual meetings tend to be more open and you might be asked just to talk through how university is working out for you. Even if there is a theme (looking at your career goals is an obvious area that comes up regularly in these meetings) you might not be required to do much, if anything, in advance. This does not mean that you should be passive. Taking time to think before the meeting about what you need to discuss, and making notes of areas that are concerning you, or of opportunities you would like to pursue, will make the time with your tutor more profitable.

INSIDER
HINT

You can be sure that your tutor will have done some preparation for each meeting, if only by accessing your record online. Academics have access to far more information than they did even a few years ago. As your tutor glances at the computer screen during a tutorial, you can be fairly sure that it is revealing your grades, your full attendance record, notes made during previous meetings, and emails of concern about you. I mention this not to worry you, but to urge you to offer the full story if you are facing difficulties. Your tutor being able to see this data is a good thing: after all, having the full picture is the best way to offer you any help that you need.

Is this the only time I will see my personal tutor?

Not necessarily. Students sometimes make the mistake of thinking that the only time they can see their tutor is during a regular, scheduled session or when things are going wrong. In fact, some of the most fruitful time you will spend with your personal tutor is when things are going well. If you have just received pleasing grades for several assignments, your personal tutor will be delighted to hear, but will also be able to work with you to think about how you could maintain this achievement. If you are thinking about choosing your next modules, or selecting the best topic for a major project, or finding some useful experience in the career market, your personal tutor will be able to help. Never hesitate about contacting your tutor if you need help or want to talk about how to maximise your progress. Sometimes an email exchange is enough, so you need never be anxious about taking up too much time.

Your personal tutor group might be as small as six people, or very much larger, and you might find the idea of any group meeting daunting, especially in your first few weeks at university. If this is the case for you, there is no need to see this as a failure, or to avoid meeting your personal tutor at all. Tutors are quite used to making separate appointments to see some of their tutees individually, so do not be put off; if you receive an email asking why you did not attend a group meeting, just ask for an individual meeting.

CAREER
MOMENT

It is surprising how often students overlook the fact that personal tutors have contacts – lots of contacts. They will know all about how to find a part-time job on campus, they will be fully aware of the skills you need to demonstrate if you want to go into a particular career (they will have professional contacts in the field) and they will remember where their ex-students are working. If you want work experience, or to shadow a successful professional, or to talk to an expert about the skills you need to develop to succeed, your personal tutor's office would be an obvious starting point.

How should I talk with my tutor?

The absolute ideal would be to aim for 'friendly, but not a friend'. You are meeting with someone whose job it is to help you, and who probably has many years' experience of helping students. If you can show that you feel positively towards the situation then this will come across as friendly. However, this is probably not someone you would see – or would want to see – for a coffee between lectures, or away from campus. If you encounter difficulties and open up to your personal tutor, you might want to keep that experience in the room, and not spend social time with that person, haunted by memories of a moment of distress.

Although I am encouraging you to build a strong working relationship with your personal tutor, I also recognise that sometimes personalities do not work well together. It is possible that you will find your personal tutor's style difficult to grasp, or you may find your tutor too ebullient or too dour to allow you to work well together. It is also inevitable that some students are allocated to a tutor who is about to take some research leave, or who works on days when the student is not at university. You may have been given the impression that you are simply stuck with your personal tutor and that there is nothing you can do about it. This is not the case. If you have good reason to want to change your personal tutor, be firm about it and ask the support team or your head of teaching to change you to a different personal tutor group. Do not let yourself feel bad about this – these things happen in life and it is not your fault.

How can I make the most of each tutorial?

Whether or not you are asked to prepare in advance for a personal tutorial, and even if the format is very open and casual, I would still offer you the same advice: prepare, make notes, then follow up.

If you have been told in advance that the meeting has a theme (such as employability, module choices or assignment information) then you will have some focus for your preparation. This does not prevent you from also discussing other issues that concern or interest you, and most meetings will be fairly open, often with no theme, so you can flex the meeting (especially individual meetings) to suit your needs of the moment.

There are some key areas you would want to consider before every personal tutor meeting. As you think about them, make a note of what you want to ask. It can feel a bit awkward, going into a meeting with a lot of questions, but tutors always appreciate it. It means that you are taking the meeting seriously and that you are clear on what help and information you need.

Checklist – for a personal tutor meeting

✓ Do you have any grade issues that are worrying you?

✓ Do you want help to do better?

(Continued)

(Continued)

- ✓ Do you want to talk about your aim for degree classification?
- ✓ Are you struggling to make sense of one topic?
- ✓ Are all of your seminar groups working for you?
- ✓ Are you finding the online virtual learning environment (VLE) easy to navigate?
- ✓ Is your home life affecting your studying?
- ✓ Is finding employment proving difficult?
- ✓ Would it help you to think in more detail about your career goals now?
- ✓ Would you like help with a placement, or work experience or shadowing?
- ✓ Do you keep receiving the same comments on your work?
- ✓ Do you understand all of the feedback on your recent assignments?
- ✓ Would it help you to talk through your future academic plans?
- ✓ Are you concerned about an additional educational need that is not being met?
- ✓ Do you know where to go for help to work out a financial difficulty?
- ✓ Would you like to get more involved in university life, but are not sure what to do?
- ✓ Would you like help to set up a reading group, or revision group, or extra lab group?
- ✓ Have you been sent an announcement by email about something in your department that does not really make sense to you?
- ✓ Is there anything else at all that is playing on your mind?
- ✓ Is there anything you would like to add to this checklist that you think is going to be relevant to you from time to time during your studies?

Take notes in the meeting, even if you feel a little shy of asking your tutor to slow down or repeat something. It is far better to take that extra moment than to miss vital information. Of course, your tutor will not mind in the slightest if you ask for time to make notes, so you will soon see that there is no reason to feel awkward. I frequently speak too fast to my students, and am always grateful when someone asks me to slow down or repeat something.

You will probably add to the checklist I have given you here, and some of the questions will be more relevant at some stages of your degree than at others, but if you work through it each time you have the chance to meet with your tutor, you will go into the meeting confident that this chance will not be wasted.

It can be a good idea to ask your personal tutor if it is acceptable to send a list of questions in advance, if you are concerned that you might not ask them all in a meeting, or if you would like to give your tutor the chance to check information for you before you meet. Only do this, though, if you feel it would help; if you only have a couple of straightforward queries it usually works well just to ask them at the time.

Source: Monkey Business Images/
Shutterstock.com

What is always a good idea is to email your tutor after the meeting, if you either need to confirm what was said, or you are not sure that you noted down some important details correctly, or if your tutor was not able to answer a query but agreed to look into it after the event. Academics are busy, and it is too easy to forget to check something that a student needs to know, even with the very best intentions. No tutor will object to a reminder after a meeting.

How do I make this a sustainably productive relationship?

The answer to this will rely, to some extent, on the sort of person you are. If the idea of having one person assigned to you, with whom you meet to talk about your progress and your university experience, does not appeal to you, then you are unlikely to see this as a relationship in which you want to invest too much time. You will probably want to go to the first meeting that is set up for you, as there may be vital information given then, but you might not want to do much more than that. That is fine, but never let that get in the way of you seeking help from your tutor if ever you need it. Academics are very used to students appearing in their second or third year wanting some help from their personal tutor.

If you do see this as a potentially productive relationship for the way you like to work, you might give some thought to whether it is working at its best for you. Throughout this guide, I mention ways in which your personal tutor could be of value to you. If you ponder it every now and then, and feel you could be working the relationship more fully, take the chance to email your personal tutor and ask for a meeting, or send an email update of your progress, or ask a question that has been niggling you.

INSIDER
HINT

Being a personal tutor is an odd job. I see some of my students regularly, and know that I will miss them when they leave. With some, I have seen hurdles overcome and huge strides made in their development; others I have never met, as they simply failed to show up to any meetings.

In the short term this might not matter too much, but I am regularly in touch with some graduates for whom I was personal tutor more than a decade ago. I offer them advice on where to go next in their careers, I recommend good books to try and, crucially, I continue to give them fulsome, glowing references each time they change jobs, because I feel in a strong position to offer a reference that genuinely reflects their current position. It is worth bearing this in mind when you are considering whether or not to go to your first personal tutor meeting.

5

Your first lectures

What are lectures all about?

Lectures can feel very alien when you first attend them. Unlike school or college, where you may have been used to classes of thirty or so students, all sitting at desks and interacting with a teacher or tutor, lectures can be given to several hundred students at a time in a huge lecture hall, and interaction is minimal. A lecture can be far smaller than this, of course, but be ready for a crowded event. This can be enjoyable; you see all of the fellow students who you only ever spot in lectures, and there is often a real sense of occasion: this is an event, rather than the less formal workshops or seminars you will attend.

Top tip

> It might be helpful to ask, in the week before the lectures begin, how large your lecture groups are likely to be. This will help you to prepare - if the lecture group is small, you might expect that you could become more involved, whilst a very large lecture group is usually less likely to be active.

The huge advantage of a lecture, as opposed to classroom teaching, is that you can sit back and just listen. No need to think up a clever question, no concerns about suddenly being asked to respond, no need to do anything at all, except make the most of the opportunity to learn. Of course, not every lecturer will necessarily allow you to approach a lecture in this way. Even in large lecture halls, you will come across the odd lecturer who likes to throw out a question or two, or ask you to talk to your neighbour for a minute about a topic that is being covered, but you will soon come to know which lecturers tend to enjoy that style of lecturing.

INSIDER
HINT

Lecturers know that all students learn more deeply if they are active in their learning, so some lecturers will deliberately ask a question, or ask you to talk in pairs for a minute in the middle of a lecture, so that you are actively thinking about what is being taught. However, we have to balance this against the amount of material we need to cover to support your learning adequately. As a basic guide, I would say remain quiet in a lecture unless you are invited by the lecturer to speak.

Where should I sit in a lecture?

This seems like such an easy, almost irrelevant, little question, but for some students it can make a difference to how well they can concentrate and how much they enjoy a lecture. Many students try to sit in roughly the same place every time they are in a particular lecture hall, and this does have advantages. It means that if you are friendly with people you tend to see only in lectures, they will be able to look out for you. If you are not there for a lecture, they will probably expect that you will be asking for a copy of their lecture notes.

There is another benefit to sitting in the same place – you do not have to think about where to sit. Again, a minor point but one about which students can get quite grumpy. If you find yourself stuck at the front of a large lecture theatre and you have to dash to another event straight after the lecture, you might feel a little uncomfortable. If you are claustrophobic, being crushed in a huge group of people trying to leave the hall might not feel comfortable. Sitting beneath a sunny window for a whole lecture would challenge even the keenest student to stay awake. So, finding the best place for you and sticking to it will probably work better.

What if I miss a lecture?

In your first week, ask whether lecture notes (or a version of the lecture, such as the slides used or a copy of the handout) will be made available to students; this is most likely to be the case. Some students need to see lecture slides before the lecture, and so they are often made available on the online VLE up to forty-eight hours before a lecture. The reason I suggest checking on this in your first week is that many students suffer from 'Fresher's Flu' in the first few weeks of term, once everyone has returned to university, bringing all of their new germs with them, so knowing that there is lecture material available even if you are ill will be reassuring.

It can be tempting to take photos of every image you see on the screen in a lecture, and record what you are hearing on your phone or similar device. I consider this in more detail later in this guide, but take time to think about it now. How much help would it be? Would you want to do this in every lecture, or just in some parts of some lectures? Too many of my students end up with dozens of images and hours of recording by the end of the first week and feel overwhelmed by it, and frustrated when they discover that all of the slides are made available to them for each lecture.

Lecture material put on a VLE, or even lecture notes taken by a fellow student, can never be as useful to you as attending the lecture. They are a fairly good substitute if you are ill, but can never be more than that. It is why, even when lectures are recorded by a university and lodged on the VLE for students after the event, attendance at lectures remains high. There are two reasons for this: you understand better if you can see and hear in real time exactly what is being taught, and you will find the passion of your lecturers for their subject inspiring.

Lecturers expect to be approached straight after a lecture by a few students who are keen to follow up on something they have mentioned, or who want to ask a practical query about a module or its assessment. If you see lecturers dashing off straight after a lecture, head down and determined to evade you, it probably just means that they have another appointment. If this happens every time a particular lecturer finishes a lecture, it might mean that they are anxious about that sort of quick interaction with lots of students after a lecture. If this is the case, try emailing instead.

Do I have to attend the whole lecture?

Usually, all students would attend the whole lecture, but if you arrive late there is no need to feel that you cannot go in because you have missed the first ten minutes. Nobody will mind. Similarly, if you need to leave for a few minutes during a lecture, this will not cause any problems for either the lecturer or your fellow students.

What should I take with me to the lecture?

Apart from your note taking tools (pen and paper or electronic device) you might not need to take anything – most usually you could expect handouts to be given out during the event. If you have forgotten to bring a text book or other material with you that you had been asked to bring to the lecture, there is again no need to leave or avoid the event. It will still be of value to you.

Top tip

> Reading this chapter (and Chapter 10 on making notes) you will need to make a decision on whether your notes will be handwritten or typed. This will not necessarily be the same for each circumstance. Taking notes from an online source lends itself well to typing notes, for example, but notes in seminars are often written down by students so that they do not have the barrier of a laptop screen between them and the rest of the group. In lectures you need to be careful. Typing notes can lead to you writing too much – some students can take down a lecture almost word for word – and then finding that you have made notes with no sense of judgement or sifting. Instead, many students perform better overall if they work hard to make a productive set of concise notes in the moment, notes that they can use easily in the future.

What will be covered in the lecture?

This is probably the most substantial difference between pre-university teaching and studying as an undergraduate. Lecturers are often given free rein when they are asked to give a lecture – they really can choose to talk on whatever takes their fancy within a topic. Teams of lecturers (working with the convenor/leader of the module/course) will then work together to make sure that you are given full enough coverage across the series of lectures for a course or module, but you need to be ready for significant variations between types of lecture.

The general lecture

You will be so glad that you went to this type of lecture. The lecturer will be saving you time by giving you all of the basic information you need to get you going on a topic. The topic itself might be quite niche, perhaps on just one aspect of your module or course, but the lecturer is refusing to 'take sides' by showing you just one approach. Instead, you are being offered a brief survey of all the main approaches that you might take, all of the ways you might tackle an area, and all of the absolutely vital information about an area that you need as you study on the module.

Top tip

> These lectures can nip along at a cracking pace, so you will need to make sure you keep up. If, in your first few lectures, you find the pace too fast for you, try to stay calm and simply add a symbol to your notes (a star, for example) whenever you found yourself losing the thread or failing to grasp the point. These are the areas you might check up on through the VLE lecture notes later; they might also form the basis of your questions in the next smaller learning event you attend (a seminar, workshop or guided lab session).

The structural lecture

This type of lecture might not be covering topics specific to the material on your module at all. It is designed to help you succeed in the module. It might be dedicated to working through what is expected on the assessment tasks on the module. Equally, it could be offering you information about choices you have to make for optional modules, or it could be offering you a structural overview of how a module fits together, or how this module fits into your degree programme as a whole.

If the lecture is on material within your module, you are likely to be offered information on reading lists and how they are comprised, or an overview of how much material to cover, and in what depth.

Top tip

> This is the type of lecture in which you might be expected to ask some questions, so remain alert to this chance to confirm what you think is being said. Never leave this type of lecture without any of the handouts that you are offered: they will be important for your long-term success on the module.

The informational lecture

These lectures can be hard work. The lecturer is sharing with you an overview of a topic area, or giving you a detailed account of one experimental approach, or theory, or piece of work by a leader in the field. This lecturer will be the expert in the subject (probably having published on it as part of academic research) and so will be keen to impart to you as much information as possible.

Sometimes, especially with a less experienced lecturer, this can lead to just too much information being offered for the time available. You will be able to spot this because, in the last third of the lecture, the academic is likely to start looking flustered, or will keep mentioning the time and assuring you that the lecture will still finish as scheduled, whilst talking faster and faster. This can be frustrating for students who are trying to keep up, but it is not a regular or persistent problem in lectures, so it will not trip you up too much.

Top tip

> Your note taking skills will be tested to the full here. There is likely to be a mass of information on offer, so you will soon become expert at condensing this into manageable notes and you will come to learn, relatively quickly, what to include in detail and what can be jotted down in the briefest possible form.

The inspirational lecture

These are usually the most enjoyable lectures you will attend. They are not designed to be reassuring or practical; they are given as an invitation to share in the vision of the lecturer. They can sometimes be startling in their pinpoint focus: perhaps just a few lines of text, or one minor but nevertheless striking theory. The idea behind these lectures is that you leave the lecture hall inspired to carry out your own research, perhaps having had a 'light bulb moment' when something has just become clear to you.

INSIDER HINT

A 'threshold concept' is an idea or way of thinking that is fundamental to your understanding of a topic area. Without grasping these key ideas, you will struggle to move ahead in a positive way with the content of a module. You can probably recall times when, even at the end of a course, there were some parts of it that you just did not quite 'get'. Those were times when the threshold concepts had passed you by.

In an inspirational lecture, you never need to worry about how many notes you make. The lecturer may well have designed the lecture so that you need no more than a brief handout; the lecturer knows that you will be leaving with something far more valuable than notes: the threshold concept.

Making the most of lectures

If your course is made up of both lectures and seminars in fairly equal proportion, you will devote most of your preparation time to getting ready for seminars, and this is the most sensible approach. However, you will not want to ignore lectures until the moment they happen. Instead, you could ask yourself some questions that will help you to maximise the effect of each lecture.

Checklist – getting ready for a lecture

✓ Read the lecture brief, if you are given one.

✓ Categorise the lecture according to the types listed here, so that you are ready for the right kind of note taking.

✓ Check the lecture slides or other lecture material online in advance if it is posted there and you think it will help you to focus.

✓ Work out how this lecture links to the next small group learning activity you have: are there certain areas that you hope the lecturer will cover?

✓ Work through any material you were given in advance of the lecture. If you cannot do this, still go along to the lecture. It is better to be there ill-prepared than not be there at all.

✓ If you have an assignment coming up, use an active learning sheet (an example is given after this checklist) to capture useful material for the assignment.

✓ If you have decided to record the lecture, give yourself enough time to set that up.

You might not be able to work through this checklist completely for every lecture, but even taking a moment with the lecture brief or thinking about the title of the lecture will help you to focus.

Active learning sheets are a good way to capture information quickly and easily. The example in Figure 5.1 shows an incomplete but developing active learning sheet:

LECTURE TITLE AND DATE:

IDEAS FOR MY ESSAY:

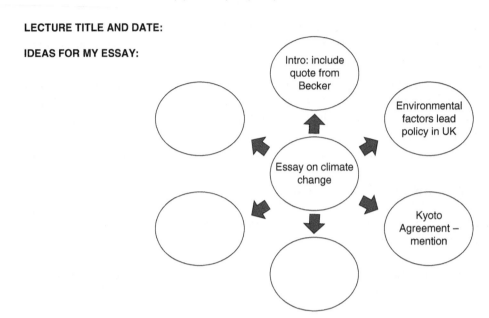

Figure 5.1   A partially complete active learning sheet

By using a sheet such as this you can force yourself to add very brief notes alongside your fuller lecture notes whenever anything is said in the lecture that you think might be relevant for your next assignment. You will want to add more circles to the sheet if the lecture is complicated and full of ideas and information that you might want to use.

In the centre circle you can give a few keywords from your assignment title or brief, to keep this in the forefront of your mind during the lecture. These are called active learning sheets because, rather than simply absorbing information and making notes in a lecture, you are, in the very moment of receiving the information, making a judgement on how you could use it, and how it fits into your existing knowledge.

Some students enjoy active learning sheets such as this so much that they use them for every lecture, either alongside or instead of a fuller set of notes (depending on what they need to get out of the lecture). In that case, you would put the lecture title in the middle circle, with your points radiating out from it in the outer circles. Note that in the top left corner there is a place to put the lecture title and date. You could also include the lecturer's name for easy reference back to them should you need to in the future. You might also consider using just one or two of these sheets over the course of a whole week, or even a whole module. These would be titled 'connections sheets' and you would use them during lectures, seminars, discussions, indeed, in any event where you noticed a connection and wanted to record it before it was lost.

Top tip

Capturing information is good, as long as you know whose information it is. Whilst you are sitting in a lecture and taking a moment to look out of the window, you might well be struck by an amazing idea, or you could make a connection that leads on to your assignment. It is both frustrating and undermining of your confidence to find that note several weeks later and not be completely sure whether it is a note you made from something the lecturer said, or if it is your own moment of brilliance. This can lead to reluctance to use it. Avoid this happening to you by noting 'MY IDEA' in the margin of your notes whenever you come up with a good idea, whether you are sitting in a lecture, taking part in a seminar or making notes from a source.

Students often like the idea of recording audiofiles of lectures, in the belief that they will then have that lecture securely captured for future reference, and sometimes also on the basis that they can then relax a little and enjoy each lecture, knowing that they fully intend to make notes from the MP3 file at a later point.

For some students this is essential, because they are unable to take notes at the time and/or need the backup of a recording of the lecture. For others, it is a complete disaster. I have seen far too many students spend their whole first year at university feeling guilty about the dozens of recordings that they always meant to work through but have never quite managed to listen to again after the lecture. Months later, it is difficult to avoid making notes that are almost word for word what was said, because you are under no immediate time pressure to make those notes, so you are also in danger of making notes that are far too long.

If you are happy using software that converts speech to text (and this may be cloud-based and available to you for free at your university) then you might see it as a useful backup, but there is little that beats note taking in the moment, if you are able to do this well. With practice you will become an expert at picking out what you need, and at the end of the lecture you can relax.

CAREER
MOMENT

In this chapter we have focused so closely on the immediate challenge of lectures that it would be easy to overlook their value to you in your future plans, but the skills you learn here will be of benefit for the whole of your professional life. By the end of your degree, you will have mastered:

(Continued)

(Continued)

- Listening and prioritising what you are hearing (essential for every business meeting, especially if you are chairing the event).
- Note taking (invaluable in meetings and at conferences).
- Prioritising of information (the building block of managing projects and processes).
- Making connections (the basis for analysis).
- Weighing up the merits of competing ideas (every sales pitch relies on this).
- Critical thinking (allowing you to assess a variety of situations).
- Working under pressure (it is bound to happen to you).
- Reworking material in the moment to produce reusable material (essential for disseminating material and arguing your case in a professional setting).
- Excellent attention to detail (something that can be hard to prove unless you use this example).

… and you just went along to a lecture: not a bad hour's work!

How do I develop my lecture skills over time?

Too often students forget to assess their lecture capture techniques, and so spend too much time and energy using methods that are not ideal for them. Once you feel you are used to lectures, force yourself to try out a new method, just to see if you might like it. This could involve moving from pen and paper to a laptop to take your notes (because you can type really fast) or moving back from a laptop to pen and paper (because you cannot resist taking verbatim lecture notes, and you then spend too long condensing them – or ignoring them).

Top tip

Try not to see your lecture notes as a final product. The more you work and rework your notes, the deeper your learning (because we learn by using material), the greater your understanding (because connections arise as you rework) and the less time you will spend later in revision (because revising from full lecture notes is exhausting and not particularly fruitful). Reduce your notes as your knowledge increases, work your notes into essay plans every now and then to test their usefulness, collate several sets of notes into one set of highly relevant notes.

You might try a completely different approach for a lecture or two. This might involve just using active learning sheets (see Chapter 5) or recording methods such as mind maps, rather than making notes in the traditional sense at all. You might try recording a lecture and then challenging yourself to reduce it to a brief set of notes within the following twelve hours. You might make traditional notes, but then add a series of bullet points at the end, limiting yourself to, say, just six key points that you have taken away from the lecture. The harder you work a lecture the harder it will work for you.

6

Your first seminars

What is a seminar?

The meaning of 'seminar' and 'tutorial' can differ depending on your university. In this chapter a seminar refers to a small group session in which an academic talks with students about topics in a module, often reflecting on the material that has been delivered in a lecture.

In a lecture you can expect to sit and listen to an academic talking to you; in a seminar you can expect to be doing much of the talking. This is only one of the reasons why a seminar differs so much from a lecture. It will also be far smaller: perhaps just a dozen or so students, and in some modules, even smaller still.

The function of a seminar is also very different from a lecture. You will expect that the seminar leader will lead a discussion, and offer useful material for that discussion, but much of the activity in a seminar is led by students. Indeed, for a seminar in which a student presentation is used to kick start the discussion, the academic might fade into the background for much of the time, content to hear students having their say.

INSIDER HINT

Seminar leaders will be academics, but their level of experience in the specific subject area under discussion might vary, and this will not matter at all. Seminars are designed to foster discussion and the sharing of ideas, so you are not relying on your seminar leader to offer

(Continued)

(Continued)

you the 'last word' on a topic, but instead you will turn to the leader to steer the seminar along a productive path.

In your first year in particular you might find that seminars are led on occasion by doctoral researchers; this can be useful because they have probably been sitting where you are now relatively recently. On the other hand, a seminar might be led by a world-leading expert in the field; a fascinating experience, but also demanding on your energy and brain power.

Seminars usually last one or two hours, and will often sit alongside a series of lectures. The basic premise of this system is that you will be offered information and inspiration in lectures, and you will then be given the space in seminars to discuss your reaction to that information, and consider how it is developing your understanding in an area. There are some modules that might be taught only by seminars; these are exciting chances to learn, but also challenging because you might be generating some of the core material under discussion.

The set-up of seminars differs greatly from academic to academic. Some will hardly need to prepare for a particular seminar, but will just write up a few provocative questions, or copy an extract from a text, or write a formula or data set on a board. They will then enjoy coming to this, like you, with a fresh perspective, because you are creating understanding between you, relying on the academic's expertise and experience and on your willingness to share your thoughts and ideas.

Top tip

> Do not be surprised if you are not asked to prepare anything at all for this type of seminar. You might not even have the chance to see the material under discussion before the seminar begins. The only expectation on you is that you will bring energy to the situation, and be prepared to share your ideas.

In some seminars it will be clear to you that the leader has undertaken a significant amount of preparatory work for the seminar. In these cases, especially in lengthy seminars, you might receive a mini-lecture at the beginning, setting out some overview material that is an essential basis for the discussion, before the seminar is opened up to all for analysis and comment. You might be asked to prepare material for either of these types of seminar.

Top tip

This is not a formally recognised lecture, and so there will be no requirement for the seminar leader to provide a handout or to lodge lecture notes on the VLE for the module. Be ready to take notes!

Another form of seminar is the student-led seminar. All seminars rely on the students in them, but in this type of seminar there will be a formal expectation that a student will lead some, or all, of the seminar. This might take the form of a presentation (ten or twenty minutes would be usual), with a set of questions offered to the group at the conclusion of the presentation, or some more material being provided by the student presenter that can form the basis of discussion.

You might not be alone in this task: group presentations are used in seminars, or there might be two or more presentations that then form the basis of discussion. The key here is to ensure that you know exactly what is required of you. Are you simply giving a presentation, or are you answering questions at the end as well? Or perhaps it is you who is to throw out questions for the group to discuss? Should you be producing a handout? How long should you talk, and will you be interrupted by the academic seminar leader from time to time?

You should have time to ask all of these questions before you present, as seminar presentations would not usually begin until two or three weeks into the module. Although this can sound like a daunting undertaking, it offers several benefits to students, not least the fact that there is probably only one week in a term when you may be nervous about giving a presentation for a particular module seminar. In the other weeks you can sit back and enjoy sharing in the work of others.

Top tip

This type of seminar can require group presentations. If this presentation is being assessed as part of the final module mark, make sure that you are clear about how this will work: will you receive a group mark, or will your individual efforts be assessed? Will any peer review mark (where you score each other's input into the task) be taken into account? A group presentation is by no means a bad thing, but you do need to know how any assessment of it is being structured.

Seminars – will the practicalities suit me?

Once you have been enrolled in a seminar group you will be reluctant, under-standably, to make any changes. However, if you find that the timing of a group does not work for you (it means dashing across campus between tightly packed events, or it means you are struggling to fit in a part-time job), you might want to reconsider your seminar time. Equally, if you find your group particularly chal-lenging, for whatever reason, you might want to make a change. Changing seminar groups is not always very difficult, and systems need to incorporate the possibility of change wherever possible, so being comfortable in your studies might include asking to change seminar group.

INSIDER HINT

However easy the mechanism for changing seminar groups, it is not necessarily going to be plain sailing. I have had students join my group just a couple of weeks into a term who never quite settle down, despite my efforts. I have also seen students who seem to 'seminar hop' from group to group, never finding a group where they like everyone and the seminar leader. It can be months before they work out that there are going to be people in any group with whom you do not feel entirely sympathetic.

Remember that seminars are designed to explore ideas, so a group will often range quite widely, moving away from the lecture topics. Seminar leaders might also make up their own assessment tasks and titles, just for their own group. This need not be an insurmountable prob-lem, but make sure that you have a detailed conversation with your seminar leader, the module convenor or your personal tutor before you take this step, just to make sure that you are clear on all of the potential ramifications.

What will it feel like to be in a seminar?

To start with, it will feel odd, perhaps a little scary, and certainly challenging even for a confident student. There are three aspects of a seminar that make it a challenge: you are being asked to share ideas, even if they are not quite fully formed, you are speaking in front of an academic who you might feel is judging your performance, and you are in a semi-social setting.

Source: Imag

50

INSIDER
HINT

We cannot escape the fact that a seminar is a social setting, even if it is a rather unusual one. For some students this triggers crippling shyness; for others, it brings out in them a need to say anything at all just to break the silence. Something that academics dread, almost more than anything else in their professional lives, is the awkwardness of a silent seminar group. As the silence lengthens, and the sense that nothing productive is happening becomes stronger, the academic becomes either bored or stressed, and everyone begins to resent the time that they are spending in this silence.

Some academics tackle this head-on by just asking individual students direct questions, but most tend to avoid this. The frustration for the academic is largely based on the knowledge that this is your precious learning time that is being lost. If you are the one student prepared to speak up, especially in the early seminars, you will get a positive, and grateful, response. I still remember students from a decade or so ago, just because they were the first to speak – they are also, of course, the students who did well in the module because they used the seminar time to their advantage.

What is the purpose of a seminar?

There are many good reasons why you might want to work hard in a seminar, and the checklist below will offer you a sense of why this might be so.

Checklist – how seminars work for you

- ✓ They save you time – preparing for an essay is far easier if you ask the right questions in a seminar on the topic.

- ✓ They reduce your anxiety – you can ask general questions about how a module or its assessment works, or about what is expected of you in terms of learning on the module, and there is plenty of time for the seminar leader to answer all your queries.

- ✓ You feel part of a learning group – this can help you feel more motivated, it can also be flipped easily into a wider reading group, independent study group or revision group later on in the term.

- ✓ They can be reassuring – rather than working alone and hoping that you are on the right lines, a discussion will confirm whether you have grasped the 'threshold concepts' from the lectures, and whether you are thinking at the right level.

(Continued)

(Continued)

✓ They regulate your workload – if you are feeling guilty all the time, thinking that you are not working hard enough, or you are exhausted from working late into the night, a seminar group discussion will offer you useful clues about how much effort you are expected to be putting into a module.

✓ They offer you expertise – there is nothing quite like sitting in a room with an expert in a field to make you feel like a 'proper' university student, which, of course, you are.

✓ You gain an insight into academic structure and methods – by seeing how your seminar leader approaches a challenge you will get a clearer idea of the differing methods you could try in your studying.

✓ You can try out your arguments – as discussion and debate are the primary purpose of a seminar, it is the perfect setting to work through an argument you hope to develop in an essay or dissertation.

Another purpose of a seminar from your point of view could be to make friends. This might seem so obvious as to be hardly worth mentioning; but university brings with it the chance to make lifelong friends, but also to make 'situational friends'. These are fellow students you are friendly with in a seminar group, with no particular expectation that you will meet outside the seminar or remain in contact once the seminar series is complete. Cultivating these very useful and rewarding friendships can be beneficial to you, offering you the chance to test your thoughts one to one, or know someone who is prepared to share notes if you are unwell.

INSIDER HINT

You might not be the sort of student who makes copious notes in every seminar. Perhaps you have decided to focus on the discussion and just note down a few highlight points in the seminar. Even if you do not plan to make any notes at all, always make sure that you have pen and paper ready (or laptop, if this is what you use) whilst you are in the seminar. It is demoralising for seminar leaders to see a student who apparently thinks it is not even worth making notes, and you may be remembered as a student who is not much interested in the subject.

It is also worth thinking about how advantageous seminars are to your career; this is something that students too often overlook. This works in two ways. By being in a seminar you are working in a formal setting, analysing and debating, and this gives you a strong indication as to how you would like to work in future.

If you feel uncomfortable in this setting, the study benefits you gain from a seminar will make you persevere, but you might want to take heed of that feeling; perhaps in your future career you might decide that you work better in a different type of situation.

The second way it will work for you is that you can demonstrate to an employer all of the transferable skills you have gained from working in seminars. They are called transferable skills because you have used and sharpened them up in one setting, and you are then in a position to benefit a future employer by transferring the same skills to a new setting.

CAREER MOMENT

Seminars are an excellent source of transferable skills:

- using new information effectively
- analysing information at speed
- teamwork and group discussions
- leadership
- sharing ideas and creating solutions
- giving presentations.

What should I do to prepare for a seminar?

You will develop a study rhythm in your first term, so that preparing for seminars becomes part of your normal routine, and you will be able to judge how much, or how little, is required of you in advance of each seminar. If you are giving a presentation in a seminar, you might work for several weeks to gather material, prepare some slides and rehearse to time. For other seminars, where you are simply contributing to a discussion or group activities, this checklist will help you to prepare.

Checklist – what to do before each seminar

✓ Read any material you were given in advance. If you have not read it, or only had time to look at some of it, still go to the seminar – better to be there underprepared than not to go at all.

(Continued)

(Continued)

✓ Check the VLE for the module to make sure that no last-minute material has been posted that you need to consider before you go in.

✓ Think of one question to ask in the seminar. This is not really for the benefit of the seminar leader – it is so that you are ready if you are put on the spot and have to say something.

✓ Look back through your lecture notes to see if there are any questions you need to ask, even if they are not directly related to the topic of the seminar. Again, this is for your benefit because it will save you time and anxiety later.

✓ Think about your next assignment – is there anything that is holding you up? Could you ask a question now that will help you progress?

✓ Does the reading list for the module work for the assignment you have chosen, or been instructed, to do? If you are given some choice, or are carrying out an independent research project, you might be able to make up a bespoke reading list just from suggestions made in seminars by your fellow students and your seminar leader.

✓ Were any discussions opened up in the last seminar that you would like to revisit now that you have the chance?

It can be unexpectedly difficult to find time to sit down and prepare for each seminar once the term gets busier. There is always a temptation to overlook the preparation and simply attend the seminar. In some cases this can work, but it can also catch you out. Missing even one seminar can make you feel so awkward that you miss the next one, and then the next …

If you are pushed for time one week and know that you will struggle to prepare fully for your seminars, there is a way around it. Put aside not the hour or so you really need, but just twenty minutes (and this can be as long as it would take you to order and enjoy a drink in the coffee shop). In this time just think about what you recall from the last seminar: is there a lingering question you wanted to ask? Then check if there is any material to read in advance of the seminar. If there is nothing to read, you now know that you are as prepared as anyone else. If there is preparatory material, skim it, so that you are at least familiar with what is being covered, even though you do not have time to read it in detail. Is there a passage or a diagram that particularly catches your eye? Highlight it and read this little section of the material in detail. You will not be thoroughly briefed for the seminar by doing this, but you will be ready enough.

You can take this approach to seminars when you are really pressed for time, because seminars are largely about the energy you put into them in the moment, rather than what has happened before the event. You may find the seminar a little less useful, because you have not prepared as well as you might, but you will have been seen to turn up and join in, and you will still walk away from the seminar room with plenty of useful material and some good new ideas.

Top tip

There is a pragmatic reason why you might want to attend every one of a seminar series, even if you cannot prepare brilliantly for all of them. Sometimes attendance is not just expected, but also credit bearing. It might be that a proportion of the marks for the module overall can be gained simply by turning up – easy marks that you will not want to lose.

How much should I speak out in a seminar?

Saying something, almost anything, in the first couple of seminars for a module will pay dividends; you will be remembered as an engaged and willing student and you will pick up some useful information early on. Beyond this, you might be strategic. You have a surprising amount of power in this situation: seminar discussions ebb and flow in direct response to the students' questions and comments, so if you have prepared a question in advance that relates directly to your assignment, you can guarantee that you will reap the reward from your efforts.

Top tip

If you have never heard your voice in a seminar room it can be slightly daunting to think of saying something. To overcome this, have ready with you, for your first or second seminar, a prepared question that you want to ask, and try to make yourself ask it. This is purely mechanical, rather than information gathering. Once you have heard yourself speak out, you will never have to worry about talking in that seminar series.

There are students who try to dominate the conversation just to hear themselves speak, which can be unproductive for the whole group, but, in general terms, the more you speak the better your seminar experience will be. As long as you are also prepared to let others do some of the work by speaking out to help move your ideas forward, you will be able to make the most of the seminar.

INSIDER
HINT

One of the peculiar things about a seminar is that it is difficult to say anything which is out and out incorrect. The basis of a seminar is to try out ideas and to talk through material, so even if a comment you make misses the mark a little, it is likely to prompt others to speak up in response; between you, you will get to the right place. Academics know how this works, so they are ready to allow almost anything on topic to be said, because they recognise that this is a productive way to move forward. This is good news for you – speak out and listen and you cannot go far wrong.

7

Extending your reach

We have covered plenty of material so far in this guide and you have risen to many new challenges. There is no need to worry if, after the first few weeks, you have not completely conquered making lecture notes, or you do not yet find that seminar discussions come entirely naturally to you: there is time to perfect all of these things.

However, you are reading this book because you want to make the most of your chances and you want to be the best you can be, both at university and in your future career. That is why, even as you are mastering this new learning environment, I am offering you some ideas about how you can move beyond the basic building blocks that we have already covered in these first few chapters.

For all students, and especially for those who plan to make the most of the time, university offers the chance to make connections and find openings that will boost their studying and also prepare them well for new challenges ahead. You might not want to explore all of these options in your first term – you are going to be very busy – but you could return to this chapter from time to time to remind yourself of what might be open to you.

Your family and home friends – are they in the loop?

It is inevitable that your family and friends from home become more distant from your day-to-day life whilst you are at university. This can be a good thing: you are living your own lives and will have plenty of news to swap and stories to tell when you see each other again. It can, however, become a problem if your family members no longer really understand what it is you are actually doing at university.

They could become embarrassed, thinking that they somehow should know all about the modules you are taking, even though you have not told them. They could also feel unnecessarily excluded, worrying about how you are settling in and not liking to ask.

The problem here is straightforward: you might be cutting off a vital source of support without even realising it until it is too late. When you come to choose modules for next year and want some advice, or when you are feeling lonely or have run short of money, your family can help most effectively if they know what is happening to some extent. I am not suggesting this needs to be lengthy phone calls or daily emails, but making a conscious effort every couple of weeks to offer friends and family some detail of what you are studying, and telling them explicitly how you are feeling, rather than leaving them to guess, can avoid this potential problem completely.

Put a note in your diary!

Refreshers Week – does this exist for you?

Depending on the structure of your terms/semesters you may be offered a week in which you can catch your breath. This might be called a reading week, a study period, an enhancement break, or any other of many such names – one of the most catchy being perhaps 'Refreshers Week'. In this week (it is usually just a week) your university might offer extra sessions, often carrying no credit but helping to support your study.

Top tip

You need not be caught out by all of these different names being offered for essentially the same thing. Your Students' Union is bound to be involved, so just go along and ask about it there, or check out the Students' Union website or social media accounts.

Think strategically here. You have already been through Freshers' (or Welcome) Week, so you need to make a decision about how involved to become in this centrally organised study break. You might find that some of the sessions on offer would be of real value to you, but you might also believe that going home for part of the week to take a break and study quietly might work better than staying on campus all week. You might be keen to join some new clubs, or to take part in sporting competitions; there might be some interesting talks on offer that could help you in your study. In short, universities might let students decide how they manage this week, or they might make a huge effort to offer you support with a long-term impact. Planning ahead will save this from being a wasted week.

Take a step back – what do you need out of this week?

Reading lists – how useful might they be?

Within a week or so of your first term you will be familiar with reading lists and how they work on your modules. Some academics take time to organise and annotate reading lists for their modules/courses so that students are guided gently through them. Others believe that it is up to students to work out which resources to prioritise in their reading. Whichever approach your lecturers take, reading lists will become the backbone of what you do.

Top tip

> If you have half an hour, take a look through reading lists for modules that you might like to choose next term or next year. If they are online, this will be easy. If they are not, a quick trip to the administration or student support office should secure them for you. You will not want to spend long on this, and you will know that reading lists can change from year to year, but a brief perusal early on in the year will help you to start mulling over your next set of study options.

Increasingly, reading lists are online, and this gives you an advantage, as you can simply click through to online resources such as journals and websites, and entire book texts can also be found online. This does not make hard copy books and journals irrelevant – they have their place and it is an important one – but online reading lists do challenge you to explore.

If, up until now, you have only looked at printed material that feels familiar to you (books and websites, perhaps) at some point during your first year it makes sense to explore a little further. Journal articles are a quick way to extract vital information to support your arguments in assignments, whilst image banks, podcasts and online artefact archives can bring your subject to life for you. There is no need to waste time trying to work out how to find the best sources in the most efficient way: librarians love nothing more than showing off these resources to students. An hour with a librarian will probably save you days of stress in the future.

Book an appointment with a librarian!

Your Students' Union – what could it offer you?

In your first few weeks at university you might be forgiven for thinking that all the Students' Union does is run some clubs and societies and offer students a social life. In reality, this is only one aspect of how Students' Unions operate in most universities. There are members involved in student representation, usually at the highest level, so your Students' Union officers will be speaking on your behalf, for example, about how the curriculum is designed, how students' work is assessed and how terms should be structured.

Your Students' Union will also be offering advice on issues that might touch your life every day: opening hours of libraries, the rights of students, student finance and wellbeing, working against discrimination at all levels. Many Students' Unions run a newspaper or radio/TV station, as well as offering some training to students (especially in study and career skills, and in wellbeing).

Top tip

Student newspapers are very popular. So many students want to work on them that it would be worth your while to have a niche in mind if you try to volunteer as a writer. You might, for example, be better suited to editing or scheduling, or you might have an idea for a new type of article that has not been tried before. If you still struggle to gain a place on the newspaper, approach your department: there might be the chance to write and publish a department newsletter instead.

So, a Students' Union is a hardworking and powerful part of your university. You might never become involved in its work, but it does open up some interesting opportunities for students. It will also be easier for you to tap into the help it offers if you have taken some time earlier on to browse around the website. You could also talk to students in the Students' Union offices – these offices are usually designed to be open to anyone who just wants to drop in, but they are not always easy to find, so you might have to search around.

Walk into your Students' Union offices and say hello!

Study advice and support – are there online courses?

Your first contact with study advice in your university was likely to have been either before you came to campus (because you have pre-existing needs that had to be met) or during your first week (when you learned about what support was available and maybe attended a couple of study support sessions). It is perhaps not surprising that the majority of students tend to put study support to the back of their minds after this, unless they have an immediate need that they recognise and that is putting a barrier in their learning. Even then, students often turn first to their tutors or seminar leaders, or look for advice on their department's website or a module VLE.

In the early days, this would be a reasonable approach, but once you feel more established, find out what is on offer to help you make the best use of the time and effort you are putting into your course. It can be difficult to find time to attend courses, but online courses and advice sites are usually available. Students often find it easier to use these when they are at home, over a vacation or in a break in scheduled study during a term. That way, you know that you are not just managing, but setting yourself up for an easier and more successful time ahead.

Schedule time for a study support course!

INSIDER
HINT

Never, ever pay for an externally provided course online unless you are certain that you need it, and absolutely sure that it is not available through your university (either the exact course you have already found or something that will serve the same purpose). It is frustrating to see how many of my students have paid over the years for courses that are available for free on a part of the university website that they overlooked.

Student/campus cards – what more can they do?

You know by now that your student identification card (or whatever it is called at your university) offers you access to buildings, or is used to register your attendance at lectures, or might double as a library card or a membership card for your Students' Union. It might also be a cashless card for purchases on campus, but it can do more for you financially than that.

Not all Students' Union cards necessarily denote affiliation to the National Union of Students, and not all student cards require affiliation to any political body. Indeed, some universities run a student society that has no purpose other than to represent the students, socially and academically, in that university. This may not matter to you at all, but you might want to know exactly what your student card represents.

Your student card comes with a plethora of discounts, some of which are not obvious when you first arrive at university. Your Students' Union (and the National Students' Union – the NUS) will be lobbying hard for discounts all the time, so more are added every year, and things that did not interest you a few months ago might now appeal.

Every three months, find out what your student card could offer you.

Clubs and societies – where did they go?

University clubs and societies can go very quiet once term begins; either they have recruited new members and are focusing on activities to keep them, or they failed to recruit and have folded. Simultaneously, new clubs and societies will be forming as a result of student demand, and this is true both of groups organised by the Students' Union and those supported by your department.

You might also have overlooked, in the rush to get settled, some groups that are nationally organised. There are also groups that only exist for limited periods (such as reading groups or independent study groups for a module, or groups of students planning a trip abroad). These are often advertised in emails, which you may have ignored because you receive so many emails and these few did not seem relevant to you.

Academics sometimes enjoy helping to set up departmental or university groups of students, because they can see how helpful they are, both to students in their university lives, and to academics who would like their students to take the lead in some of their learning. If you wish that there was a film viewing group for your module or course, or you would like to join a reading group to help with your wider reading, or you know that a revision group is going to be essential to your success later on, approach some academics to see if they could help to set it up and publicise it for you.

If you are not the sort of person who much enjoys organised group activities, you might not rush at the chance to get involved in them. It is more likely that you will think through their value to you in other ways than the purely social, and make your decision based on that.

Make a firm plan – which group will you join, or abandon, and why?

If you enjoy groups and feel that you have time to join more, or you are disappointed in the groups you joined at the outset and want a change, the weeks just before or after the winter vacation are a good time to do some research on what is available.

Social study spaces – when should you use them?

We all tend to be creatures of habit, to a greater or lesser extent, and this can be advantageous. If you know that you work better on your own, you will tend to do that as much as you can; if you prefer to work in a library, resource centre, department study room or similar social learning space, you might be happy with that arrangement. However, it could be useful to try switching your pattern every so often. Research shows that a change in environment can be helpful, particularly for brief periods every now and then. So, a Friday afternoon spent in a social learning space when you are used to working alone in your room might offer a helpful change of scene, whilst an occasional study weekend in your room could see you plough through vast amounts of work.

Top tip

Social learning spaces are called that for good reason. There is an expectation that you will meet other students there and talk, for at least some of your time there, about your studying, and life at university more generally. This might be the space where you can work on a group presentation within the comfort of familiar surroundings, or where you might find a fellow seminar student who you have not talked to before.

The other benefit of social learning spaces is that they are often open long hours – sometimes they offer twenty-four-hour-a-day access. This is in recognition of a variety of student needs, but it is also a hint to students. It is only when you have been at university for a few weeks or months that you can reliably analyse when you work best. Use your library to experiment. If you go there at 9 p.m. or at 7 a.m., even though you would never normally work at those times, you could be

Whoever said you could not work brilliantly at midnight, or 6 a.m.?

encouraged to find that there are other students there and you might be delighted to find that there is much more space – this could become a very effective study time for you.

Socialising – is it helping or hindering your efforts?

This guide is not designed to go much beyond your studying life at university, but there are two aspects of your social life that might impinge negatively on your studying, so they are worth mentioning here.

Your hall of residence or other student accommodation will have been arranged for your first year before you started your course, but the second year of your course might leave you open to the confusions – and the pleasures – of finding your own accommodation with friends. Even if you are offered a second year in halls, you might still want to make changes to exactly where you live within them. It is amazing how early plans for this move begin. I have seen my students discussing their plans before they have even reached the winter vacation, so you might want to be thinking about this earlier than you might have expected. Students worrying about their accommodation hinders their studying, some-times for months, so making early preparations makes sense.

INSIDER HINT

I have seen all sorts of different living arrangements being organised by my students, and, overall, those that seem to have the most beneficial effect on studying are arrangements where the students who share accommodation are friendly with each other, but not close friends. This seems to offer space to grow and change, and explore new options, with people you like around you.

The second aspect of socialising that can have a severe impact on studying is social media. We have all heard horror stories about online bullying and people living their lives through the bubble of their social media image, but from the point of view of studying the main threat from social media is the sheer amount of time it swallows up in your day. You are also likely to receive multiple 'virtue signals' on social media – students who appear to be working hard and succeeding, which only serves to make you feel worse about your own social media distraction time.

You may not want to take the radical step of retiring altogether from social media, as I have seen some students do, but you can limit your time on there. Giving yourself certain times of the day when you refuse to look at social media seems to have a limited effect: you feel teased to go on there as soon as you have told yourself you should not do it. Instead, try to avoid social media when you are undertaking a specific task (I will not look at social media until I have finished making notes on this book or until I have completed this essay). This approach seems to work better for most students.

Decide how much control you need to take over social media, and get help from your university support services if you need it.

Modules – what next?

As soon as the relief of finally choosing your modules wears off, you begin to evaluate. Did you make the right choice? Do you like this way of working? Is this subject area all that you hoped it would be? Do you think the assessment will allow you to shine?

All the time you are learning more about yourself and how you work best, and this will help you to start thinking about next year's modules. You will have months to go before you have to make a formal choice about modules for your second year, but you will not want to miss the chance to explore them in more depth, especially once you realise that the chance is fleeting and could easily pass you by. However much information is offered online or through reading lists about a module, there is little better than sitting in on a couple of the lectures for that module to get a good sense of whether it might appeal to you.

Top tip

If the course or module you are interested in is large, with lectures to dozens of students, there is no need to ask permission to attend: you could just turn up and listen. Of course, if you would like to talk to the lecturer in more detail, perhaps to check whether there are any major changes to the module being planned, you might email first and then see the lecturer straight after the lecture to share your interest and ask any question you have.

You will not base your choice entirely on attending just two or three lectures, but it is likely to have quite a significant impact on your decision making.

Your compulsory modules, if you have any, will have been designed to cover the essentials for your first year; beyond that, you can usually range quite freely. You might have selected your first year modules with an eye to the challenges of the second year, perhaps even with the shape of your degree overall in your thinking, but most students tend to focus just on what appeals to them most in their first batch of optional modules. There is space during this first year to think forward a little, to see how your first and second year modules might link together.

Once you have settled into the first year and feel that you have a good idea of what each of your modules is offering, and demanding of you, take some time to extend your thinking into second year modules.

Top tip

Thinking ahead can be a pleasure, but some solitary thinking at this point can be advantageous. Talking to groups of friends about future module choices can leave you swept up in the moment as they all express strong opinions, and it is easy to find yourself registered on a module that is not really your choice. Taking time to think about future options now can avoid this problem: you will already have formulated some ideas before the discussions begin.

Checklist – thinking forward on modules

✓ Are there subject areas that you want to jettison in your second year?

✓ Is there a subject area that you love so much that you would like to extend your knowledge through an advanced module in that area next year?

✓ If you tried to choose modules that supported each other and linked together, how well has that worked?

✓ If you chose disparate modules with very few strong links, did you enjoy that sense of ranging widely in your degree subject?

✓ Are there any problematic gaps in your knowledge that are becoming obvious and that you feel you need to fill through your second year modules?

✓ Are there any assessment tasks that you really enjoy, or in which you excel?

✓ Thinking towards a final dissertation, or extended project if you have one, are there any modules that might help you in this, or that you should avoid so as not to risk assessment overlap?

✓ Does any particular lecturer's style really suit the way you like to think about and approach a topic? Is that lecturer teaching on a module next year that appeals to you?

✓ If you are covering a very wide base this year, are you being asked to specialise next year? If you are, which area of your degree is calling to you most loudly?

I am not suggesting that you make firm decisions now about what modules you will take next year, but making some provisional choices can be useful. It would allow you to talk to your personal tutor and other advisors about how the modules might work for you. It would also, just as importantly, give you the chance to see links across modules and towards the future.

CAREER
MOMENT

Making choices for your second year will be based on what interests you. If you are making strategic decisions you are also likely to be thinking about how your choices affect your workload or your assessment marks. Give a moment, though, to thinking about the impact your second year module choices could have upon your career. Does your degree course require you to specialise early? What careers might your choices lead you towards? If you are planning a career that links only tangentially to your degree subject, or if you have no idea yet what your career might look like, you will be able to move ahead without too much concern: your enthusiasm for an area, and the checklist above, will steer you in your module choices.

Slowing down – will you get the chance?

The first year in many degrees is designed to keep students hard at work throughout the entire year, with teaching and term-time assessment closely followed by batches of exams. The whole year whizzes by and, almost before you know it, *Second year planning could start now!*
the summer vacation has arrived. Some students enjoy this approach. They made all the big decisions in the first weeks of the academic year, and then all they had to do was knuckle down and work hard.

However, many term schedules offer lulls in activity, a week when you can pause, review your progress and recharge your energy. This might be a formal study/reading/enhancement week (see earlier in this chapter) or a slower week that is not centrally designed into every student's timetable but that crops up for your individual selection of modules.

This slightly less pressured time in your study year tends to come at the end or at the beginning of terms, and academics often have no idea that it is happening. They know, for example, that they are giving the students on their module an easier time in the week or so before an assignment is due in, or at a point in the term when they require independent research and study, but they might not think beyond this. This means that they have no clear sense that their colleagues have made similar choices in the other modules you happen to be taking. This means that it will be up to you to judge whether and when there is a lull coming up (which is why students often miss the chance it offers, because nobody has told them to expect it).

It may be that you are too tired to want to do more than take this lull gratefully and catch up on your rest, and this would be a reasonable choice to make if you have had a hugely busy and challenging term. This could work to your advantage, giving you some mental breathing space before the next set of challenges. It could also disadvantage you, though. If you have a set of exams coming up very soon after the end of the teaching year, or you have a series of class tests in the last couple of weeks of term, you will want to be prepared, so you might want to use this lull more industriously.

You will not need to throw yourself into a full-on revision schedule in this small lull, but you could undertake some less taxing activities for which you would be grateful to yourself later on. You will probably not want – or have time – to carry out all of the tasks in this checklist, but you can choose those that appeal to you and will be most useful.

Checklist – using a lull in study time

✓ Have you mastered the library system?

✓ Have you tried EndNote or EverNote, or similar study skills packages?

✓ Do your notes need tidying?

✓ If you recorded any lectures, would now be the time to work through those recordings?

✓ Are there any study skills courses you could attend in person or take online?

✓ Could you reduce even a portion of your notes to a much briefer set of notes – perhaps just a series of bullet point lists of key information – to save you revision time later?

✓ Are you sure that you know every assessment task that is coming up between now and the end of the year?

✓ If there is any reading you promised yourself you would do some time ago, could you do it now?

✓ Are there any placement opportunities in your department or university that you would like to explore at this stage?

✓ Now that you know what you are doing, is there anything that is taking up too much of your time without much benefit?

Free training – what is out there?

If you have not yet had the chance to take on any additional training at university, this will not matter at all, but it could be an expensive oversight if you do not find out what might be available to you for free. This might be a specialist course that is not required but could help you hugely in your modules or future life (a basic introduction to a classical language, an additional support course in sociology, a one-day presentation skills course). It might also be career related (such as creating a CV, or trying out a psychometric evaluation test).

Assess your situation – consolidate and drop where you need to!

More specifically, if you are not sure about what might be on offer for you, you could ask your personal tutor. Beyond this, go to your student support centre or resource centre and ask where to look: be ready to trawl widely, as information on courses is not always held in one location.

> ### CAREER MOMENT

The most expensive time for training is often when students graduate and realise, too late, that they will be required to use data analysis software, or even quite basic IT such as spreadsheets. Being able to use social media can give the illusion that you have skills in technology, but this is often not the case. It is surprising how many students stick to basic packages, and have very little experience of cloud-based software or the more advanced professional software they might encounter in their professional lives.

Extending your reach is likely to be something for which you are aiming: reading this book suggests that you want to do well at university and beyond. That is why I want to take some time with you now, at the end of the first part of this guide, to think about what all of this activity means for your job prospects, and how you can capture all that you have done so far, ready to present yourself to the career marketplace in future.

Degrees can be expensive – save yourself future expense where you can!

8

What graduate attributes have you now acquired?

Looking back – what have you achieved?

It can be difficult to grasp, at first glance, just how much you have achieved in the first stages of a degree course, so it is helpful to take stock. When you use this chapter will depend on how much progress you feel you have made. As you are now at the end of the part of this guide entitled 'Getting Started', I feel safe in assuming that you have worked through the material so far (and probably returned to it a few times, as things progressed) and that you feel confident in much of what you are doing. If you do not yet feel ready to consolidate your progress by identifying your graduate attributes, you could just skim read this chapter and return to it later.

There is no need to worry if you do not yet feel that you have mastered university life in all its aspects, or that you are studying at your absolute best. You have plenty of time to develop and explore your strengths – that is what university is all about. That being accepted, making a note now of how well you are doing will not only boost your confidence, it will also direct your next steps.

Although I have listed some graduate attributes and some transferable skills for you during this first part of the guide, now is a good time to look more closely at what they mean.

Top tip

You do not have to reflect on these issues by yourself. Although there is guidance here to help you assess where you are and how best to move forward, your Careers Service is there to help you. At university it will be a free service, offering knowledge of the graduate job market both at home and abroad and a wealth of experience and expertise to help you make best use of your time at university as you consider the career marketplace.

Transferable skills

These are fairly straightforward – they are things that you can do in one setting that can be transferred to another setting. In your case, they are the things you have learnt to do, in your studying but also from any other area of your life, which an employer would want an employee to be able to do.

Graduate attributes

These are more complicated – they are part of who you are. They encompass the approach you tend to take to challenges and situations and the attitude you take when you are asked to achieve something; they also include personal qualities that you will have developed over time, such as your ability to prioritise and analyse, as well as determination, team playing and attention to detail.

Graduate attributes will have developed as a result of your time at university, but this does not mean that they are only applicable to careers that link directly to your degree subject. There is debate around how relevant all of your experiences at university are to your graduate attributes (experiences such as work placements, or leading a society, or undertaking extracurricular professional training) but, for the purposes of this guide, I will be including every experience you have at university as moulding you into a graduate with an impressive set of graduate attributes.

Turning skills and attributes into benefits

Transferable skills can only benefit an employer to any great extent if your personal qualities (part of your graduate attributes) enable you to be particularly good at something. If this aptitude comes together with an enthusiasm for using a set of skills, then you have something powerful to offer to an employer.

This has to be more than a set of words on a CV, though; you need also to be able to demonstrate that your skills and attributes will come together to offer a quantifiable benefit to an employer. Sometimes this can be done by demonstrating that you have conferred a similar benefit elsewhere (which is where any work experience comes in handy) and sometimes you demonstrate that you understand what benefit is being sought, and that you are the right type of person, with the right set of skills, to offer that benefit.

Formula 1:

A set of skills + graduate attributes that allow me to excel in those skills = benefits

Your success is going to rely on being able to demonstrate each aspect of this equation, and we will return to it later in this book; some examples will help to keep it clear in your mind:

Example 1:

IT competence in spreadsheets (skill) + enjoying attention to detail (graduate attribute) = accurate and useful data analysis (benefit)

Of course, this only works if you actually find giving attention to detail satisfying. If you have had to master it for your course but it was the least exciting aspect of the work from your perspective, then you probably want to move away from spreadsheets in your future career.

One of the most challenging aspects of university life is learning what you *do not* want to do for the rest of your life. You may be used to family, friends and teachers telling you that you are good at something, but your time at university gives you the opportunity to decide whether you enjoy something enough to want to spend the rest of your working life doing it. You may also enjoy so many different aspects of life and your skill set that you do not anticipate just having one job role or career sector in your lifetime. If you have no real passion for something, it can be difficult to develop beyond a certain level, and you may find yourself in a career that you do not enjoy as much as you had hoped and expected. Moving on, we can consider an example for a student who enjoys one aspect of study life:

Example 2:

Excellent presentations (skill) + leadership qualities (graduate attribute) = effective leadership of a team (benefit)

This might look straightforward, but it only works if you can prove to an employer that you can bring this benefit, so now you need to add another factor to your equation:

Formula 2:

A set of skills that I enjoy using + graduate attributes that allow me to excel in those skills + evidence/proof = benefits that I can demonstrate

Looking at how this might work will make this clearer:

Example 3:

Excellent presentations (skill) + leadership qualities (graduate attribute) = effective leadership of a seminar team presentation (evidence/proof) = top mark awarded (benefit)

This would look impressive on a CV, and you have certainly demonstrated that your skills and attributes have produced a benefit, but you might also be able to push this further by the time you graduate. You might be able to map your achievements far more firmly onto benefits that you know an employer needs:

Formula 3:

A set of skills that I enjoy using + graduate attributes that allow me to excel in those skills + evidence/proof = benefits that I can demonstrate and that relate directly to my chosen employer.

The formula is now complete, so we can see how it might work in action for you:

Example 4:

Excellent presentations (skill) + leadership qualities (graduate attribute) = effective leadership of a study trip to Sweden = participant numbers doubled on the previous year (benefit to an employer)

This would be persuasive to an employer – as long, of course, as you know that your target employers need this benefit. If they are not asking for an employee who can enthuse others in order to increase participation in a scheme, you might be looking for other evidence or examples.

This is all positive, as long as you can prove, clearly and directly, a benefit that a potential employer wants to derive from employing you. However, if this is not possible, there is no need to despair. You can show that you have recognised and understood that an employer would be hoping to gain a particular benefit from employing you, and that it is plausible to assume that you would be able to deliver this benefit. So, in the example above, if your target employer is looking for someone to act as a section lead and motivate a sales team, you would be able to extend your example to show not just that you recognise this, but that the employer can be confident that you can deliver:

Example 5:

Excellent presentations (skill) + leadership qualities (graduate attribute) = effective leadership of a study trip to Sweden = participant numbers doubled on the previous year because students were excited by the way the trip was presented to them (benefit to an employer)

Although this is fundamentally the same example, here you are making it very easy for your employer to see how a piece of evidence apparently unrelated to that employer's needs is actually highly relevant. By helping the employer to make that link, you are doing all of the hard work and making it easy for the employer to choose you.

The formulae I have offered you so far show the skills as the first variable; there might be times when your research into an employer or a position suggests that showing off a graduate attribute first might support your efforts better. If an employer is looking for a strong leader for an archaeological dig that is open to volunteers and students alike, you might choose to flip the formula:

Formula 4:

Graduate attributes that allow me to excel in certain skills + a set of skills that I therefore enjoy using + evidence/proof = benefits that I can demonstrate and that relate directly to my chosen employer

By using this flipped formula you could offer several examples that all link back to one aspect of a role, and in which you can show a series of benefits. In the examples I give below I am assuming that the student is targeting an employer who is looking for a candidate who can introduce new working practices into a small business team:

Example 6:

Team player (graduate attribute) + excellent presentations (skill) = successful launch of new range in a retail outlet, leading to increased sales (benefit)

Example 7:

Team player (graduate attribute) + excellent time management (skill) = efficient management of a study retreat for sixteen sixth form students (benefit)

Example 8:

Team player (graduate attribute) + excellent analytical abilities (skill) = prompt delivery of curriculum analysis student study report, leading to change in the design of assessment with no student or staff complaints (benefit)

If you choose to work in this way (and it will all depend on what you are offering and the role/organisation for which you are aiming) you can be easier on yourself in terms of evidence. Some of your evidence (in examples six and eight) will demonstrate a benefit that maps directly onto the needs of the employer, but some (in example seven) will be of a more general nature, relating back to an achievement of which you are especially proud, rather than linking directly to the employer. This might be something, as in example seven, that you hope to be able to discuss at an interview.

You will also notice that I have sneaked a 'real world' example in here. The student is using experience from some retail vacation work to prove a benefit to this potential employer. Later in this guide we will consider in more detail how any work experience you have had fits into your career plans, but it is important to recognise that you possess more than just graduate attributes. You are also likely to have professional attributes that have been acquired through other activities in your life, such as vacation work, or professional placements, or being involved in organisations away from your university. Nothing you have done need be wasted as you pursue your perfect career.

This is all about research – on yourself, so that you know what you are happy to offer and how you might continue to develop and excel in future, and research on an employer to know exactly what benefits will most appeal. This research might not need to be very detailed at this stage of your journey but getting to grips with the idea of skills, attributes and benefits as a career trio will help to guide your steps now.

Top tip

You can only think about the person you want to be in your future career if you are prepared to let go, just a little, of the person you have always been expected to be. This might be difficult for you, and confusing (even painful) for your family, but it is important. Parents often tell me that they knew their child was going to be, say, a teacher, from the age of eight, and they are then amazed to find that their graduate child has decided to become a change process manager. They will still be proud, naturally, but they might need help with understanding what this new career is, and you might need help moving away from a present path into one that will make you far happier.

Recognising your value

You will notice that the skills and examples I have used here might be specific to your degree, but they could also have arisen from a degree in another subject. They will also map onto a whole series of careers, many of which will not be related in terms of content to your degree subject, but which will be open to you because your skills are transferable, whatever your career choices.

This can be the most difficult reality for many undergraduates to believe: employers need the skills you have, and they will pay dividends for the graduate attributes you have acquired, and many will have very little need to concern themselves with the specifics of your degree subject area.

This is good news – in fact it could not be better news for you. Students who come to a subject such as English Literature often start their degree course sure that they will go into what they think of as the only career paths to follow with that degree: teaching, publishing, marketing and journalism are favourites with incoming students. In fact, many of the graduates from this degree will enter banking, business or politics, or will undertake a law conversion course and become lawyers.

This move away from 'traditional' careers expectations does not arise because students cannot make up their minds about what they want to do. It is because they come to realise that a startlingly wide variety of employers value what they have to offer, and that their career options are far more diverse than they ever imagined. When you come to think about it, it makes perfect sense. To succeed in banking you need some mathematical aptitude, of course, but it is just as important to be able to grasp complex ideas around financial systems and human responses to those systems, to lead teams of people who have to make difficult decisions and to talk to people about money, having analysed the available data. This sounds very like an English Literature graduate to any academic who has taught one.

Finding your graduate attributes and skills

Once you begin to consider the skills you are gaining and the graduate attributes that you are acquiring, you might quickly be overwhelmed. You will realise that you have a wide skills base even at this relatively early stage of your degree, and you have developed graduate attributes almost without noticing that this is happening to you. Let me offer you just a few examples of what a couple of commonplace university situations might produce in terms of skills and attributes:

Checklist – skills and graduate attributes from lab work

From a laboratory session with a small team investigating the properties of a material, ready to report back to a study group, you could expect to be working on the following skills:

✓ understanding a detailed brief

✓ being aware of health and safety conditions

✓ working within specified lab hours

✓ acting as part of a small team to analyse the material

✓ making minute observations and recording them accurately

✓ producing a report and giving a group presentation on the results.

You are also potentially acquiring, to a greater or lesser extent, the following graduate attributes:

✓ attention to detail

✓ team playing

✓ time management

✓ presenting a persuasive argument.

As you probably notice from the earlier points in this chapter, the skills are degree specific, whereas the graduate attributes are not.

Another example will serve to show a similar pattern of achievement:

Checklist – skills and graduate attributes from a seminar

From a one-hour discussion on material unseen before the seminar, structured as a ten-minute analysis in pairs, following which each pair feeds back to the group, the following skills will be honed:

✓ working under time pressure to grasp the essentials of the material given to you

✓ analysing material effectively

✓ working with a partner

✓ articulating your ideas effectively.

The circumstances might differ from the lab work, and the exact nature of the skills you are acquiring might also alter slightly, but the graduate attributes remain the same:

✓   attention to detail

✓   team playing

✓   time management

✓   presenting a persuasive argument.

Being selective

The fact that you can pull out such important skills and positive graduate attributes from just a couple of examples from the many situations you will face at university (and, naturally, from any professional experience you are developing) leaves you with what might be an unexpected challenge. You no longer have to think in terms of *whether* you will gain transferable skills at university (you will) or *how* you can acquire graduate attributes (your course is designed to achieve this). Your challenge is to be selective.

Checklist – how to select skills and graduate attributes

You need to ask yourself the following questions if you are going to present your best and most effective face to the world:

✓   What skills do I enjoy using most?

✓   What skills would I rather downplay or jettison entirely in future?

✓   Which graduate attributes feel most valuable to the way I want to be?

✓   Which graduate attributes sit less comfortably with me?

✓   Of my many skills, which are my strongest?

✓   Where do I need to develop my skills further?

✓   If I could map my 'ideal future self' as a professional, what might that look like?

The easiest way to tackle this checklist is to work out where your skills and graduate attributes are coming from, and how strong they are, from several possible selections. Using a chart such as Figure 8.1 after a particular event might help:

Situation + skill (S) or graduate attribute (GA)	Strength of skill/attribute					
	1	2	3	4	5	6
Lecture – note taking (S)				✓		
Lecture – making connections (s)						✓
Lecture – time management (S)		✓				
Lecture – analysing material (S)					✓	
Lecture – preparation (S)	✓					
Lecture – attention to detail (GA)			✓			
Lecture – concentration and focus (GA)						✓
Lecture – team playing (GA)	✓					

Figure 8.1   An example of a skills checklist

This is a student who finds the business of lectures a bit cumbersome, often forgetting exactly when and where they are, and not preparing for them especially thoroughly. However, once in the lecture hall the student uses active learning sheets and finds it easy to focus on the task in hand, making useful connections and absorbing the material well. The lecturer asks students to work in pairs for brief, intense analysis of a situation at several points during each lecture, so the student puts this in the chart, but in this case there was only one chance to do this.

All of these skills and graduate attributes are available to every student, but each student will have a different pre-existing skill set, will have a different approach and set of preferences and personal qualities, and will be at a different point in their journey in developing graduate attributes.

Making charts such as this for a variety of your university everyday situations will help you to analyse where you are in your own journey. You need not restrict yourself to formal learning situations. If you are part of a club, or a study group, or you are working on a student project – all of these are situations that are adding to your impressive list of skills and attributes. You need not ignore your professional experiences, either. I have used similar charts with students as they decide between different possible types of vacation or part-time work. It can make a tremendous difference to know that you are not just earning money, but also boosting your skills set and putting into action your newly developing graduate attributes.

You might find it easier to make a judgement on where you are if you were to present the material in the form of a 'radar chart' (also sometimes called a 'web chart'). For the example above, it would look like this for the skills:

What graduate attributes have you now acquired?

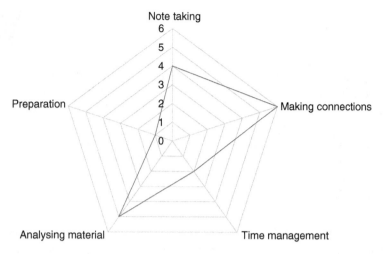

Figure 8.2 An example of a radar chart for skills

It would look like this for the graduate attributes (Figure 8.3):

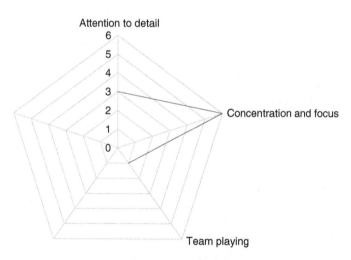

Figure 8.3 An example of a radar chart for graduate attributes

These examples are based on just one event: you might choose to produce charts such as this for a series of events. As you progress through your degree, this would give you a good guide as to where you excel, and can prove it to an employer, and where you need more development, assuming that the skill or graduate attribute in question is one that you really want to use in the future, or that you believe you will need from time to time in your ideal career.

INSIER
HINT

I keep stressing this, but it bears repeating. I have seen so many of my students trying to develop every possible skill to the highest degree in order to secure what they perceive to be a good job, but they are overlooking the logic. If you hone a skill that will make up a large proportion of your target career, but you really do not enjoy using it, you had better rethink – is it really the right career for you? If you excel in a skill that does not particularly appeal to you but you know that it will only form a small part of your work life, that would be a far better position to be in, and will lead you down a more satisfying career path.

As we reach the end of this interlude of looking back, you would be forgiven for feeling a bit rushed. So far, we have been thinking together about university firsts – your first seminar, lecture, module choices and so on. Now we seem to be jumping ahead to your career moves after graduation. There is no need to worry.

I have introduced these ideas to you early in your time at university because that is where they most properly sit. If you leave it until your final year to think about what skills and attributes you have, and what you might need, you will join the thousands of panicking students who struggle to achieve all they want to in their final year, before anxiously entering the career marketplace. You are clearly not going to be in that category. Using this guide will ensure that you think about these matters early and so can plan and make preparations for your perfect career as an integral part of your university life – so much easier, and so much more effective.

Looking forward – what next?

If you have no very clear idea of your future career in the early stages of your time at university that is not a bad place to be. If you have a sure idea of your career path, you might need to keep an open mind – your degree experience might confirm it, but it could turn it on its head. That is one of the purposes of university. It gives you the chance to interrogate all of your existing ideas about yourself, who you are and who you want to be. It also gives you a fantastic opportunity to look around and see what else might be open to you.

Top tip

The ideal position to adopt during your first year at university is open to options, not too set on one career path, and keen to explore as you move forward.

Until this point, you may, or may not, have carried out research into a particular career or set of careers. You may, or may not, have had a job, and you may, or may not, have undertaken a professional placement or work experience. Whatever your position, you now have the chance to find out far more about the reality of a whole host of careers.

It is only at university that you are likely to be offered tangible evidence about potential career paths based on what past students on your course have actually done in their professional lives, as opposed to national or more general statistics. It is also your first opportunity to hear the details of those graduates' career stories. By finding out more about the graduate career destinations of people who have completed your course, you will be getting a proper sense of what is open to you. You will also, I hope, feel more adventurous about breaking moulds and trying out whole new career paths that have not been tried before.

INSIDER HINT

Many university departments have set up schemes that allow you to hear more about the career journeys of their graduates and, in many cases, to talk to those successful professionals. In my own case, one of my English Literature students ended up being a scuba diving instructor in the Maldives. She told me that talking in seminars and getting her point across was the perfect training for an instructor. Just the fact that she did this has inspired several more students to think far more widely about their career options.

The other facet of university life that might be crucial to your successful career is the new friendship groups that you are making. It is not unusual to find that graduates have no idea what their friends, relations and wider friendship group from home do for a living, yet these are the very stories that you want to hear. You also need to know why your fellow students have chosen to pursue particular career paths in the future – what attracted them? What research have they done? Do they have contacts in that area, professionals you might talk to or shadow? Do they know of anywhere where you might be able to undertake a placement or professional internship?

When I see students working together on their careers with this type of networking I am always delighted to learn how fruitful it is. You are all at a stage of your lives where friends and relations are keen to help get you – and your fellow students – on the right career path. You could not find a better time to get help.

Top tip

> You cannot leave this type of networking to chance. Arrange with your fellow students for a group of you to talk about what you all know about different careers, and what insider information or contacts you might be able to use.

The idea of working with a group of friends you trust to see if you can network and help each other does not remove the need to find some solid and useful information on career options, and this is where your university's Careers Service will be able to help. You will need to decide, though, just how much help you need, and of what type.

There are two types of enquiry you are likely to make at your Careers Service in the early stages of your career: how can you get a part-time or vacation job, and what career might you pursue long term? There is another question that is not often asked, but should be: How might the part-time work I undertake link to my long-term career goals? More of that at the end of the next part of this guide.

If you walk into your Careers Service building and ask for some general help in thinking about careers, you will certainly be offered plenty of advice and information, but you could find it more useful to work out more precisely what you want. A trip to the Careers Service is a bit like a shopping trip in this sense: the more you plan in advance, the better the chances of getting exactly what you need. It is also like a shopping trip in another sense: if you leave yourself open to inspiration, you might find yourself pleasantly surprised.

Checklist – questions you might ask about part-time or vacation work

- ✓ Are there any student jobs available on campus?
- ✓ Are there any academic-related jobs that might be open to me, such as supporting an academic in research activity?
- ✓ Are external jobs advertised on campus? Online or on a board, or both?
- ✓ Who are the key employers for students in the area?
- ✓ Would a direct approach be useful?
- ✓ How do different types of contracts work? What safeguards should I look for?
- ✓ What type of job would best suit my study needs in terms of hours and other commitments?
- ✓ What type of job would call for my existing skills set?

✓ What guidance can I get with my CV?

✓ What jobs might help me to enhance a particular skill that I will need in future?

✓ Can you help me with practice aptitude tests?

✓ Can you give me some interview practice?

Checklist – questions you might ask about your long-term career goals

✓ Is there an employability scheme run by the university?

✓ Is it rigorous and certified?

✓ What other training is on offer?

✓ Do you offer work experience schemes, such as professional or academic placements?

✓ Do you administer psychometric tests?

✓ Can you work with me on my skills set and graduate attributes?

✓ Do you have information on the career paths of previous graduates from my degree?

✓ Can you give me an idea of what types of careers might be open to me?

✓ Do you run an employers' fair (a graduate recruitment event)?

✓ Can I just talk to you about my ideas so far, to see what you think?

You could take a two-stage approach to this. When you have some time, check out the Careers Service website to work out exactly what help is on offer, and also browse through other careers information sites in case you pick up some ideas there as to what you might do in future. Then visit your Careers Service to talk to an advisor about how you can move forward.

INSIDER
HINT

I have noticed that students often feel faintly guilty once they have made their first trip to the Careers Service, as if they believe that they should have done more in the past, or that they should focus continuously on their career from that point onward. Neither of these will be true. It is perfectly sensible to consider your career in short bursts every now and then during your degree. Indeed, many would argue that this is the best way to approach it, both in terms of enjoying the moment at university and also mulling over future possibilities without any sense of rush.

There is no reason at all why you should hesitate about engaging with the Careers Service, except perhaps for immediate pressure on your time. Even if you have no idea of what you want to do, and have no work experience, and have only the vaguest sense of your skill set, they will still be able and eager to help. Working through this guide will also mean that you have identified some of your skills and had some structured thinking time about what you want to do. If you plan your first trip to the Careers Service at a point when you know you will have a brief lull in your studying (maybe a mid-term study break or one of the natural lulls that can arise in any teaching term), you will be best placed to respond constructively and actively to what is being said.

Top tip

Always make an appointment with your Careers Service in the first instance. There might be brief drop-in sessions available, or limited help available at a reception desk, but you have prepared for this and need to make the most of it. If you time going to the Careers Service at the perfect point in your studies, and then find that you have to wait a further three weeks to get an appointment, you will be frustrated and will have missed the best moment.

This chapter may have been hard work for you. It fosters plenty of new thoughts about how you might go about finding the perfect career for you, and the chance to carry out some searching analysis on what you have to offer, what you might like to offer, and how you might improve that offering over the course of your degree.

You will not be able to do all of this overnight, so there is no need to feel too stressed. Just dart back to this chapter every now and then to see if there is anything you want to take from it. The skills and graduate attributes charts, for example, would be exhausting if you tried to produce one for every experience, all in one go. You might like to leave it until you have completed a whole project, to see how the project overall helped your development, rather than analysing each element, or you might want to analyse one situation at a time, every now and then.

You have plenty of time to develop in a way that is productive and targeted, and your work on considering where you want to be will allow you to use that time most effectively. Steady in your purpose, open to ideas and targeted in your efforts: these are the essential factors both in succeeding at university and in securing your perfect career.

EFFECTIVE STUDYING

As we move on to the second part of this guide, you and I know each other a little better. I have offered you some 'insider hints' so that you know something of my experiences as a lecturer, and the fact that you have reached this second part and are still keen to learn more shows me that you are willing to try out new ideas and determined to succeed.

In this part, we move up a level in terms of what you are aiming to achieve. We will revisit a few of the areas that have been touched on already, but the emphasis will be on how to maximise your success. This is no longer about hitting the ground running as soon as you arrive at university; it is about becoming the best student you can be, so that you can achieve your study goals and face the future with confidence.

Learning styles

I am introducing the idea of learning styles to you at the beginning of this part of the book because it might have a bearing on all of the activities described afterwards. There is much debate around learning styles and how much impact they have on student achievement, with some research suggesting that they should be abandoned as a useful way to categorise the learning process. There are also some discrepancies around how they are defined. Some academics would include learning styles in this section that I will not mention, and others would be keen to remove a style or two from this list.

None of this need concern us here, as long as this section is approached in the right spirit. If you find thinking about learning styles useful in deciding how you could approach certain tasks, then the time you spend reading through and thinking about them here will have been worth it.

If you do not already know your preferred learning style, and if my very brief explanation of how students with a particular learning style like to learn is not enough to help you decide which learning style is most applicable to you, it is simple to find out. If you type 'What is my learning style?' into an online search engine you will be faced with a nice array of quizzes and charts that show in more detail how a learning style might affect the way you like to learn. Ignore the fact that some of these sites will try to sell you things that you do not need; just have fun with the quizzes and see if you can find an approximate fit to how you like to learn.

It would be most unusual for any student to have just one learning style: this is all about preferences. Most of us tend towards liking to work in one or two of the ways described here, but we can function quite happily working in many different ways if the occasion demands it. It can also be fruitful to challenge yourself to work in a way that is outside your usual learning habits, as I suggest from time to time throughout. However, as this guide is all about making best use of your time and effort, if you do recognise yourself as having a marked preference for a learning style, you are in a good position to adapt your learning environment and activities so that you achieve the best results for you.

For each of the styles I have chosen to list, I will give you an idea of how you like to learn, and the impact that this might have on some of the situations you will face as a student. In the following chapters I will refer to the effect of learning styles from time to time, with suggestions as to how you can optimise your performance.

Although you might be sure of your most preferred way of learning, you would still benefit from reading through each of these lists. The advice offered to overcome hurdles (the arrows show you these) have been given for particular types of learner but they can, from time to time, be useful to any learner.

→ If your style is **aural** you will enjoy listening to things being explained to you and you might prefer to say things out loud in order to hear if they make sense to you.

Checklist – for the aural preference student

☺ In **personal tutorials**, you will find it reassuring to talk through your issues.

☹ You might need to ask the same query of several people so as to confirm answers.

o   This need not be a problem, but reminding yourself to make a note will help.

☺ You will enjoy listening in **lectures** and find it easy to grasp what is being said.

☹ You can become so engrossed that you forget to make detailed notes.

   o   Use the VLE material that supports each lecture as a supplement.

☺ You will love **seminars** and really enjoy the way they allow you to express yourself.

☹ You sometimes forget to notice that you are monopolising the time and space.

   o   Make notes in each seminar – that way, you have to take a small speech break.

☺ You will find **lab work** in groups a pleasure because you can talk through your progress.

☹ If there is nobody in the room to talk through instructions, you might find it tedious.

   o   Finding a regular lab partner early on will be helpful in all sorts of ways.

☺ You will find it useful to talk through your **reading list** requirements with a librarian.

☹ You might find a huge reading list daunting.

   o   Give yourself a set amount of time, not too long, for an initial assessment.

☺ You will find **notes** software that allows you to capture your spoken thoughts a great help.

☹ You can find the **notes** that you create that way overwhelming.

   o   Make a date every three days to ruthlessly prune what you have.

☺ **Presentations** will offer you an excellent chance to excel in what you do.

☹ You might struggle to stick to the time and the topic.

   o   Use prompt cards to tell you when you should be halfway through.

☺ You will find **study groups** highly energising.

☹ You might be tempted to spend too long socialising rather than working alone.

   o   Ask everyone to be clear about what they want to achieve during each session.

→ If you are a **kinaesthetic** learner, you like to be active, even in a small way, as you learn. You use movement and your body to reinforce the learning process.

Checklist – for the kinaesthetic preference student

☺ You will find **personal tutorials** helpful, as long as they are not too long.

☹ Group personal tutorials might feel a little restrictive to you.

    o   Try working a small piece of modelling clay or adhesive putty as you listen.

☺ You will benefit most from **lectures** that incorporate brief pair discussions or breaks.

☹ You might struggle to listen attentively in lectures that do not allow for any activity.

    o   Set up an active learning sheet before the lecture: filling out sections can inspire.

☺ You will find the physical space in **seminars**, allowing for some movement, helpful.

☹ You might feel inhibited by those around you.

    o   Most kinaesthetic learners have found small, unobtrusive movements that are hardly noticeable can help them to focus, such as rolling a pencil.

☺ You will find **lab work** in groups a pleasure because you can move around and explain.

☹ You might be disappointed when you formally present your findings on paper.

    o   Plan in detail, so that the writing becomes a less laborious task.

☺ You will probably keep your **reading list** handy on a mobile device.

☹ Sitting still for ages looking through a reading list might bore you.

    o   Alternate your reading lists tasks between assessing, sifting, viewing and reading.

☺ Making **notes** will not worry you, as you can take short breaks and move about.

☹ The notes you create need to make sense to you, so traditional methods might not work.

    o   If anything is unclear, check online for demonstrations and examples.

☺ However nervous you might be, you know that **presentations** allow you to shine.

☹ Explaining yourself this way works well, but you might forget to reference the slides.

    o   If you include plenty of examples you are more likely to want to use the slides.

☺ You will find **study groups** useful, especially as they explore new ideas.

☹ You might be exhausted at the end of a study group session.

    o   Ask people to demonstrate an idea if they can, so that you take it in swiftly.

→ If you have a preference for **visual** learning, images and diagrams help you to understand and absorb information. Information you have heard might not always stick with you, but you can glance at a plan and use it quickly and effectively.

Checklist – for the visual preference student

☺ In your induction meetings with your **personal tutor** you will find the handouts and diagrams helpful.

☹ A chat with your personal tutor might leave you anxious because it feels so ephemeral.

- o Record each meeting in whatever way works best for you (perhaps a flow chart to show your next steps, or a visual plan of your next essay) and share it with your tutor by email.

☺ You will take copious notes in **lectures**, often in the form of diagrams or mind maps, happy that you have captured the material ready for later.

☹ You might find yourself overwhelmed with too many notes, because you prefer to keep a visual record in every learning situation.

- o Give yourself time each week to look through your notes and, where you can, reduce them down to manageable visual aids.

☺ **Seminars** will give you the chance to capture extra learning.

☹ If the discussion moves fast, you might worry that you are not recording enough.

- o Mind mapping is a diagrammatic way to capture seminars quickly and without needing to take time-consuming notes.

☺ You will be happy with **lab work**, especially if you record your progress in a flow chart or similar form.

☹ You will want clear instructions and will find it stressful to be told too briefly what is expected of you.

- o Explore the VLE for any diagrammatic instructions before your lab session, and give yourself regular quiet time to think through what you are learning.

☺ **Reading lists** will not faze you, and you are likely to want to make notes on them as you progress through a module.

☹ Occasional references thrown out by lecturers, to reading you might like to do, will probably irritate you.

- o Always have your reading notebook nearby so that you can keep track of casual reading recommendations.

(Continued)

(Continued)

☺ You will find **note taking** a pleasing way to think through concepts and material, although your notes are unlikely to take the form of text throughout.

☹ You might find yourself getting tired, making so many notes to support your learning.

   o Find other ways to record, such as active learning sheets, mind maps, diagrams and so forth. You might find organisational software that allows for visual thinking both useful and fun.

☺ Your eagerness to share your information will support your aims in a **presentation**.

☹ You might find yourself lost in your presentation if you are relying on a script.

   o Presentation slides with images, charts and diagrams can be used as prompts for you as well as your audience.

☺ **Study groups** will work well for you as long as you can make a mind map as you go along.

☹ If the group is too vague or chatty, or goes off at a tangent, you might find it less useful.

   o Groups of students with similar learning style preferences often work extremely well: this might be a deciding factor if you choose to start up your own study or revision group.

→ Those who gravitate towards **verbal** learning prefer to rely on words; they enjoy learning through reading and talking.

Checklist – for the verbal preference student

☺ Meetings with your **personal tutor** could be important to you: the opportunity to talk through your plans and ideas will always be welcome.

☹ You might struggle to keep to time, so that you do not make the most of each meeting.

   o Write down in advance what you hope to cover, with specific queries, and email this to your tutor or take it with you to the meeting.

☺ **Lectures** will always keep your attention; you will especially enjoy those lectures in which space is made for brief pair conversations.

☹ You will absorb information so well that you might then struggle to remember that you need to look at other, opposing viewpoints.

   o A study group will help to shake up any rigidity in your ideas.

☺ The discussions that take place in **seminars** will give you a firm sense of learning in action. You will also be happy to speak up and try out new ideas.

☹ You might find that the seminar becomes a conversation between just you and the seminar leader. This might not be a problem, but you might find that you are missing out on good ideas from other students.

    o   Ask a fellow student to let you know if you are dominating the seminar room.

☺ You will see the benefit of **lab work**, and it will be a powerful learning experience once you have recorded your activities and mulled them over.

☹ You might be inclined to favour scientific accounts of experimental work over the experience of undertaking lab work yourself.

    o   This need not impede your progress: lab work will be a scheduled activity within your course and, for optional lab sessions, work with fellow students who are happy to talk through what is happening as you work.

☺ You will see **reading lists** as a promise of guaranteed new learning.

☹ You might try to read so many of the texts on your lists that you do not leave enough time for other activities.

    o   Annotate your reading lists and use a reading notebook to record how well you are working through the reading for your course – and to warn you if your reading schedule is fuller than is sensible in the time you have available.

☺ You will find **note taking** both affirming of your learning and a good way to think through ideas.

☹ You will make copious notes and you need to control them.

    o   Try talking over your notes with a fellow student so that you can both then reduce them to revision style notes.

☺ Being assessed by a **presentation** could be a gift for you.

☹ You might try to speak with no rehearsal at all, or talk over others in a presentation group: neither action will gain marks.

    o   However confident you are in your ability to talk through your ideas, work closely with your group so that you come to feel part of the group effort.

☺ Joining several **study groups** will appeal to you, as they allow you to talk with like-minded students.

☹ You might not find it easy to keep to the point or keep to task, which would diminish their value to you all.

    o   Make an agenda and practise sticking to it: a valuable professional skill as well as useful for your studying progress.

Whatever preference you have in your learning style, there is one aspect of your personality that will have an overarching effect on how you might use your study time. You are likely to be either a **social** or a **solitary** learner or, perhaps, a mixture of both in differing circumstances.

A social learner will, as the term suggests, prefer to work in a group or with a learning partner. These students will gain energy from having someone alongside them in their study journey. Sometimes this means that they struggle to be alone at all, but there are times when solitary study is necessary and they will have to interject that activity with opportunities to boost their confidence and wellbeing by being with others.

Solitary learners enjoy taking time to themselves to process ideas and contemplate what they have learnt. Their most productive time tends to be when they are working alone, and in some cases being in a more social learning environment can cause them anxiety and irritation, because their learning pace slows down. However, this does not mean that they do not contribute to, or benefit from, social learning; they just need to factor in some solitary time as well.

Your learning style will direct, to some extent, the way that you respond to the material in the coming chapters; so too will your circumstances. In this part of the guide the focus is on developing yourself as a student so that you produce good results; you will want to return to certain sections repeatedly as you face each challenge. It would be unfair to expect that you would read Chapter 10, on making notes, and then transform into an expert overnight. With this in mind, I have included words in bold throughout the text, so that you can make a brief revisit to a section when you are facing an assignment, or checking another new reading list, or trying to improve your seminar performance.

9

Reading lists

Reading lists have already been mentioned several times in the first part of this book; now we are going to explore how useful they can be. There is plenty of advice here to help you throughout your time at university, so you do not need to rush through it all at once. Take your time: you will probably return to this chapter several times during your course.

How do I find my reading list?

You will know from earlier chapters that university reading lists are increasingly being hosted online. This offers you many advantages:

Checklist – advantages of online reading lists

☺   You can access your reading list from any device.

☺   You can usually access any reading list, so you can check out reading lists for optional modules as you consider them.

☺   Much of the material is available directly and online, so you can go straight from your reading list to work on the study material without any interruption.

☺   Your university would have paid a licence fee for scanning original material and so you will be offered texts online that you might otherwise have had to buy.

☺   You can see at a glance the full range of material you are expected to explore, not just books but also journal articles, online pieces and videoclips.

(Continued)

(Continued)

☺ Your material might well be organised online to show you a week-by-week set of study materials, so the reading list becomes far easier to follow.

☺ Your lecturer or module convenor might make notes on the reading lists, so you get a good sense of the relative importance of different sources.

☺ An online reading list is very easy to update, so lecturers might be more inclined to add material and references during the year.

This is all to the good, but there are also some potential disadvantages:

Checklist – Disadvantages of online reading lists

☹ If your lecturer does not keep in touch, you might find that the reading list has been updated without you being made aware of it.

→ Regular checking will avoid this problem.

☹ It is so easy to put material and references into online reading lists that they can become unwieldy unless they are rigorously organised.

→ You might need to take charge of your online reading list and create your own, bespoke version.

☹ Reading lists are created well in advance of a module being taught. If a hard copy reading list is not being given out in class, a lecturer might overlook changes that need to be made to it.

→ The first thing you might do is to spend a few minutes taking an overview of the reading list online: does it seem to you to match up well with what is actually being taught on the module?

☹ If you cannot get online, you cannot access your online reading list.

→ In reality, this might be momentarily annoying but it will not be a serious problem. University systems rarely go down for any great length of time.

☹ Some students prefer paper copies of reading lists, because some people find pieces of paper that they can carry around in their bag, and scribble on when a thought occurs to them, far easier to use, and reassuring.

→ Give online a chance, but if you need to print off study material, or indeed an entire reading list, in order for it to make sense to you, then that is what you will do. Online resources are intended to speed up studying and make it easier; if printing off some of the online material is actually what makes this speedier and easier for you, that need not be a problem.

Top tip

As with so much else at university, you need to recognise how you like to work best as a student, and you need to remain aware of possible changes as they happen. Although this can feel unnerving when you first study at university, it becomes a habit of working soon enough, but you might find it helpful to make a note in your study diary or online calendar to check updates on reading lists every few weeks.

Might there be multiple reading lists for my modules?

Yes, and no. There would usually be one **core reading list** for your module, which will be offered to you on paper or online. If you find slightly different versions, one online and one in hard copy, it is probably the result of your university only recently having moved to online reading lists, and it is a simple matter to check with the module convenor exactly which one to follow. You might also notice stray reading lists that appear in your VLE for a module. If this is not a link directly to an online reading list system, but rather a link to a PDF of a hard copy reading list, treat it with suspicion if your university is using an online reading list system.

CAREER
MOMENT

Students can struggle to navigate through multiple reading lists, with the module convenor having no idea that several rogue versions are still hanging around online and in seminar rooms. If you are the one student who emails to check which reading list is the current version, not only will your lecturer and fellow students be grateful, you will also have saved yourself time by not going off on a tangent with the reading for the course. Long term, taking proactive steps such as this becomes the normal way you expect to work. You become recognised as an organised and cooperative student, and long term, your normal work practice involves taking the lead when needed: a highly prized graduate attribute.

Beyond the core list, there may be other reading lists that are offered by academics to support lectures and seminars on a module. These should be taken as **supplementary reading**. You will work on these only as much as you need to in order to understand a topic and prepare for assessment. If the area under discussion in a lecture or seminar is not one on which you will be focusing for assessment (and this can happen, depending on the assessment tasks for a module), you may make only the most minor foray into these supplementary lists, out of general interest in the topic.

Lecturers design modules with a very clear idea of how the learning outcomes match to the assignments being asked of students. Knowing this will help you manage your reading lists creatively. By recognising that you might not be assessed formally on every scrap of information offered on a module, you can decide where to read widely and where to take a light touch approach. This is not about avoiding work, it is about using your time wisely: this makes for a happier, more successful student.

Although you will probably expect to be offered a reading list for each module you study, do not be overly concerned if it does not exist. Occasionally, a module convenor will decide that all of the essential reading material for a module can be offered in printed form in seminars. It might also be that a module is diverse in its coverage, with assignment titles that are created by students from a wide list of optional areas. In this case there may be **no formal reading list**, but rather a bespoke list of recommendations made to each student as the need arises during the module delivery.

There will also be **ad hoc reading lists** that develop as you study. They will not be obvious (or even exist) at the start of a module. They are, in effect, hidden reading lists, and you will need to keep a look out for the chance to create them. You might use the following clues when compiling a hidden reading list.

Checklist – hidden reading lists

✓ Names of authors and books that are thrown out during a lecture and that you scribble down in haste, to check on later.

✓ Small reading lists associated with one task on a module.

✓ Reading lists that develop from the bibliography (references) sections of books or journal articles that you have found particularly helpful.

✓ References mentioned in conversation during study groups or over a break in a seminar.

✓ Reading offered to you by an academic during a tutorial on some work you have submitted.

✓ Passing mentions of material that you hear in the media and need to hunt out.

There is a danger to making reading lists such as this: they can make you feel guilty all of the time. You have heard of a resource that you feel you should look up, but you have not found time to do it; or, a lecturer mentioned a text in passing in a lecture, but you cannot recall exactly what the title was and you feel that you should have listened more attentively. Worse than this, you constantly feel that there is a huge pile of texts and online resources lurking somewhere that you should tackle.

INSIDER HINT

Part of what makes you feel weighed down by your reading lists is the fact that academics tend to get a bit carried away from time to time. We go to a conference and are inspired in an area of our work, or we have a spare afternoon and decide that we are going to follow up on our best intentions and make a really good reading list. Sadly, this often becomes a really long reading list, which makes the academic feel good and the student feel overwhelmed. A huge reading list with a clear set of guidance notes can be a blessing, though, as long as you are prepared to take it for what it is: an excellent overview of an area with expert help to navigate it. It is better to be faced with a long list that you have to tame than to be offered no reading list at all, which can be undermining and rather scary.

There is a simple way to fix this for yourself: buy an A5 hardback notebook and keep it near you when you are studying. It could be a virtual notebook on a mobile device, but most students seem to prefer to use a hard copy notebook for this. Every time useful material is mentioned, or you find a reference to something that looks helpful from a source such as a website or bibliography, jot it down in this **reading notebook**. That way, you can relax knowing that it is safely stored in there.

Top tip

If you intend to use a virtual notebook of some sort, you might find it useful to explore OneNote or a similar software package that is designed specifically to help with organising your material in a way that is most useful for your needs. This type of software might be available for free for all students at your university.

Whenever you get some spare time, look through the notebook and see if you can fill in the gaps: looking up the title of a book that you did not quite hear in a lecture, but you know the author and subject matter, or finding the URL of a website that keeps being talked about as a valuable resource. In these brief sessions you probably will not have time to work through the text or online material, but you will be further forward in your detective hunt for good resources.

Source: Rawpixel.com/StockSnap.io

Top tip

This is a great way to while away an hour if you are tired or stuck in your progress on a project or essay. It is not difficult brainwork to look up some references, but it is satisfying to do and it can make otherwise frustrating, tired time into a much more productive hour or so.

You are now creating a reading notebook that has full references in it, built up from a variety of sources and filled out by your detective work. Now is the time to be firm. Make sure that each entry in your reading notebook has an initial note, then several lines left blank ready for you to add bibliographical details when you can find them, but also leave a margin to one side of the page. When you can put aside time to have a session online and/or in your library or resources centre, be ready to make decisions. If you come across a resource that is not helpful to you, be decisive and write 'NO GOOD' in the margin. When you find material that might work for a particular assignment, write the details of that assignment in the margin. When you have made notes on material that is of general use on a module, write 'DONE' in the margin and, if you would find it helpful, the module code as well.

By making these prioritising decisions, you break down a mass of reading lists, from various sources, to a controlled and useful set of resources that you are using to best effect. Figure 9.1 is an example of a typical page from a reading notebook such as this:

DONE: MODULE AT116	*Archaeology: An introduction* – Kevin Greene 2010
NO GOOD	How to read a dig site: Bridgelworther 2018
	Journal article on classical theatre and archaeological finds in Athens? In department resources room – red cover
DONE: ESSAY 4	*Human remains in archaeology: a handbook* – Charlotte A Roberts 2008
NO GOOD FOR NOW	*Raising the dead*, www.raising the dead Redfreet article from 2004
DONE: MODULE AF889	*Archaeology: theories, methods and practice* – Colin Renfrew, Paul G. Bahn 2016
	Swardsty gave a talk on burial practices at the local history society talk in March – find out if he put it online?
DONE: EXTENDED RESEARCH PROJECT??	For introduction: *Archaeological theory today* – Ian Hodder 2012

Figure 9.1   Example of a reading notebook

You can see that this is a work in progress. The student has yet to find all the details of a couple of items: that will come another day when there is time to spare. You will also see that some initial sorting has been done, so the student has made notes on some of the material, and allocated it to either a module in general or an assignment in particular. Even when this categorisation is not firmly decided (as the question marks reveal), the student will feel content that at least some possible material for a large assignment, due n several months, is ready to be used if it is needed and seems relevant at that time.

I am not suggesting that you transpose your entire reading list for every module into your reading notebook, although I have known students who have done this. Standard reading lists can be used as they are: your reading notebook is additional, for stray references that you want to capture. It is also a useful place to bring some references from this year's reading lists that you think you might want to come back to next year.

The fact that some resources have been designated as 'NO GOOD' does not necessarily mean that they are in themselves no good, but rather that they do not fit the needs of this student. An article online might not have been thoroughly researched, and so a student might not want to use and cite it, but it might lead to other resources that have been more rigorously reviewed, with full citations. A resource might be excellent in itself, but simply not relevant to the topics under discussion in the module that this student is taking. Be clear and firm on this – shelve as many resources as you need to with your 'NO GOOD' label. They will still be there in the reading notebook if you need to come back later because your studies are taking a new direction, or if you realise that a text you found unappealing in its style actually turns out to be essential reading for your studies.

You might not have expected to be in a position, as a student, to dismiss important books and articles, but you are. I have known academics who are superb in their field but who readily admit that they write in a style that is difficult to grasp. If it is an essential text, you might have to work through it, but if you have a choice of several key texts, there is no need to labour through one when there might be another that suits your style of learning and thinking much better.

Am I expected to read all of the texts on my reading list?

Very rarely. If you are given a list entitled 'Essential Reading' and there are just a handful of texts on there, it would be reasonable to assume that you would read them all, or at least the relevant parts of each. For most reading lists, you are expected to be selective. This will become obvious to you if the academic who made the reading list has offered guidance notes, as is often the case. The selective nature of reading lists is determined partly around assessment (you might choose to delve deeply into just one or two topics) and partly around resources. If hard copy books or journals are being offered, there is sometimes not enough time between seminars for every student to take every item out of the library, read and return it, so several possible sources are offered.

Top tip

If you are given notes on a reading list, with comments from a lecturer about the relative value of a selection of texts for different purposes, take the hint and follow that guidance. Too often students spend hours trying to range across a selection of texts with very little sense of purpose.

Although you might not be expected to read and make notes on every single item on a reading list, this does not mean that you should not *explore* every item. A few minutes spent looking through a resource to see whether it suits your purposes can be fruitful. If you like it, you will read it more fully and make notes; if it is interesting but not relevant at the moment, you might put it in your reading notebook for further consideration later.

Primary vs secondary sources

It can feel awkward if people around you are talking about **primary and secondary sources**, and you are not entirely sure about the difference between them. A primary source is anything that you are seeing at first hand (a novel, a verbatim account of a speech, a play, the results of a piece of research). A secondary source is how you encounter these sources at second hand (a critic's book on a novel, a newspaper commentary on a speech, a director's account of a play, the analysis of a piece of research).

With online sources this has become more complicated than in the past. A website, for example, is a primary source in itself, in that it has been created by someone and therefore can be subject to your scrutiny. However, if it includes quotes from a newspaper, it becomes a secondary source of that particular piece of material. The newspaper is still the primary source; the website repeating the words originally printed in the newspaper is a secondary way to view those words.

You can see from this example why academics are keen to direct their students to primary sources. The website might misquote the newspaper article, or quote from it so out of context that its original meaning is obscured or skewed.

INSIDER HINT

There is a danger in relying too heavily on secondary sources: you might become confused over who is doing the thinking. Academics are used to navigating sources. We are always aware of whether we are commenting on original material or evaluating someone else's comment on that material. For students this can be a blurred area. You see a quote on several websites and also take in all of the analysis and commentary that surrounds it. After a while it becomes difficult to remember just what the original intention of the text was, and whether this matters, and what context produced it, and whether the ideas about it that you would like

(Continued)

(Continued)

to use in your essay are yours or those that you encountered on the websites. If you can start with the primary material, even if you first learnt about it through a website quote, you are in a good position to make your own academic judgement and then take into account the analysis of others, always with a clear sense of what is primary (and so fixed in terms of what it actually is, whatever is said about it) and what is secondary.

It can be bewildering to try to keep firmly in your mind the difference between primary and secondary sources, and so be clear about how you might use them. It does become easier with experience, so you will find that, in the later stages of your studying, you will be happier with this differentiation. Never worry about asking for help in this area: you will be handling so many different types of material that some uncertainty is only natural.

CAREER
MOMENT

Knowing the difference between primary and secondary sources, and basing your judgement on that knowledge, is valuable beyond your studies. When you are working professionally and presenting your findings and professional recommendations, your colleagues and/or clients will want to know how valid and reliable your material is, and being able to distinguish clearly between primary and secondary sources will be part of that judgement call.

How do I make the most of a reading list?

Exploiting the value of reading lists is usually about following the same set of steps every time you face a **new list.**

Checklist – conquering reading lists

✓ Locate a copy of the reading list for each of your modules as soon as you can.

✓ Check that you have the right list – if it is online, are you looking at the right year's list?

✓ If you have been given a hard copy list, does it match the online reading list for the module?

✓ If you are able to, work on the reading list before the term gets too busy.

✓ If there is no written guidance, and the list seems long and/or confusing to you, make an appointment to ask for some pointers so that you can make best use of the list.

✓ Take a first look at the reading list when you have at least half an hour to spare so that you can explore it and make some decisions: categorising, making plans, adding items to your reading notebook if it will help.

✓ As soon as you receive details of your assignment, make sure that the reading lists supports the work that you are being asked to do.

✓ If you are asked to make up your own assignment title, talk to your lecturer about the resources you will need: you might need to go off the list.

✓ If you feel uncertain at any point, you need not waste time worrying: go straight to a librarian or study advisor and ask for help.

✓ Make sure you are clear on the functionality of an online list. You will probably be able to make notes on it and indicate priorities around your reading. If you make it your own in this way, it becomes a useful tool rather than a daunting list that is difficult to access each time you approach it.

Can technology help?

Technology can save you vast amounts of time, just when you need it. If you use **bibliographical software** (such as EndNote) you will be storing and sorting information as you research, plan and write an assignment. In this way you can avoid the frustration of desperately trying to create a bibliography (reference list) for an assignment just at the point at which you want to submit it. It also means that you will have a searchable and fully cited list when you come to tackle your next assignment and need to use some of the material in that context.

Where is the best place to read and study?

There is often an assumption amongst students that they will always work in the library or resource centre, because that is just what students do. This is a mistake. You need to make absolutely sure that it is the right space for you before you commit to working there. For a short time, whilst you are making some brief notes or between lectures, working in the library might be convenient, but beyond that you need to examine how and where you work best.

Top tip

To make the most of software such as EndNote you will probably need some training, and usually this is available to students through their library service or resource centre. Although you could work your way through it without any help, you would probably miss useful functions; it will save you time if you get help early. It will also mean that, when all of your fellow students are panicking about how to use the software, right at the last minute, you are one of the few people who actually knows what they are doing.

Deciding where you work best will depend on a series of factors:

Checklist – where to study

✓ If you have a study group, you will all decide together where you will meet, and a central location such as a study pod in your library might be most convenient.

✓ If you are easily distracted by visual interruptions, such as people moving about or walking by you, a library is probably not the best environment for you.

✓ If you share accommodation and it gets noisy, the library can be a good escape route, but if you are not naturally someone who enjoys working in a library, think about it more closely. Is your accommodation noisy all the time, or could you alternate between there and the library?

✓ You might choose the library as a way to regulate your time. Some students like to know that every Tuesday morning they have their regular slot in the library, perhaps even at the same desk, so that they can build a comforting routine into their study life.

✓ You might work in the library for an hour or so each evening, or for a morning each weekend, so that you are not tempted to abandon work.

✓ Libraries can help you focus. If you plan to use the library study space for some specific activities, such as preparing a learning journal, or making notes for one of your modules, and you use other spaces regularly for other specific study activities, it can help you to get into the swing of studying faster. The location helps you to gain focus on that particular module, or study task, because the location reminds you of the last, similar, piece of work you carried out there.

✓ Libraries can save you time. If you are working through a reading list and it involves looking at hard copy material, or if you prefer to sift through material in hard copy as you decide what to make notes on and what to discard, you will want to be in the library.

✓ You can ambush yourself into a very productive week if you sneak some time in the library. Promising yourself thirty minutes in the library before four of your lectures each week might seem like a waste of time, because it feels like such a short study opportunity. In fact, you will be training yourself to concentrate hard in that time, each time, and you will have won yourself two hours of focused study time each week with very little effort.

✓ Some students find that libraries lend themselves to particular types of activity. They will use libraries to look at any visual study material that is being offered, such as videoclips or lecture recordings, but prefer to work elsewhere for other tasks, such as making notes on primary texts.

INSIDER
HINT

Across many universities I have noticed, in recent years, a marked trend towards reading lists which should probably be called 'reading/viewing lists'. Academics are often keen to harness the power of the visual, and so film clips lodged online, or the use of screencast or screencapture software, are becoming more popular. It would not be surprising if you found that your lecturers offered you short films, clever screencasts or even animations to help you learn. I use all of these, and students seem to enjoy the break away from reading, and benefiting from other ways to learn, so look out for resources such as this.

Your relationship with reading lists is going to undulate during your life at university. At times you will hardly think about your lists, because you are using them steadily and have no immediate need to check a specific area. At other times they will be at the forefront of your mind, as you receive a new list, perhaps, or as you face an assignment. As long as you have mastered the principles of reading lists and how to exploit this important resource to the full, you can happily let this natural rhythm develop, knowing that a useful reading list is never far away.

10

Your first sets of notes

Notes that you make in a variety of situations are going to form the bedrock of your study success; as the ability to record information efficiently is also crucial to many successful careers, it is an art to be mastered early. Although many of the same judgement skills are going to be needed whatever the source material for your notes, there are different techniques that you can employ, depending on your circumstances and the purpose of the notes.

I will be offering you plenty of 'insider hints' in this chapter. I have done this because it is easier to understand how notes can work, and their value, limitations and complications, if you have seen hundreds of students making them in a plethora of styles and formats, and then using them in a range of ways.

Do I need to make any notes at all?

It becomes a standard reflex amongst students to whip out a notebook, tablet or laptop the moment anyone says anything in an educational setting. This is perfectly understandable, but you could save yourself time and improve your experience if you ask yourself each time whether you actually need to make notes.

In a **lecture**, you may find that you are being asked to consider some extremely complex concepts, and your lecturer wants you to think, rather than scribbling with your head down.

Lecturers are often expected to make their lecture material available to students in advance of the event, either through the VLE or in hard copy. This might take the form of the slides for the lecture, or a brief list covering the main points of the lecture. So, you do not need to worry overly about the basics escaping you if your mind wanders for a moment or if you have decided to make only a sparse set of notes and then you need more detail later. It is worth noting that lecturers can revisit this material, so sometimes you will find that they offer more detailed notes just before the exams or assignments, or they add material in response to questions that were raised in the lecture. Never assume that what you saw on the VLE the day before the lecture is all that will ever be there. Check periodically on any new material that might have been posted after the event.

Because lectures can take different forms (as was shown in Chapter 5) you will be making different sorts of notes for each type of lecture, and inspirational lectures in particular will challenge you. You are unlikely to want to come away with no notes, but you will want to absorb the information and ponder it rather than just writing everything down. One way to achieve this is to produce 'progressive notes'. These are notes that you can make during one event, to which you intend to add later. You may use different colours for subsequent learning events, so that you can easily track back to source for any queries you want to raise later. Students often find progressive notes reassuring, because they can become fairly substantial and give a clear sense of purpose and progress throughout a module.

In a **seminar**, it is easy to forget just how much understanding is shared in a look, or an encouraging smile, or a questioning glance around a room. Seminars present a particular challenge – you can expect most of the material to be created as a discussion takes place, so you might miss out on the depth and the chance to join in and develop your understanding if you take copious notes. At least for the first few seminars it pays to trust the seminar leader and only take down brief notes of essential points: your main energy needs to go into the intellectual experience of the seminar.

It is similar with **study/revision/reading groups**. Very often you will want to record the event and the points that were made in detail, so that you keep pace with the discussion and do not miss anything that is referred to later on. However, if you choose instead to work from the assumption that these notes can be brief, because you are contributing throughout the event, you will be in a good position to gain from these groups. Taking ten minutes afterwards to write down a list of key points might serve you far better than coming out with pages of notes, most of which you do not need.

INSIDER
HINT

I often ask groups of students to organise material for a practice report. I give them the scenario – which is no more than a couple of sentences – and then I give them instructions about how each group might work. Even though I reassure the students that I am about to give out a piece of paper with full details on it, some still cannot resist writing down that two-sentence instruction. However, doing this seems to increase their anxiety, rather than reassuring them, so I would urge you to give yourself the chance just to listen from time to time if you possibly can.

You would reasonably expect that, if you are examining primary or secondary **written or visual sources**, you would automatically be taking notes. This is true, as long as you know that the sources are worth the notes. Just because something is included on a reading list does not mean that it necessarily meets your particular needs, or that you need to record it in detail.

For example, if you are asked, as part of your preparation for a seminar, to watch a three-minute screencast and a two-minute YouTube clip, and to listen to a four-minute section of a podcast, making notes on them could be a complete waste of time. The nine minutes you spend engaging with the material will give you the overview you need, and the seminar will give you ample opportunity to delve more deeply and take notes. The extra time you spent making notes to which you never refer after the event will feel like a frustrating waste of your precious study time if your seminar leader asks you to do this each week.

You might assume that if a text is recommended on your reading list as being valuable for a module, you would need to take notes, and this is largely the case. However, Chapter 9, on reading lists, has cautioned you to be independent minded and bring your own judgement to bear on each potential source. If it is not essential to you, because you have already covered an area, or because it is not accessible for your way of working, and you have been offered several similar sources, you will want to skim through before you commit to making notes.

INSIDER
HINT

Although there is an assumption that all students today only work online, and type up notes directly from sources presented to them in various online formats, the reality is that many of my students prefer hard copy sources and hard copy notes. Especially in their first year, students

(Continued)

(Continued)

can find this more reassuring and, oddly, more restful. If you feel this way, never let yourself believe that you really should work only in a virtual world: hard copy notes that you can print out, or write by hand, still have a place in studying.

Notes for **assignments** are likely to range from very full and detailed notes from some courses or modules, to a few stray notes from a lecture that you put on an active learning sheet (see Chapter 5, where I write about your first lectures). You might make a set of notes specifically for the assignment, or simply high-light those areas of your existing notes that you want to use. You might check with a tutor early on in the process on your first few assignments, to make sure that how you are approaching this is the most efficacious way to work in this context. This might also give you the chance to glean a few more references from the academic.

INSIDER HINT

Academics want to help their students, and so they can sometimes be tempted to offer mate-rial even though they cannot quite recall the title of the website or text that is in the back of their mind, or they might enthuse about a source that helped them enormously on a project, not realising that it has been updated or superseded since then. I once spent nearly an hour looking for the 'big orange book at the end of our usual shelf in the library with a picture of a reclining nude on the cover'. I found it, eventually, on a completely different shelf. It took me five minutes to check and then put it back because it was irrelevant: my lecturer was thinking of an entirely different book and had confused it in the haste of a corridor conversation about my assignment.

As long as you are clear about what is being asked of you, you are unlikely to take notes that you do not need; unless, of course, you are very nervous and just making notes to make yourself feel better. This is not always a bad thing if it helps, but over time you will find that you become sharper in your notes for assignments and this will streamline your studying.

Revision notes will be made, worked and reworked as you approach your exams, but one of the first things I will be urging you to do in Chapter 22 (on exams) is to discard any notes that you realise, in hindsight, you no longer need.

Sometimes this will mean discarding notes that you never really needed in the first place, but this can be satisfying, as you will see how far you have come in your note-taking abilities. You will hope to find that you made fewer irrelevant notes as your first term went on; if this is not the case, revision can provide an excellent prompt to make you think more strategically about your notes.

INSIDER HINT

You might not have expected that a university lecturer would be urging you to make fewer, rather than more notes. I have come to see over many years – and many different students – that it is not the quantity of notes that makes the difference, it is how well they are used.

How reliable is this source/situation?

A **lecture** will give you fairly much guaranteed reliability around sources. The 'fairly much' in that sentence is because of the way lectures work. If you are being given a lecture from a series of slides and it is clear that you are simply listening and trying to understand, you can be sure that the lecturer will have checked and double-checked every citation that is made. That is, if the lecturer refers to ('cites') a particular work, it will be an accurate reference. If, however, you are in a lecture that is a little more interactive, with the chance for a question or two, or a brief discussion in the middle, then a query from a student might throw up a rather more vague reference. It would make sense to check with the lecturer that you heard correctly and that the description of the book has led you to the right book, before you go ahead and spend time making notes.

INSIDER HINT

Academics usually love words and images, which means that they have rooms that are full of books and articles, often with posters on the wall explaining theories or sharing nice quotes. This can make for an inspiring place to learn: it can also lead to confusion. Academics keep favourite books and posters for decades, so if you see a text, or any other material, in an academic's room that appeals to you and that you think might be useful, check that it is up to date and reliable before you go to the library to find a copy.

The purpose and structure of **seminars** leads to variable reliability in the material you gather in your notes. Your seminar leader will be offering you theories, concepts and material, all of which should be reliable. You might also notice books or journals in the seminar room that could be helpful, and you will note down the titles (perhaps in the reading notebook you might have made after the last chapter). Of course, you will also hear, and make, comments, ideas and suggestions throughout the seminar of varying quality and reliability.

It is easy enough to sift through seminar material by listening carefully to the seminar leader's response to any students' comments and making an immediate judgement on whether you are happy to note it down as a good point, or put a question mark beside it as a little more dubious. With practice this type of judgement sifting will become very easy. What is equally important, but not nearly so easy, is to remember to write 'MY IDEA' beside any brilliant idea you have thought up and made in the seminar. This is crucial, because you will be looking back on these notes for ideas to include in assignments, or presentations, or to use as pointers to future research and study. You can only pursue any of these avenues with confidence if you know that you are following your own idea, rather than mistakenly picking up someone else's idea. It is not that you will not use other people's ideas, but you will want to cite your source and being uncertain of this will leave you stranded.

Top tip

Not being able to cite material correctly because you cannot recall exactly where it came from can be immensely frustrating, and a huge waste of time as you hunt around, online or in your notes, to find the source and so the correct reference. Being unsure of whether or not an important thought is yours is more than frustrating, it can be very upsetting. You long to include it, you know it will gain you extra marks, and you really want to share this great idea or clever connection. Avoid this ever happening to you – MY IDEA could be one of the most useful notes you ever make.

Each student, in each seminar, will produce notes that are slightly (and sometimes significantly) different. This is a positive result, because it means that the students feel confident about what they need from each seminar and how they are going to use the material in the future. Try not to put pressure on yourself over this. During your first four to six weeks at university, try out different ways to make notes in seminars and you will find what works best for you.

Study group notes will rely on two very different sources: the texts/lecture slides/academic handouts under discussion, and the comments and ideas shared by students. The notes of the study group might also look forward in several directions – towards an assignment, looking forward to the next seminar, looking back to consolidate your learning. By using colours and margins you can categorise these notes as they happen, and this is the easiest way to save time later.

Source material, either online or printed, might seem like the most reliable material from which to take notes. Even here, you need to check that the material is reliable. First, remind yourself of the differences between primary and secondary sources (from Chapter 9 of this guide). If you are making notes on a primary source, you are dealing with first-hand material and, whether or not you agree with the opinions stated, it is at least reliable as a source. Secondary material can often feel more useful to you because you are seeing what others think about a primary source or a situation. It is in the secondary material that you will see academics and others working through material, concepts and theories. These might or might not be of value to you, depending on what you are aiming to achieve in your notes, but make sure that you check a few points as to reliability before you begin to make notes, by asking the following questions:

Checklist – reliability of source material

✓ Are you sure that you know whether you are working with primary or secondary material?

✓ How old is the material? If it is from some time ago, does this matter?

✓ Has the material been superseded by something that is more reliable/current?

✓ If you are planning to use material that uses quotes from other sources, can you find your way back to the original material?

✓ For online material, was the material lodged on the site by its originator, or is there a chance that it is a paraphrased or inaccurate copy of original material?

✓ If this source is reliable and valuable, does the bibliography or references section of the text, or reference on the website, lead to other, similarly valid material?

The reliability of notes for assignments and revision will rely entirely on the reliability of the original notes you made, if you are using your own notes to create a new set of briefer notes to prepare for an assignment or an exam. If you have worked these notes in advance (that is, you have checked them for reliability as you made them, or checked for their reliability with an academic after the event) you can move forward with no qualms.

If you are working towards an assignment, there can be a tendency to amass piles of new notes so as to alleviate your anxiety. To some degree this can serve a useful function, but there is a better way to approach these notes. Rather than endlessly scrolling through books or journals, or reading pages and pages of web material, force yourself to print off what you think is going to be useful. This is time consuming, so you will be encouraging yourself only to print off material that you believe will actually be useful. Then judge the material a second time: use a highlighter pen to highlight those passages that relate specifically to your assignment. This will help you make fine critical judgements, and you might discard some of the material as irrelevant. You will then be left with core material that positively supports your assignment: this is what you will use as you move ahead.

Reliability will obviously be vital when you come to consider **revision notes**. When we discuss revision and exams in Chapter 22, more help will be offered on how to make this judgement. At this stage you can safely assume that the primary function of revision notes is to reduce material to manageable chunks, ready for recall and effective use in the exams.

By the time you get to the end of your first term, you will have noticed that your notes, both their detail and style, will have developed. You might never need to read through this entire chapter again, but you could usefully return to it from time to time if you feel that your note-taking skills are starting to slide.

CAREER
MOMENT

'Note taking skill' sounds like something you would abandon as soon as you leave university, and many students simply overlook how valuable a skill it is to employers. Making a good set of notes from a client meeting, or during a conference or public event, or as you prepare material in your work, will not only support excellent professional results, it will also mean that you can produce results faster and with more certainty. It may seem like a mundane skill now, because you are using it daily, but it is highly prized by employers once you point out to them how good you are at making, reworking and using notes and the benefit this would bring to them.

As you will see from the guidance throughout this chapter, notes are rarely static. Most usually you would be reworking your notes, and there might be several reasons for this:

Checklist – reworking your notes

✓ Once you have checked whether your sources are correct.

✓ After a study group, to condense your notes to just key points.

✓ After a lecture or series of lectures, if you prefer to consolidate your ideas in a cover sheet that lists just the most important/relevant points.

✓ After any learning activity that relates to an assignment, so that you can make a list of those points that are relevant, or colour code your notes with highlighter ready for the assignment.

✓ When you are preparing for exams, so that you can reduce full notes to briefer revision notes and then, perhaps, to revision cards or lists.

What is the best design for these notes?

Notes do not need to be lines of text, handwritten or typed. Being more creative (such as diagrams, lists of points, mind maps, bubble charts and tree charts) can lead to note taking that is more productive and, usually, faster. It may be that you decide to stay with the traditional form of writing out notes for much of the time, and only venture into other formats for particular purposes. This can work well, as it helps you to focus on the reason for your notes as the format and design you choose will be serving that purpose.

INSIDER HINT

Some of my students need to make notes in the first instance simply to help them under-stand a topic. Particularly for verbal learners, notes are the gateway through which they learn efficiently. If this is the case for you, reworking your notes will be helpful, and you will still want to reduce them as you prepare for exams, but you need not worry about always aiming for succinct notes. Brief notes to which you have to add to later in order fully to grasp a topic would be counterproductive.

How can I sharpen my notes?

Throughout this guide here is an emphasis on time: saving time and using your time wisely. Having worked through this chapter, you have several options for achieving both of these things. Vacation time is important in this context.

You might be working on assignments over your vacations, and you might also be studying to prepare for new modules in the coming term, but try not to overlook the value of consolidating your notes over these breaks in teaching.

Some of my students work me very hard when they return from vacations because they have worked through their notes and now have a series of questions, or they have perused a series of active learning sheets and want me to add to them. It is hard work on our brains for the hour that I see them, but it is hugely satisfying, and the student comes away having saved significant amounts of future effort.

This vacation work will involve looking back – have you reworked notes as you need to, so that you are clear on everything? Are they all stored away (in hard copy or electronically) in a way that makes them useful in future and easy to access? Do you need to check any references, or add possible new sources to your reading notebook? Can any of the notes be set aside in an archive somewhere, because you do not think you will need them again now that you have completed some part of your studying?

This process of consolidation also involves looking forward. Should you make some cover sheets for any sets of notes you might need for future modules, so that you can access them easily when you need them? This will not take long, as it will all be fresh in your mind, and it will save you time later. Do you need to rework any of these notes because there is an assignment coming up later for which you are likely to need some of the material in a targeted way? Could you produce brief revision notes ready for exams, especially any which are quite some time away? Is there any material that you would like to extract now ready for a presentation? Have you made any active learning connections sheets that you now want to revisit, either to bring several sheets together or to think through the implications of what you recorded in this way?

This is, perhaps, the most challenging chapter we have worked through so far. There are plenty of ideas here, and some insider information to help you along the way, but there needs also to be a word of warning. If you have always made notes in a particular way, and it has served you well, you need to bear that in mind as you put the advice here into action. Trying to make wholesale changes is both demanding and, potentially, counterproductive. You could lose confidence if you change everything at once, or lose heart and simply give up on trying to improve your note taking. Little by little is the answer here.

One way to achieve this little-by-little approach is to have a 'random notes' page beside you as you make notes from any source. You will not designate any particular purpose for this page, but you will jot ideas down on it as you work through source material (as you become more adept at this you might also use this page as you take notes during lectures and seminars). If, at any point, you spot a way that the material can be used, such as for an assignment that is coming up, or you spot a connection between two ideas or topics, or would like to look over something again, note it down on this sheet. Keep this sheet in your mind's eye and, whenever the chance arises, follow some of the leads on there. This is a good way to relieve stress and it ensures that you are making the best use of the time you spend making notes.

I would not be surprised, or especially concerned, if you were still putting some of these ideas into practice during your final year at university. Knowing that note taking is a lifelong skill makes the effort worthwhile, whenever you make it. Developing the way that you use that skill only serves a function if it actually improves your study life. If you make a change to the way you make notes and, even after a few weeks of trying, you find that it is making studying harder rather than easier, walk away from it and try another way forward, or revert back to what you have always done. If you find some methods that work for you, enjoy them, knowing that it was worth trying out something new.

11

Your first presentation

In the last decade or so, presentations seem to have become more popular in universities as a way to encourage students to explore ideas and also as a means to assess students' knowledge and understanding. This is, in general, a good move for you. It gives you the chance to show off your knowledge in a way that does not rely solely on an exam or a lengthy essay, and you are awarded a mark on the spot, or very soon after the event. My students usually say in their feedback that they like to 'get part of the assessment out of the way' during the term by giving a presentation, so that there is less pressure on them when it comes to written coursework or an exam.

This is a strange chapter in terms of career moments. Although in many aspects of your studying you will be able to modify your skills as you approach a career, every part of this chapter relates directly to your future career, assuming (as most of us must) that presenting, in one form or another, will form part of our working lives. When I can relate one particular aspect of presenting to a specific type of professional situation, I will, but other than that you can assume that this chapter in its entirety will help you later in your life.

Of course, having to give more presentations is only a positive move from your viewpoint if you are confident about your ability to give a good presentation and receive a high mark. Interestingly, even students who did well in school or college presentations can find a university presentation unnerving at first. This is partly because it feels more important, and partly because of the variety of ways in which presentations are used in university situations.

INSIDER
HINT

Although academics do not always reveal this to their students, it is the case that, for nearly all students, simply giving more presentations makes you a better presenter. The suggestions in this chapter will help you get better faster, but you will improve regardless of how scared you might be before your first presentation, or how frustrated you might feel if it does not go perfectly on the first attempt.

We will be considering together four types of presentation in this chapter: seminar presentations, assessed presentations, informal presentations and non-academic presentations.

Where and when might I give a presentation?

Seminar presentations can be expected of you nerve-wrackingly early in your time at university: the second or third week would not be unusual. This is probably a good idea, as it helps students to get into the swing of seminars from the outset; it can also be daunting. A seminar presentation will not necessarily be a long presentation though: ten minutes or so would be usual on many courses.

CAREER
MOMENT

On a vocational course where it is thought that students will be called upon to give presentations frequently in their future careers, presentations might be longer than this, and might become progressively more lengthy and demanding as a course progresses.

Lecturers will not know how experienced or confident each student in a seminar group is around presentations, so students in the group might be asked to volunteer for the topic/week in which they will give their presentation. The presentations are held informally, in the seminar room: although you are unlikely to feel very informal when it comes to your turn to present, of course.

INSIDER
HINT

It is easy to make the mistake of putting off your presentation by volunteering for the last possible opportunity. Students come to see me each term, explaining that they feel far more confident about a topic being covered earlier in the term, but that they are too worried about presenting to volunteer for a presentation slot early in the term. Once you have seen your first seminar presentation you will know everything that is involved and need not hesitate to volunteer for whichever topic appeals to you most.

Seminar presentations such as this are not assessed as part of your module mark, although you might be given a mark or grade to show how well you did; this is usually called a **formative mark**. Being marked, even in a formative way, can put students off presenting in the first two or three weeks, so you might need to make a strategic decision: do you present early, and so have no presentation stress later in the term, or do you hold back until you feel more confident in the subject area? Only ever base this decision on your knowledge of the topic, not on your feelings about presenting.

Top tip

> If you know that you are going to be asked to give a seminar presentation in three of your modules, decide how you might spread this workload over the term before you are asked to volunteer. It might seem a minor point, but avoid sitting at the end of the group if you have a plan of when you want to give your presentation in a seminar: this might give you first choice as a sign up sheet comes around, it might leave you last and with no options.

On the surface, **assessed presentations** can seem identical to standard seminar presentations, but they will feel different. You might be in the same seminar room, and in front of the same students, but your seminar leader might be joined by another academic who will also be marking your presentation, and they might both be looking down to make feedback notes from time to time.

If the situation is altered for assessed presentations – if you are expected to be in a different room from your normal seminar room, for example, this need not concern you too much. Students often find it helpful to be in less familiar surroundings for an assessed presentation, as it makes them feel more formal and ready to perform well.

INSIDER
HINT

The single most common point of failure in an assessed presentation is a student's inability to address an entire audience. In your eagerness to do well, your eyes can be drawn inexorably to the markers in the room, ignoring all of the other audience members. Being aware of this so that you can avoid it is a simple fix that could give you dozens of extra marks during your time at university.

You might assume that **assessed presentations** come only at the end of a module, but this might not be the case. Some academics decide to devote only a small proportion of the module marks to the presentation (maybe 10–20 per cent) and then ask students to give their presentations each week from weeks three or four of the term. This is good news for you – the marker will also have to give a relatively high proportion of the marks (up to 70 per cent would not be unusual) to your preparation (your slides, handout, how well you seem to have prepared your argument) so as to compensate for the fact that not every student will be accomplished in giving presentations.

INSIDER
HINT

It is possible that you will be marked not just on your presentation, but also on your engagement as an audience member. Listening well, asking relevant questions and giving productive feedback to your fellow presenters is good practice anyway (you will want them to do the same for you) but if it counts towards your grade, you will want to make doubly sure that you are fully involved in the event.

In this context, I am taking informal presentations to be those that you might give to a study or reading group. These might happen anywhere and be of varying lengths of time, but it pays to approach them in a similar way to any other presentation. Aspects of a presentation that your audience will care about will still pertain no matter how small or casual that audience. Use the following checklist as a guide:

Checklist – informal presentation checklist

✓ Keep to time – others will want to speak.

✓ Make your slides clear and legible – this shows you care about the group.

✓ Offer a handout, even if brief – this will help you to marshal your thoughts.

✓ Begin with an overview of your structure – however brief the presentation.

✓ Give everyone time to make notes – they need to feel their time is well spent.

✓ Let everyone know when to ask questions or discuss your points – keep control.

Your expectations of university might not have included **non-academic presentations**, but these arise quite often, especially if you are involved in the wider life of your university. Working on a club or society committee, being elected to office in your Students' Union, acting as a student ambassador or advisor: all of these activities will require you to present from time to time.

CAREER
MOMENT

When you come to face the career market, presentations are going to remain important not just in gaining a job, but also in being successful. Actively seek out the chance to gain as much presentation experience as possible whilst you are studying.

Who will be watching?

An **assessed presentation** might be given to your tutor alone, or to your seminar group, perhaps with your tutor and another marker present. However, your tutor might decide to invite a wider audience, with a group of academics coming along, or students from another module or seminar group joining in to see what you have learnt.

None of this will get in your way, and you do not need to change how you behave at all, but you do need to know in advance so that you can ready yourself for the right audience.

INSIDER
HINT

It is sometimes possible to give an assessed presentation just to your seminar leader, rather than to the whole seminar group. Nervous students often want to do this, but, almost without exception, those who do it tell me afterwards that they wish they had simply given the presentation along with everyone else. This is because they have had to keep worrying about it when their peers have achieved it and moved on, and also because it is more difficult to give an effective presentation to just one person.

How long might a presentation last?

Although this is probably an unanswerable question, as it depends on your discipline area and the purpose of the presentation, it is worth noting that **seminar presentations** are often fairly short (say, ten to fifteen minutes) if the expectation is that they will be used as a spur to a wider conversation. If that is the case for your seminars, make sure that you know in advance whether you are expected to lead that wider conversation or whether your seminar leader will take over at that point.

Assessed presentations will usually be a little longer: perhaps twenty minutes or so (although it would not be out of the realms of possibility for you to be asked to present for twice this length of time).

Informal and **non-academic presentations** are often the most challenging in terms of timing, because you are not given a strict time limit, yet there is probably an expectation around roughly how long you will be speaking.

Top tip

Be pushy here if you can. It is not a pleasant experience to turn up to a study group or university event expecting to talk for the wrong amount of time, so you have a right to be given some sense of what is expected of you. People will recognise that your questions about the detail of the presentation reflect how seriously you are taking it.

CAREER MOMENT

For job interviews, you will be given a very strict time limit, and you absolutely must work within it. Running over on time makes what you have said almost irrelevant: if you cannot manage your time you are unlikely to be an appealing candidate.

Will I be presenting alone?

Not necessarily. You might be put into pairs or a group for presenting, or you might be given the choice between presenting alone or as part of a group. If you are given the chance to decide, think about it carefully. If you have any doubts (you do not know how the other people tend to work, you prefer to keep control, you might struggle to meet up regularly, you do not seem to agree on how to approach things) then present alone. It might seem more daunting, but it allows you to shine without any possible glitches from others. If you feel confidence in the student(s) with whom you will be presenting, working as a pair or in a group can be easier as you can play to each person's strengths and rely on each other for support.

It might seem counterintuitive to carry all of the work of a presentation alone rather than dividing it between a group, but group work of this type brings its own challenges and can be harder than simply preparing a presentation for yourself. I have had such mixed results with group presentations that I try to avoid offering them as an option for formal assessed work.

If you are given no choice but to present as a part of a group, or if you have the chance to present with a group of people with whom you know you can work effectively, here are some 'golden rules' that you might follow:

Checklist – group presentations, questions to ask

- ✓ Decide at the outset how you will communicate: meetings, email, calls?
- ✓ How will you divide the presentation between you?
- ✓ Do you all have to speak?
- ✓ Would your weakest speaker prefer to introduce you all and then sit down, and/or field questions at the end?
- ✓ Would you work better if one person made all the slides, or would you prefer to have one person collate and check the slides produced by everyone else?
- ✓ Are you each going to move your slides forward, or will one person be in control of the lights and the slides?
- ✓ How often will you need to meet to prepare the material?
- ✓ Can you each rehearse separately and then give yourself an afternoon, or whole day, to work through it together?
- ✓ Would you prefer your group to present first?

As you work together, you should find that you become more effective as a group. If you find that one group member is not joining in and helping, and you have no idea why, try not to leave it for too long. Give that person one chance to explain and, if you are not satisfied, contact your lecturer and ask to have that person removed from your group or marked at zero. If the person turns up on the day, you can then ask your lecturer to tell the student not to try to join your presentation at the last minute.

Top tip

> If you are presenting in a pair or small group and you know that you are going to struggle to get together to work on your presentation, it is possible to decide to look at distinctly different aspects of a topic, then email your presentation slides to each other well in advance and just have a rehearsal together. As long as you explain on the day that you are going to present on these different aspects, this can work well.

When it comes to presentation day, there are just a few things to remember in particular if you are presenting as a group:

Checklist – groups presentations, on the day

✓ Everyone must have a copy of the presentation slides on a memory stick, or as a URL or attachment in an email, and in hard copy in case of emergency.

✓ If you have handouts, make sure that one of you is responsible for producing the right number.

✓ You might dress in a similar style, if this would help you work as a group: similar styles of clothing (all smart, or all casual) and similar colours can help you feel confident.

✓ Make sure that you have chairs arranged so that you can all sit facing the audience, slightly at an angle so that you can also be seen to be interested in the presentation.

✓ For every moment of the presentation, every member of the group must look fascinated by what is being said: no fidgeting, no staring out of the window, no frown of disagreement.

✓ Smile at the audience as a group at the beginning, as you pause ready to start your presentation.

✓ When you hand over to each other, be very formal, stating again the name of the person who is to present next, with a sentence explaining how that section's material connects to yours, and then smile as the next person comes across to take over and you sit down. This level of formality reassures the audience of your professionalism.

✓   Decide ahead of the event who is going to field questions. If this is you, make a genuine effort to pass questions on to the relevant person, rather than allowing yourself to answer every question.

I have seen students who pass responsibility for group presentations around the group to the point where nobody has prepared anything much; I have also seen groups produce astoundingly good presentations. Either is possible, and you have the collective power to choose how high your group presentation mark will be.

CAREER
MOMENT

Although there can be challenges with group presentations, there is one huge advantage to taking up this option: there is little doubt that you will have to present in a group as part of your professional life. Learning how to present well in a group will be of great value to you as you move ahead professionally.

Will I be using technology?

It would be unusual not have access to any technology as you present, but make sure that you check in advance exactly what will be available. You might well have a choice about whether or not you use it. It is possible to give a highly effective presentation with no more than a handout or a model/demonstration, and if your audience has just watched six presentations with densely packed presentation slides, it can be a relief to sit back and just listen to someone.

Find out at the outset exactly what is expected of you in terms of technology; you can then use the checklist below to decide, from your options, which technology would best suit your purposes.

Checklist – presentations and technology

PowerPoint advantages:

☺   It is familiar to most of us.

☺   It looks professional.

(Continued)

129

(Continued)

☺   It offers you reliable templates.

☺   There is a neat progression from slide to slide.

PowerPoint disadvantages:

☹   It is so familiar we can get bored easily.

☹   You might be tempted to rely on it too much.

☹   The range of features can make it distracting.

Cloud-based software (such as Prezi or Google Presentations) advantages:

☺   It looks fresh and new to many audiences.

☺   Prezi in particular is hugely creative and can tell a good story.

☺   It is intuitive in its design.

Cloud-based software disadvantages:

☹   Downloading to a memory stick is not always easy.

☹   If the internet fails on the day you could be stuck.

☹   Some people find it difficult to watch as you swoop back and forth in Prezi.

Internet advantages:

☺   You can click onto a clip or page that someone else has made.

☺   You can tap into expertise efficiently.

☺   A screencast or videoclip can add interest to a presentation.

Internet disadvantages:

☹   The internet has to be working on the day.

☹   You have to manage your time more tightly.

☹   The material was not designed for a presentation.

Audio equipment advantages:

☺   Using a videoclip with sound appeals to audiences.

☺   A microphone ensures that you can be heard by everyone.

☺   Music playing softly as you wait to present intrigues an audience.

Audio equipment disadvantages:

☹ A silent videoclip, if the technology fails, is frustrating.

☹ A microphone can distort your voice and you probably do not need it.

☹ Too much sound can look pretentious, or as if you have nothing to say yourself.

Conference software advantages:

☺ You can widen the scope of your audience, if they are calling in.

☺ You can give a presentation from a distance, if you are calling in.

☺ You can easily record the event.

Conference software disadvantages:

☹ It seems always to break at crucial moments.

☹ The audio can be persistently problematic.

☹ It takes some getting used to, and this can be distracting.

Top tip

> You will have noticed that several of the disadvantages around presentation aids lie with the potential failure of technology. Always, always have a backup of some sort ready that does not rely on technology.

As you can see, there is plenty to consider when you are making a decision about presentation aids and technology. To be fair to technology, I should perhaps also acknowledge the weaknesses in old-fashioned presentation aids:

Checklist – presentations without technology

Handouts advantages:

☺ Technology is not needed.

☺ It gives your audience members something to look at whenever they like.

☺ Audience members have something tangible to take away.

(Continued)

(Continued)

Handouts disadvantages:

☹ It takes longer than you expect to hand them around.

☹ You might be tempted to put too much information on there.

☹ You cannot control when an audience member looks at information.

Physical example advantages:

☺ You can prepare the object in advance to make it perfect.

☺ Audiences get excited about seeing a physical example of what you are saying.

☺ It is striking and so helps the audience understand your points.

Physical example disadvantages:

☹ It might be too small to make much impact.

☹ Only part of your audience might be able to see it properly.

☹ It might be a distraction after a while.

Demonstration advantages:

☺ Audiences usually love them.

☺ It shows your energy and enthusiasm.

☺ It can save you time just to show rather than tell.

Demonstration disadvantages:

☹ If you are nervous, your audience will be nervous for you.

☹ If it fails, you will feel embarrassed.

☹ If someone else gives the same demonstration before you, yours would have less impact.

Luckily, you should have the chance to try out all of the different options described here, so you will not need to have a set preference for one type of presentation aid that you always use. It is more a case of trying them out and then using each type of aid where you think it is best suited to what you are trying to achieve.

CAREER
MOMENT

It might seem odd to you that I am including technology such as conference software or cloud-based presentation slides, especially if you do not expect to do more than give brief presentations to your study group. Even though you might not need to use this technology, you are in the ideal place to try it out as you study. Giving a Skype presentation from the room next door to your study group will feel funny, but it will give you vital experience in this type of remote presenting technology; this could be vital if you are later interviewed for jobs in another area or country.

What about making presentation aids?

We could spend hours together thinking about preparing the presentation aids that you might use during your time at university, but that is not the best use of our time in this guide. If you are inexperienced or anxious about making aids that work well, you will no doubt seek help from tutors, study advisors and other guides. For our purposes here, I will offer a few 'golden rules' for making presentation aids.

Checklist – golden rules for presentation aids

✓ Work on them early, otherwise you might panic and overfill them.

✓ Always ask someone to check them for you: little errors look huge on a big screen or a handout.

✓ Always have a backup ready in case technology fails you.

✓ Make sure that they are accessible to all members of your audience. Produce additional material if that would help.

✓ For handouts, decide in advance at what point you will hand them out, and then leave enough time for everyone to get a copy.

✓ Always allow more time than you expect for people to look at them.

✓ Look at the screen yourself as you change slides, as a prompt and to remind yourself to give others time to take in the information on the slide.

✓ Other than that, try to avoid looking at the screen.

✓ Handouts do not have to be boring: keep them brief and engaging; use colour and images; try a larger size font to increase impact.

(Continued)

(Continued)

✓ Think about what you can offer your audience to take away: a handout with links to your online material, perhaps, if you are relying solely on slides.

✓ For slides, avoid using colours that fade in light (such as red and yellow) and make sure the contrast between background and text/image is high enough.

✓ Use large font sizes (20 point as an absolute minimum).

✓ Avoid too much punctuation on slides and avoid crowding them.

✓ Creating a first, introductory slide with your name, student number and topic is useful, especially if a marker who does not know you is in the room.

✓ Slides or handout pages throughout your presentation that offer an overview of what you intend to cover overall, or what you plan to discuss next, are always appreciated.

✓ If you are intending to talk for some time with no aid, reassure the audience that you are not going to refer to the handouts for a few minutes, and/or use a blank slide in your presentation.

✓ If you have to skip over material for which you have a handout or slide, do it deftly, mentioning to the audience that the material was prepared for them to read later (and that you will send out a copy of the slides).

✓ Once your aids are perfect, rehearse with them in play, so that you get used to the timing and rhythm of your presentation with its aids.

✓ If anything goes wrong, press F5 (the 'refresh' key) and *smile*. Key F5 does not always fix the problem, but it does give you a chance to turn away from the audience as you decide to move ahead without the slides, and pressing F5 always seems to make us feel better in these situations!

What is the best way to rehearse?

Top tip

Whenever you practise your presentation, even if you are just testing to see if it works to time, make sure that you stand up to deliver the presentation. The reason we talk about 'giving' or 'delivering' a presentation, is that it is intended as a gift to your audience members. You are offering them your thoughts and ideas in a formal way, and you need to stand to achieve this. If you sit down and rehearse, you will inevitably speed up and lose your sense of how much time it will take on the day. Always rehearse to no more than 90 per cent of the time you have been given: it usually takes longer on the day, and nobody would worry if you were a little under time.

Whether or not you are presenting alone or in a group, you can run through this sequence of rehearsals to make sure that you are confident and ready, but not so over rehearsed that you sound bored or uninterested in your material.

Checklist – sequence of rehearsals

✓ **Rehearsal for material**: read through your material, either from a script or from prompt notes or cards, to see if you have enough material, if it fits well together and if it achieves your purpose.

→ Cut the material down or add to it between this rehearsal and the next.

✓ **Rehearsal for time**: present your material, this time at a slower pace as if in the real event, and check that the timing is right.

→ Adjust the material again if the timing does not work, but from now on, rehearse only from prompt cards, or very brief notes on one piece of paper that you can put down, or from your slides. Throw your script away.

✓ **Adjustment rehearsal**: now that you are working from prompts your timing might alter; this rehearsal should reassure you that you are on track.

→ If you have been miming looking at the screen each time you would show a slide, now is the time to use the real slides. From now on, always use the slides, or refer to real handouts, as you rehearse.

✓ **Presentation aids rehearsal**: this rehearsal, using your slides, demonstration, online material and/or handouts, will feel very like the real event. If you possibly can, this would be a good time to rehearse in the space in which you will be presenting. Even if it is a familiar space, like your seminar room, it can feel quite alien once you are standing up and speaking in it, so a rehearsal in the space is useful.

→ You will not expect anything much to change from now on, except your audience. If you can ask friends to come and listen to your next rehearsal (they need not be expert in your material), this can be a great help.

✓ **Final timing rehearsal**: you will hope that your timing has not drifted too far, and hopefully you will have a rehearsal audience of friends and supporters there to make it all feel real. Ask your audience broad questions, rather than worrying too much about the detail of your content. Can they read the slides? Are there any errors on the slides? Can they hear you from where they are sitting? Does the flow of the presentation work?

(Continued)

(Continued)

→   You might be happy to leave it at that. You know that your material works and that you have a strong argument and/or a clear message. You are happy with your presentation aids and you know that the timing works. If you find your nerves getting the better of you, you might want to undertake one final rehearsal.

✓   **Stress reduction rehearsal**: you must approach this rehearsal on the assumption that only small details will change. It might be that you rehearse to calm your nerves in a room near your presentation room in the hour or so before you give your presentation, just to boost your confidence. If you spot a minor error on your slides, it will not be too late to change it; if you find that the timing is not working quite as you planned, ignore it.

CAREER
MOMENT

The value of working through this list now is that you will see how well it suits you. Perhaps you prefer to allow a good amount of time between one rehearsal and the next, or maybe you find it helpful to run through two or three of these types of rehearsal in a row, as you find your way into your presentation. It might be that, when working in a group, you would rather not undertake all of these practice runs together, but rather work alone to start with and then come together for the final rehearsals. All of this is important knowledge: when you present professionally you will be confident about how you prepare best.

What if I get nervous?

Good. You need to be nervous if you are to perform at your best. Not so nervous that you cannot speak and you feel ill, but nervous enough to allow the adrenaline to help you think faster and react well in the moment. Now that you know improvement in presentation skills relies largely on just giving plenty of presentations, and working on getting a little better each time, you are unlikely to avoid them even if you are nervous.

CAREER
MOMENT

Within an academic setting, and often within a commercial setting too, audience members are not fazed by nervous speakers. It is a commitment to them (they matter enough to make you nervous), it shows the importance of what you are doing (because you are doing it despite your nerves) and it spreads a feeling of goodwill (partly because the audience members are relieved that they are not having to speak). As long as you smile, to show that you are nervous but also keen, well prepared and determined to present, nerves will not be a problem for you in terms of the grades you achieve or the professional impact you make.

If you get so nervous that you need adjustments to be made (that is, if you have a documented anxiety problem or similar) then your tutor will be able to do this for you, but even those students who suffer from anxiety often still choose to give their presentations, knowing that they will feel more confident by achieving this.

There are relaxation and anti-stress exercises you can try and techniques you can use to help keep your nerves under control. Here are some practical steps you can take if you are worried about how nervous you might get:

Checklist – presentation nerves

✓ Avoid taking rapid deep breaths – this can leave you feeling dizzy. Slow, longer breaths are better.

✓ If you can, be the first or second presenter. Academics would rather alter the order of presentations than have a student suffering, or unable to give a presentation.

✓ Never use a script, however nervous you are. It will encourage you to look down at it and talk fast and quietly.

✓ Use prompt cards with bullet-pointed notes to help you keep on track, and/or slides that will help remind you of where you are in your presentation.

✓ Avoid notes on pieces of paper – shaking is obvious with a noisy, shaky piece of paper, and it is too easy to hide behind it. If you have made some brief notes on a piece of paper to help you, put it firmly on the desk in front of you and anchor it with something so that you are not tempted to pick it up.

✓ Although you might not expect it, being nervous most usually slows us down when we present, even though we might feel as if we are dashing along. Always make sure that you rehearse to a few minutes under the time allowed, especially if you are nervous.

✓ Make a deliberate effort to smile every now and then: note this on your prompt cards if you might forget. A smiling, if nervous, student, can expect all of the goodwill of the audience.

Source: Rawpixel.com/Shutterstock.com

A presentation is a strange thing in many ways. It can feel important and formal even in a familiar setting; it can be exciting but also nerve wracking; it can feel like a disaster even when everyone has enjoyed it. However, one of the most important features of presentations is one that is rarely mentioned by academics: you will get better each time that you give a presentation. This might not be obvious to you, because we all have a tendency to focus on where we could have improved, but it is true.

With this in mind, it makes sense to take a few minutes immediately after each presentation you give, and then again the following day, to think through what happened. What did you do well? How are you improving? Where might you need to expend more energy next time? When you receive feedback on your presentation, see how well the list you made and the feedback points match. This will give you a sense of how objectively you are able to judge your performance and also give you a clear idea of any areas of presenting that you need to work on next.

With all of this hard work, the central premise still stands: you will get better each time you present, so find as many chances as you can to stand up and give it a go.

12

Study groups

Study groups will tend to pop up from time to time during your studying. They can be more, or less, formally composed and they are usually convened for a specific purpose. As you will be giving them your time, it makes sense to consider a variety of these groups, to think about what value they might have for you, and to develop strategies to maximise their effect on your studying and achievements.

The lecturer appointed study group

These are short-lived and useful in helping you gain the most from lectures. If a lecturer decides to offer a 'flipped learning' lecture, you could be asked to view a short screencast of the lecturer giving you the main points before the allotted lecture time. This might be around twenty minutes of film for a traditional hour's lecture. You might also be asked to look at supporting material or at additional online resources.

When you turn up at the lecture hall for your lecture, there will not be a traditional lecture on offer, but instead the lecturer will either answer a series of questions that students have sent in advance in response to the material, or will ask students to work in pairs or small groups to talk through their findings and thoughts and then feed these back with questions.

There are two ways in which study groups might be used here: you might be in a group in advance of the lecture, looking through the online material, or you might be grouped with other students in the lecture hall to talk through what you now know, and the questions you need to ask.

Checklist – for flipped learning preparation work groups

✓ If you are in a new group to prepare for each new lecture, decide straight away how you will communicate – meeting virtually online or in person?

✓ In your first group session, make a note of what works for you: each taking a section of the material from which to raise questions? Explaining sections to each other? Making individual notes and comparing them?

✓ In every subsequent group, whatever the membership, try to follow this same system if it has worked well for you.

✓ Appoint a spokesperson to ask questions or make points in the lecture from your group: you do not have much time to feed back, so one person talking makes sense.

✓ Other groups will ask a similar range of questions, so you will receive plenty of material regardless: make sure that your questions relate to an area you find tough, or to your assignment.

Checklist – for flipped learning lecture groups

✓ If you are already working with someone on a project for the module, sit beside them in the lecture so that, when you are paired up, you can ask questions relating to your project, if they seem relevant.

✓ You will not have much time, so focus your attention straight away to make sure that you have questions and comments that will really help you.

✓ If you do have a few spare minutes, talk about other opportunities. If you do not know the other people in the group well, find out what they are doing in their studying: this is a good way to find extra study groups, or good places to work, or useful source material.

✓ Make a conscious effort to move away from people you know for at least a couple of lectures. That way, you will meet new people who might appear again in your next seminar group.

> CAREER
> MOMENT

I am always impressed by how many students make excellent professional networks in these briefly formed groups. They spend those few spare moments talking about their plans and, before they have left the lecture theatre, they have a contact for a placement, or a lead for some summer work.

The peer learning group

Every study group is, in a way, a peer study group; that is, it is based on your fellow students, your peers, talking with you about your areas of study. In universities a peer study group can, however, be a more formal set-up, with students volunteering to join a scheme that is run centrally and offers training. Students with experience of a module, or a skills area (such as presenting, or using a learning journal) are allocated to a seminar or study group and asked to support the group members in their learning.

Student peer supporters/mentors are not going to be teaching you, or marking your work, but they will be helping you to understand each new challenge on a module and they will guide discussions on areas of your topic that you have been asked to work on, either in the seminar itself or in a related group outside the seminar.

> **CAREER MOMENT**
>
> If your university runs a peer assisted learning system, volunteer to be a peer learning supporter as soon as you can. The training for this position is usually extensive and useful, and you will gain impressive skills in mentoring, instructing and supporting. All of this looks fantastic on your CV, but students often miss this chance because they have overlooked how valuable it is to them for their future.

Checklist – for peer learning groups

✓ Be clear from the start about exactly what the peer supporters are offering to do for your group: lead discussion? Offer you questions to help you think through an area? Demonstrate technology or lab protocol? Watch as you practise a presentation? Explain how something works?

✓ If the timing of the peer learning group does not work for you, rather than give up on it check whether you can join another of the groups.

✓ Treat your note taking as formally as you would a seminar with an academic. If you cannot attend a session, ask for copies of the notes.

✓ When you are preparing for an assignment, be bold in asking for help to think through what might be expected of you in general terms.

✓ Your peer supporter is only concerned with your studying; if you are feeling unhappy with your course overall, or with life at university, you will need to seek help from your tutor or central support system.

(Continued)

(Continued)

✓ Peer supporters are not academics, and so will not feel confident in helping you with certain study areas, such as the detail of academic English, or the minutiae of a niche area of your topic. That does not in any way diminish their usefulness, but it does mean that you can expect them to point you to experts from time to time.

The student-led study group

Source: Franckreporter/Getty Images

This term can cover a multitude of activities, from a presentation group whose members disperse as soon as the presentation is over, to groups who get together to find more time in the lab and help each other, to students/societies linked to a subject area. If you do not see any of these prominently advertised on notices or online within your department, ask your personal/academic tutor or your peer supporter, if you have one. Do this regularly: many of these groups will only exist for a few weeks each year, in preparation for exams, for example, or around a one-off event such as an overseas study trip.

Student societies linked to a subject can sound quite casual, with a focus on socialising (for example 'The Chemistry Geek Club', 'The Italian Film Club', 'The Politics Department Student Debate Group'), but this often obscures some very useful academic work that goes on. There will usually be social aspects to such a club or society, but there might also be the chance to meet a study partner, or to pick up free books from past students, or to get hold of specialist material that is held only within the club archive.

Checklist – for student-led study groups

✓ Make your interest known so that academics or support staff tell you if a group already exists or if a new group in your area of interest is set up.

✓ Be clear about what the group offers, and what you are expected to do once you join.

✓ Let everyone know when you can attend meetings of the group. If you cannot make every session, the group can plan around that if needs be.

✓ If you are not online all the time, or if you are struggling to keep focus and trying to cut down on your online activity, let everyone know when you will be available for online activity.

✓ In a newly formed group, decide (and note down) what you aim to achieve, when you will get there, and how you will communicate.

✓ If you feel the need for a study group in an area of your work and it does not exist, set one up yourself. It is easy to do, especially if you can enlist support from a seminar group, or join with a friend to arrange it, or ask your personal tutor or seminar leader to support it.

✓ Explore funding if your group is going to be long standing and have an impact across a department or several modules. Money might be set aside in your department to fund study trips, or student conferences, or resources such as DVDs or cloud-based software registration.

CAREER
MOMENT

The importance of the funding that can sometimes be made available to formally constituted, student-led, subject specific study groups should not be underestimated. It can give you access to career boosting experiences, such as organising a conference or poster event, and also to expensive training and software that might be on offer only to this type of group in your university.

The revision study group

This might be one of the most useful groups you find, but it also has the potential to be the most destructive study group you join. I have seen students have their confidence ruined by working in revision groups where they are made to feel stupid; I have also known students who have become so terrified as a result of ludicrous rumours about exams in revision groups that they were simply unable to face the exam. As you can tell from these examples, revision groups must be treated with caution.

Checklist – for revision study groups

✓ Consider first whether you want to revise with your friends; it can be unhelpful to mix study and socialising in this formal way.

✓ How large do you want this group to be? If you have been put in a revision group by a seminar leader, would you rather split it up into smaller groups if this works better for you?

(Continued)

(Continued)

✓ Is the group guaranteeing to cover the areas in which you need revision help?

✓ After your first two revision sessions, analyse how long you have spent actually covering revision. Is it worth your time?

✓ Would you rather prepare for each meeting thoroughly, or do you find it more helpful to be faced on the day with questions and discussion?

✓ Is your group happy to spend some of its time together on the mechanics of exams, such as planning, multiple choice question techniques, essay structure and so forth?

✓ Do you need to ask an academic to join the group once or twice, so as to answer your questions, or perhaps to respond to queries by email or online?

✓ Would you want to meet the group after the exam to celebrate, or do you think this might encourage unhelpful or worrying speculation about what you did and how well you have performed?

Although revision study groups can be problematic, they also have advantages: bouncing ideas off each other, reassuring the group that you all have the same essential material on a topic, testing each other and providing moral support. For these reasons, a revision group should not be dismissed without giving the idea consideration.

Virtual study groups

Online study groups (either in chat rooms or via Skype) can be potentially useful if you are away from university and still want to work with other students, or if you want to collaborate with students on another campus or in another country. For some students, they never seem to quite gel: perhaps the technology gets in your way, or you prefer to sit with someone face to face. For other students, they work very well because they allow you to compartmentalise the group within your study life. You could be online with the group members only during agreed times and there is little possibility that you would ever bump into them casually. This could be ideal for you: fellow students with whom you have much in common, but who will not necessarily become everyday friends.

Checklist – for virtual study groups

✓ This chance might not come up as an automatic part of your study – are you prepared to make the effort to start a group, given the benefits that might accrue?

✓ If you have issues around mobility, or you live at home during term time, might this give you the chance to become even more involved in campus life, remembering that virtual study groups might operate on your own campus?

✓ Do you struggle to stay on task? Might this type of group lead you into wasteful hours spent online when you could be using your time more wisely?

✓ If you know that you want to limit the time you spend with the group, especially when you first join it and are evaluating its value to you, can you make this clear and stick to your good intentions?

✓ Do you feel comfortable using videoconferencing equipment? Could you try it out before you commit to joining a virtual group that meets that way?

✓ Does your VLE offer the functionality to create a virtual group within an existing module area of the VLE?

✓ Would you want to remain separate from academics, or would you like them to join you online from time to time?

✓ Are you as sure as you can be of the identity of members of the virtual group? Does it feel safe?

✓ If anyone is trying to sell you essays or in any other way ask for payment for cheating in the group, do you have a mechanism for removing them from that online area?

✓ If the group is successful working within its initial remit, could you work together to decide how else you might study as a group in future (such as supporting each other in your dissertation research)?

> CAREER
> MOMENT

When considering joining or forming a virtual study group, look beyond your immediate study needs. Students often find their opportunities to study aboard in these groups, or make contacts that give them vacation work options in other countries. After graduation it is often the friends in these groups to whom members will turn for both national and international professional contacts.

You will have noticed that this chapter includes plenty of 'career moments'. That is because study groups often run parallel with your studies, and so employers are impressed by your participation in them. Your study groups might be centrally organised or arranged by students, and it is relatively easy to bypass them altogether or simply not engage. This is always a mistake. If a particular study group is not offering you enough help for the time you spend in it, and you are not in a position to change it, you should give it up, but beyond that you will always gain from these groups. In the short term, your studying will be more time effective and your understanding will become deeper. As importantly, in the long term you will have something persuasive to talk about at interviews, because study groups offer you an easy route to skills that it can be hard, and time consuming, to achieve elsewhere.

13

Your first doubts

What doubts might I have?

It would be unusual, although not impossible, to go through your entire university life with no doubts at all about what you are doing, or how well you are doing it. For most students, an element of doubt creeps in from time to time, and it is only natural that this happens. Human beings reflect on their actions all the time, and this can allow doubts to arise. So, the first thing to remember is that you do not need to doubt your choice in going to university just because you are experiencing some confusion or anxiety.

Misgivings will come and go, and for most students, most of the time, they are just a mildly unsettling part of their university experience. For others, the anxiety grows, sometimes to the point that they simply cannot study at all. The problem for you is that it is difficult to tell in advance how you will respond to feelings of unease whilst you are at university, which is why this chapter is worth reading, even if you do not anticipate having any problems.

It might be useful here to outline what I mean by 'doubts'. Although I recognise that your doubts might be around emotional or mental health issues that are far wider than the scope of this guide, by focusing in this chapter on your study challenges, we can at least work together to ensure that your studying remains a positive part of your life. The list below is not exhaustive, but it does show the types of study doubts students at university tend to encounter from time to time:

- Should I even be at university?
- Am I clever enough?

- Did I choose the right subject?
- Did I choose the right module?
- Why do I not enjoy seminars?
- Why is my workload overwhelming?
- I am getting behind with my work – what should I do?
- How am I going to cope with a presentation?
- Why are my grades not improving?
- I have no clear career goal – what is the point?

There is a process for addressing doubts such as these:

- deal with doubts early (pushing them away is unlikely to fix them)
- spend time pinpointing as closely as you can what the problem is (identifying the problem clearly will allow you to get the right help speedily)
- never assume that you have fully identified the problem before you speak to someone else (if you reflect with someone, ideally a member of staff, you will confirm the exact nature of the problem)
- work out a solution that involves a clear plan of action (again, never hesitate to ask for help if you need it)
- keep to the plan (if it goes wrong, ask yourself if you misdiagnosed the problem, or if you just need to reschedule the plan a little)
- when you start to feel better, keep going with the plan to the very end
- move on decisively, safe in the knowledge that you have conquered this doubt at this point: that is enough.

The last point in this process is often the hardest. It is so easy to see yourself as 'someone with a problem' or as a student who has failed in some way, but that simply is not the case. Overcoming a problem, facing your doubts and dealing with them, that is the true success story of many students.

INSIDER
HINT

One of the most peculiar aspects of students doubting themselves or their study choices is that, when I speak to them, a surprisingly large proportion of them have no real doubts at all. They are tired, or homesick, or lovesick, or simply not eating and drinking enough. It might sound unlikely, but it is true: make sure that your doubts are not just a natural response to physical or emotional problems that have little to do with studying. I once let a distressed student have a daily nap in my office for a week: all of her huge doubts about her abilities and her choices simply melted away.

How might these doubts feel?

Although a list such as Table 13.1 cannot cover every possible study problem you might encounter, I will offer you here some different ways in which each of these doubts might present itself, so that you can recognise what might be happening.

Table 13.1   How doubts might present themselves

Doubt	How you might be acting or feeling ...
Should I even be at university?	• Checking out old school friends on social media and feeling envious of those who did not go to university. • Worrying far more than usual about how much it is costing. • Feeling uninspired about your assignments.
Am I clever enough?	• Fretting about the grades your fellow students achieved at school or college. • Freezing when you would normally happily ask a question in a seminar or study group. • Becoming upset as soon as someone questions your view on a topic.
Did I choose the right subject?	• Enjoying being in clubs and societies more than your module groups. • Feeling that something is missing, somehow, as if you have missed the point somewhere. • Worrying excessively about your career goals.
Did I choose the right module?	• Feeling that lectures are not making things clear enough to you. • Becoming anxious about the assessment tasks from the very beginning of the module classes. • Being angrier than you would expect at not being given a place on your first choice of module.
Why do I not enjoy seminars?	• Hating getting up early for seminars and/or struggling to sleep at night. • Being irritated that the people in seminars are not giving you the chance to talk. • Failing to make any notes in seminars, even when you are interested in the topic.
Why is my workload overwhelming?	• Finding no time to relax properly. • Slowly finding your enjoyment of your course ebbing away. • Longing for the vacation to start, but dreading the deadlines you have to meet before then.

(Continued)

Table 13.1   (Continued)

Doubt	How you might be acting or feeling ...
Why am I so behind with my work?	• Repeatedly checking the practicalities of your course, worrying that you might have missed a deadline. • Not being sure where all of your notes actually are – feeling that you are becoming less organised each week. • Being unclear about exactly what assignments are due.
How am I going to cope with a presentation?	• Believing that you are just not good at presentations. • Wondering if you have an anxiety disorder. • Focusing only on the moment you will give the presentation rather than preparing the handouts or slides you will be using.
Why are my grades not improving?	• No longer bothering to look at a marker's comments – they always say the same thing. • Looking over and over again at every comment, becoming more upset each time. • Being embarrassed because you do not really understand what a feedback comment means, and you are not sure who to ask.
I have no clear career goal – what is the point?	• Feeling that university might be a waste of your time. • Believing that every student you meet has a perfect career plan and you are being left behind. • Becoming convinced that you do not have any decent skills or experience to offer in terms of your career path.

The reason I have offered you such a detailed chart to show how you might feel or act is so that you can identify what is likely to be the root cause of your problem. I have already mentioned how often feeling unwell can lead students to believe they have a study problem that, in reality, is purely a physical malaise. You can see in this chart how easy it is for students to assume that they have made a major mistake in their course choices, or that they have the beginnings of a mental health condition, when in fact there is a simpler solution.

It would be wrong to suggest that students do not have many and various deep-seated problems that can affect their study life and, perhaps, their entire future. However, finding the true cause of a problem is the best start to fixing it; if you have a problem or a doubt that can be resolved fairly straightforwardly, this chart will be a good starting point.

Doubts are nearly always confusing; they rise up and make you feel negative about all sorts of things. It might seem strange to you now, but students regularly present a problem to me, and are clearly really anxious about it, but find, when we explore the situation, that they have missed the real problem entirely.

Problems that are deceptive

These are real problems that have been brought to me by students. I am including them here to show you how difficult you might find it to analyse your doubts; I hope it might persuade you not to keep your doubts to yourself, but to ask for help in working out what is actually wrong.

1. **Apparent problem** → carrying out a research project away from university would not give me the grade I want for this module, because I am not very good at independent research.

    Actual problem → the only project I have been offered is in London and I am not sure I can afford to commute, and I am uncertain about whether I have any other options.

2. **Apparent problem** → I have missed several lectures because I do not find them useful; I think I might have chosen the wrong modules this year.

    Actual problem → I recorded the first few lectures, intending to make notes later, and now I have hours of recorded material that I cannot find the time to revisit.

3. **Apparent problem** → I struggle with early seminars because I tend to oversleep; if I liked them better I suppose I would make more effort; maybe I am not a good fit for university.

    Actual problem → I work a late shift so I am usually up until 2 a.m.

4. **Apparent problem** → I suffer from seminar stress; it is making me very despondent.

    Actual problem → I have fallen out with a housemate who is in my seminar group.

5. **Apparent problem** → I need extra time for exams because I suffer from attacks of anxiety.

    Actual problem → I have never been taught any exam techniques so I cannot think straight as soon as I see the exam paper.

6. **Apparent problem** → I want to transfer to a university nearer home because I have found a degree course that I much prefer.

    Actual problem → I am really homesick but I do not want to burden my parents by asking them for the train fare so that I can go home more often.

None of the 'actual problems' in these examples are any less real or important than the 'apparent problems' that were presented to me in the first instance, but they are a very different set of problems than seemed to be the case. Also, in all of these real life examples, the actual problem turned out to be easier to fix than the apparent problem. That is why working with someone else (a fellow student, an advisor, your family and friends or an academic) is so important. Academics in particular are useful for this conversation, because they have seen so many different doubts and problems amongst their students.

Top tip

In their eagerness to help you fix a problem, the people in whom you confide might naturally rush towards identifying the problem. The time spent on analysing the problem is as important as the time you then spend on finding a good solution, so it is a good idea to talk to several different supporters when you are trying to work out what is wrong.

The first thing you might be interested to know is what the students in the examples above did to resolve their problems:

1. There was a webpage offering research project opportunities and the student had not noticed that there were two links for information, one for projects in London and one for projects outside the capital. The student clicked on that second link, and the academic relabelled the links to make them clearer.
2. The student returned to the slides that had been put on the VLE for all the earlier lectures, made notes from those and his memory of the lectures, giving himself a strict time limit of half an hour for each set of notes. He then just deleted the recordings of lectures.
3. The student changed shifts: this was not a perfect solution, because the money was not so good, but it did mean that he enjoyed university far more. I had offered to move his seminar groups to avoid those earlier seminar slots, but talking together made it clear that changing shifts and being less tired all the time was a better solution overall.
4. I was tempted to offer a new seminar group to this student, but I knew that each seminar group was taking a slightly different study path and I was worried that we might be creating a bigger problem if we went for this solution. Luckily, the student was so relieved to have worked out the actual problem that she chose to tough it out and get on with the seminars. It was just as well – they had made up their differences three weeks later.

Top tip

When you are trying to work your way through a problem or a time of stress remember that your university will have invested in a wide range of support, which might include welfare officers, study advisors, life coaches, counsellors and student support teams. The help will be there, and it should be signposted clearly online. If you cannot see it easily, your Students' Union would be a good place to start.

5. This took some time. The student worked with study advisors, online resources and published guides to learn about exam techniques. Although this was not a quick fix, it was better than allowing the student to believe that she had a serious problem with exams, and arranging for her to be given extra time in every exam.
6. As is so often the case, the student's parents were only too happy to pay the train fare: they had been agonising at home about why their child seemed to hate university.

How can I make my doubts go away?

Accept → that doubts will creep in every now and then. Before rushing to fix anything, just give yourself a few days to make sure that you are not under par physically for some reason. If the doubts disappear after a few days, you have learnt a useful lesson in how life as a student tends to develop a rhythm of its own.

Recognise → that if your doubts still linger, there may be an underlying problem that needs to be fixed. Once you have recognised this, doing nothing would be a mistake. Getting help early on is far better than letting a problem fester.

Slow down → although you will benefit from solving problems at the earliest possible stage, try to resist jumping to judgements early on. Time devoted to analysing a problem will be time well spent.

Reflect → on whether you recall similar feelings from an earlier point in your life. Just because you are in a new place does not mean that all of your feelings will be new. If you suffered from anxiety in your early teens, for example, you might be so surprised that it has resurfaced when you least expected it that you simply fail to recognise it.

Share the problem → ideally with two or three people you trust, one of whom should be a lecturer, a tutor or a member of your university's counselling or welfare team so that you can gain a university perspective on what you are facing and the help that will be readily available.

Find an expert → it is important to note that I am not a medical expert and so the advice offered here will only help with common study problems, not with more serious and fundamental mental health anxieties or issues. Your friends and family are probably not medical experts either but your university will be able to help you find the right expert.

Identify the solution → bearing in mind that it might be far more straightforward than you had expected, even if it takes some time to fix.

Give yourself a time limit → if, when you looked at the solution with your tutor or your family and friends, you all agreed that your doubts should be resolved within three or four weeks, and yet you have seen no real improvement in that time, ask for more help.

Share the reward → it is easy to overlook how much your supporters worry about you (including your tutors and seminar leaders) so making sure that they all know that the problem has been fixed will reassure them. It will also remind them to make sure that you are not put in a position where you face a similar problem in future.

Move on → even though, oddly, this is sometimes the most difficult part of the whole process.

How do I move forward from my doubts?

This sounds crazy, I know, but you can move forward best by taking time to stand still and reflect. This can be a powerful moment, when you recognise, with relief, that you are back on track and your doubts have been resolved. It will also be instructive: giving yourself even a relatively short time to remember how it felt to have those doubts – and to remind yourself of what you did, step by step, to overcome the problem, and also what you have achieved despite the doubts – will give you your best defence against that doubt undermining you again in future. Some students with whom I have worked have taken the trouble to write down their thoughts and reflections at this point, and also to record their plans for avoiding the problem in the next stage of their studying.

You have to move forward. If you fail to take the next step away from your doubts, you risk not really believing that you have overcome them and labelling yourself as someone with an intrinsic 'problem' even though you have taken successful measures to eradicate the hurdles. Put as much energy as you can into this stage, even though you might be tired from the work of fixing it all. Sometimes you can put this reflection on hold for a short while until you have time to ponder, if, for example, the vacation is only a couple of weeks away and you need the peace and quiet of home to think it all through properly.

Once you have carefully considered your doubts and how you overcame them, and perhaps recorded what has happened to you – even jotting it down fairly briefly – you will be ready to take the next successful step in your studies.

> CAREER
> MOMENT

The interview question 'tell me about a time when you faced a difficulty, and explain how you overcame it' is a moment in interview that is often dreaded by interviewer and candidate in equal measure. Even if the candidate has prepared the answer in advance, if often comes across weakly, as a made-up or exaggerated problem chosen purely to highlight a hidden strength. Whilst you will not want to share your innermost fears and doubts with an interviewer, the reflections you jot down in response to study doubts may offer you excellent examples of genuine and thought-provoking challenges that you have not just overcome, but also learnt from in a positive way.

14

Managing your time

Using your time well at university has been touched on throughout this guide, but here, towards the end of the second part, it will be considered more fully. This is partly because it is only once you have reached a point of some confidence in your studying that you can begin to take a well-rounded overview of your time management. It is also because this chapter relates directly to your career. Indeed, what you learn at university about making best use of your time will not just stand you in good stead when you begin your career, it will be an aspect of your professional life that you are likely to work on for many years.

You are likely to return to this chapter repeatedly not just as an undergraduate, but also for ideas as a professional, so see your study time as a chance to master the basic time management ideas offered to you whilst you are an undergraduate, then you will be able to finesse the way you use these techniques as each new professional challenge arises.

INSIDER
HINT

I once had a student who kept a record of the steps she was taking to manage her time more efficiently. She returned to her notes regularly, to remind herself of the methods she needed to employ; she also noted down any time management techniques she came across, ready for future use. I thought at the time that she might have been getting a bit too serious about it all, but she kept in touch and, more than six years later, she told me that she was known as a lawyer who got things done, just because she reused, repurposed and refined the techniques she had learnt at university for each new situation she faced.

How do I know if I need to work on my time management?

You do. It is as simple as that. You do, I do, everyone does, because every day throws up new challenges and a multiplicity of demands upon our time. To do well at university you have to maximise your opportunities and work in the smartest way you can, so that you use your time to allow you to shine.

A note of caution before we go any further: wasting time is one of the great pleasures of life, and it is also, surprisingly, essential to successful studying. Whilst you rest, your mind mulls over what has been learnt recently; taking a weekend off can sometimes be the most productive option. With this in mind, this chapter aims to help you control your time so that you can work well, but also take the time you need to recuperate and let your brain quietly process information.

How can I make more time?

It sounds too good to be true, but you really can give yourself more time each week to study, or relax, or learn a whole new skill. You make time by working out where you are losing time. Just for one week (mainly because this is so tedious to do that you are unlikely to last longer) make a note of how you use each hour in each day. You will find the results startling and fascinating. You probably have no idea, say, that you spend one hour and ten minutes each lunchtime doing nothing much. You might have no clue that you waste twenty-five minutes four times a week between lectures and seminars because it has never occurred to you to study in that time. It is easy to work out that in an eleven-week term this is nearly fourteen hours of time that has given you no use and little pleasure.

You might not have very long at all between activities, and so it is useful to keep a list of brief tasks you need to do, each perhaps fifteen to twenty minutes long. This is the list that will show your most impressive time management: you might be amazed at how much you can achieve over a week from this list alone. It is also a list that will help you manage some of your more challenging tasks. If you feel anxious about a study assignment or a project, take time to break it down into manageable chunks (ideally, some of these will take no more than twenty minutes to complete). The task will be more approachable once it is broken down, and your determination to complete it will increase with each chunk that you can tick off your list.

Time management cannot be about using every spare moment, but it is about putting yourself in the position of knowing where those spare moments are and then deciding what to do with them. If the spare moments actually turn out to be spare hours that you had not noticed you were losing (you always get talking between midday and 2.30 p.m. on a Tuesday, waiting for your regular lab slot, but then you always have to work on Tuesday evenings when you are tired) then you will have made a quick win just with one technique.

Finding useful gaps can be relatively easy to do and will make you feel good straight away. Exploring the other way in which you could make time might be far less easy, and it will not necessarily make you feel good in the short term. Understanding, and then reducing, the ways in which you procrastinate will always offer you the potential to find more time. Procrastination is the art of putting things off. For most students this does not mean doing nothing and simply not working; it means doing anything – anything at all – that does not involve work. The best procrastinators I know are also usually the busiest people I will meet each day.

Human beings seem to have a natural talent for procrastination, and it is important to know the difference between useful and unproductive procrastination. As I have been writing this section I have also been reheating a pasta sauce, which apparently needed the addition of fresh tomatoes, and then a sprinkling of paprika and then, for no apparent reason at all, I nipped to my kitchen just now and added fresh cream. Why? Because I am trying to think how best to express the help I hope I can offer you, and that is not always an easy task, so I procrastinated several times.

This is probably an example of useful procrastination, because I am reheating a sauce and thinking furiously at the same time. Later this evening I plan to have a delicious dinner and to mull over what I hope will be a helpful section of this guide. If I were making the sauce from scratch, and spent an hour in the kitchen doing it, that would simply be me putting off the task rather than introducing a few minutes of space to think.

One way to value your productive procrastination is to recognise it for what it is. You will probably already have some procrastination habits that you have used for some time: putting on some washing, checking your emails, reordering the books on your shelves, organising and rearranging your calendar. The following checklist offers you some useful study procrastination tasks. Each of these will take longer than me reheating a pasta sauce, but they will give you a break of no more than half an hour.

Checklist – some useful procrastination study tasks

✓ Working through your reading notebook to check references.

✓ Reducing a set of lecture or seminar notes to essential notes for revision later on.

(Continued)

(Continued)

✓ Going over any connections sheets you have made to see if you can add more connections.

✓ Looking through your latest reading list to plan your next library trip.

✓ Proof reading the assignment you have to submit later in the week.

✓ Looking at two or three screencasts or online videoclips that support your learning.

✓ Preparing some notes for your next study group meeting.

✓ Thinking of useful questions for your next seminar.

✓ Checking out the descriptions of modules you might choose next year.

✓ Skimming through some online or journal articles to decide whether you need to print anything off and work on it.

✓ Starting work on the first few slides for a presentation later in the term.

Each of these tasks might take you far longer than thirty minutes, so you will need to practise sticking within the time limit that suits you for productive procrastination (it may be less than thirty minutes if you struggle to get back to the principal task). One way to do this would be to set an alarm on your phone so that you recognise when your allotted time is up. Some students find this helpful because they can let themselves become absorbed by the productive procrastination knowing that they cannot overrun on time by mistake; other students hate it and feel too pressured by the alarm. Maybe try it and see how it works for you.

> **CAREER MOMENT**
>
> This habit of deliberate, productive procrastination will be reassuring to you when you begin your professional life. It is a work rhythm that feels comfortingly familiar, and you know it works. In every professional situation productive procrastination tasks abound, and they can be hugely satisfying as well as time saving.

You will find many ways to procrastinate, both good and bad, so you will always need to look out for unproductive procrastination, whilst appreciating the productive procrastination that you have also introduced. The downside of unproductive procrastination activities include the following:

Checklist – unproductive procrastination activities

✓ Help you to avoid a significant problem in your study life.

✓ Regularly swallow up more than 10 per cent of your study time.

✓ Become so absorbing that you struggle to return to your principal task.

✓ Distract you so that you cannot focus properly when you return.

✓ Make you feel guilty because you know that the procrastination activity is becoming more important to you than the main task you are trying to do.

How can I save time?

You will, naturally, be saving time by employing the studying methods advocated in this guide: that is one of its main purposes. You can also save time – and give yourself some time to relax – by making clear (to yourself and others) what you plan to achieve. You can do this by producing an action list for each day, or week or half semester/term.

Source: Amirul Syaidi/Shutterstock.com

Top tip

It works well if you let yourself be flexible about this: sometimes you might need a task list for each day of the week, because there is so much that is pressing, whilst at other times you might feel quite content to produce a weekly or monthly task list.

Dividing your tasks into categories can help give you an overview of the time that lies ahead of you: maybe you have plenty of reading to get through, or your main focus is an assignment, or there is an intensive series of long lectures coming up. By seeing the shape of the next spell of studying you will, without any conscious effort, be preparing yourself to learn.

When you try to devise a task list, take a few minutes (maybe more) to think through the types of task that you face in the next week: it is usually easiest to do this for a week in the first instance. These types of tasks will vary from course to course, but most of the following are likely to apply to you:

Checklist – types of study task

✓ Reading: books, journals, other reference material, either online or in hard copy.

✓ Revisiting: lecture/seminar/study group notes you have made, to see if they need reducing for ease of use, or if you could highlight certain key points or areas. If you are nearing an assessment such as an exam, you will also include practising and/or self-testing within this category of task.

✓ Researching: working on an independent research project.

✓ Preparing: for your learning events.

✓ Producing: an assignment, seminar, talk or presentation.

✓ Polishing: attending training courses to brush up on your skills.

✓ Attending: lectures, seminars, lab sessions, workshops.

✓ Actively seeking help: by seeing a study advisor or librarian.

✓ Assessing: where are you now? What might your task list look like next week?

✓ Getting organised: by working through reading lists and your reading notebook.

✓ Getting ahead: looking at the next study choices you will have to make.

✓ Giving yourself a break: this is as important as the other categories.

Two types of activity have not been included in this checklist because they are so important that they need a little thinking about separately. The first is your life away from university. Although your family and friends will want to support you in what you are doing, within a few weeks they will probably have very little idea of what you actually do each day. Even if you have siblings who have been to university, your routine (and the words you use to describe it) will be different enough for it to be tricky to follow for anyone not actually there with you. That is why it is so important to make a regular note in your task list to keep in touch with your family and check that they understand what is going on with you.

INSIDER HINT

I regularly find myself talking to students – and sometimes their families – about what seem to be huge problems that are, in fact, little more than miscommunication. A student recently moaned about a seminar presentation and the family thought their child might be about to leave university, simply because the student did not explain that the seminar presentation is not formally assessed and is just the particular challenge that popped up in conversation, and the really upset tone was purely coincidental.

The second task to highlight as important in your task list is to make your own 'career moments' regularly, just as I have been creating them for you in this book. You do not always need to know in advance what exactly you will be doing to further your career plans, but including 'career moment' as an action in each plan you make will give you the chance to take tiny steps, regularly, rather than allowing a career leap to remain as an unformed burden up ahead of you.

> CAREER
> MOMENT

For the vast majority of students, I am not sure that it is possible to sort out your entire career vision and make a workable plan to achieve your career goals over just the last few weeks of life as an undergraduate. Equally, I take the view that coming to university with an absolutely firm conviction of exactly what your career will be, and refusing to budge from that, brings dangers with it, as you will miss opportunities to interrogate your career plans as you develop. Without doubt, you can achieve a tremendous amount in the last weeks of a degree, but taking an incremental approach to your career plans, little by little each term, will give you the best chance to face the career marketplace with a solid and well thought out vision and a workable plan to success.

Career moments in this guide are being used to demonstrate how your career is not something that happens to you separately from university, but rather it is joined up with your studying life. By thinking about your career, from time to time, throughout your time at university, you will be able to see the strong connection between what you are learning now and what you will be achieving in future. It is simply a case of recognising what those career moments might look like for you. In the following checklist there are well-defined career tasks you might undertake, but you could also just add 'career moment' to many of your task lists, reminding you to take a moment and think about how what you are doing might relate to a future career, and how you might make the most of that. The list offered here is not intended as a 'one-hit fix': you will be returning to these tasks repeatedly, so you need not feel that any of them represent a huge amount of time. Little and often is the best way with this.

Checklist – career moments in your action plans

✓ Attend a drop-in session at your Careers Service.

✓ Check out any life skills sessions your university runs – these often translate well into graduate attributes.

(Continued)

(Continued)

- ✓ See if your university is offering career tests online, such as finding your perfect career, or psychometric tests.

- ✓ Ambush yourself with your CV, if you have one: a quick glance, imagining you are an employer, can be very revealing.

- ✓ Browse around the university, Students' Union and Careers Service website for a short while: what is on offer?

- ✓ Carry out some research into a career that you have heard about recently.

- ✓ Make a checklist of what you absolutely do not want from your career.

- ✓ Go back to your career radar charts (Chapter 8 on graduate attributes) to see if they have altered.

- ✓ Read through a section of Chapter 8 again to see if it prompts you to any other actions.

Although every student will, of course, produce a different task list for each week, the example offered in Table 14.1 will give you a sense of how yours might look for one week towards the end of a term:

Table 14.1 Example task list

Task type	Task	Done?
Assignment	Decide on essay title for module ST1CGH	
Reading	Journal article for Tuesday seminar – URGENT!!	✓
Reading	Reading notebook scan in Monday break?	
Attending	Lecture Monday 9–10, Room 249	✓
Polishing	IT skills session Monday 3–5, Room G90	✓
Attending	Lecture Tuesday 2–3, Room RF55	✓
Attending	Workshop Wednesday 10–1, Room 84	✓
Attending	Seminar Wednesday 4–5, Room 84	✓
Organising	Check out references from last lecture for reading notebook – Wednesday	✓
Home life	Home Thursday night – Make next week's task sheet beforehand	✓
Career	Sign up for CV workshop	✓

As you will see, this shows the task list at the end of the week. Most tasks have been completed, but a couple ran away from the student, and that is fine – they can be included in next week's list.

Top tip

The point of a task list is not to work yourself into the ground each week. It is about being able to assess what is coming up and how you might handle if. That is why it is fine to include tasks that you know you might not complete. In the example above, the student chose to have lunch with a friend on Monday, rather than scanning through his reading notebook to check on some references. This will not be a problem at all – it can be transferred to next week's task list – but it means that he was able to make a positive choice to have that lunch break, rather than walking around with the uneasy feeling that he was falling behind with something.

You might wonder why 'Attending' tasks need to be included in this list. After all, they are already on your student online timetable. Apart from the fact that time-tabling systems go down from time to time, reminding yourself in this format of when and where you need to be, can be a useful way to see the shape of your week. Seeing that both Wednesday events are in Room 84, which happens to be in the building next to the library, will remind the student that Wednesday is a good day to work in a study space in the library – that is why the reading notebook task is in there for Wednesday. In this example, the student also used to struggle to attend the 9 a.m. lecture on a Monday. Although this is no longer a problem, including it in the task list reminds him of its importance to the overall shape of his study week.

There are also some very easy tasks in here: signing up for a CV workshop is a matter of moments online, and he is unlikely to find it difficult to go home for a long weekend. They are on there, even though they are easy, because that way the student has a record of what he has done, and also has the pleasure of some 'easy ticks'. On weeks when study life is very busy (and this is not one of them) he will appreciate being able to feel a sense of achievement with some easy tick tasks.

It is clear that not every category of task I gave you in the earlier checklist is included in this task list. That is because not every student needs to be covering every aspect of study on a weekly basis. This is a relatively light week for the student, and so he has decided to make the most of it by reducing his task list to a pleasant level of activity, ready for his weekend at home. This list – alongside his previous and future lists – reassures him that he can afford to give himself this slightly easier week.

Top tip

> You might find it useful to manage your timetable on your smart-phone using an app. Be careful that whatever app you are using works correctly: occasionally students create an app for their university and its interface with the central timetabling system is unreliable.

How can I best use my time?

Source: VLADGRIN/iStock

You will need to consider two aspects of studying in order to make best use of your time: how do you work best each day, and how long can you focus? As I mentioned in Chapter 1, there is no reason to believe that you will become a new person just because you are at university, and this is to your advantage in using your time well. If you know that you prefer to work in the early morning or late at night, or that you like to take a nap each day, university allows for all of this. The systems that support you (your timetable, opening hours for your library or resource centre, even the availability of key tutors) will have been designed with this in mind.

All you have to do is remind yourself of how you like your day to work, and then aim to accommodate that in the way you use your tasks list and in the time you set aside for hard work study, easier study tasks and time off from studying altogether.

Top tip

> If you are not already aware of the time of day you study best, you could think more generally about your life when you are not studying. Do you naturally wake up early, or fall asleep on the sofa at 10 p.m.? Do you find that you can spend longer on any task in the middle of the day, perhaps, or late at night? All of these clues will help you work out your best daily routine, and trial and error will do the rest for you. It will not take more than a week or so for you to decide upon your best study routine.

How long you can focus on a task is not usually about how clever you are; it is more about a habit of working. You might be amazed and delighted to find that, during the days it takes you to write a lengthy assignment, the time you can spend on just sitting writing increases dramatically, so that you can sit for three hours at a stretch after just a week. You might then be disappointed to discover, when you face your next assignment some weeks later, that you lose focus after just thirty minutes or so. This can be disconcerting, but it is a clue as to how we all perform.

Concentration is about habit as much as anything else. The ability to sit for long periods and focus on a task comes with practice and, sadly, tends to leave us again if we are not required to keep up the habit. You need to recognise your optimal focus time so that you do not waste any of your potential study time. If you can only work productively for forty minutes, setting aside an entire after-noon to write an essay is pointless. You will not produce as much as you had hoped, and you will be disappointed and a bit confused. If you knew that your optimal focus time was forty minutes, you would have been able to set aside an hour a day for five days to write the essay.

The hour I mentioned in that last paragraph is important. Although you might discover that forty minutes is your optimal focus time, you can expect that time to increase quite quickly as you work on a task over time. It would not be sur-prising to find that you had increased your optimal focus time to an hour within two to three days and perhaps one and a half hours by the end of the week.

There is a simple way to ascertain your optimal focus time. Take a repetitive study task and count how much you achieve in twenty minutes (say, how many paragraphs in a journal article you can read and make notes on, or how many pages of lecture notes you can reread and condense ready for future use). Repeat this for the next twenty minutes, and the next … in one of those twenty-minute slots you will find that your work rate drops like a stone. You will have covered perhaps half as much as you were able to manage in the previous twenty-minute slot. So, now you know your optimal focus time – it is the end of the twenty minutes when you last managed to keep up a good work rate.

It is frustrating if you lose focus just at the point when you want to drive forward, especially if you have not given yourself quite enough time to complete a task with a deadline, but there really is no point in pushing yourself beyond your optimal focus time. You will produce substandard work that you will then have to rework and revise. Much better to give yourself a complete break and return to it later, even if it means working a longer day and taking your relaxation in breaks throughout the day and evening. If you return too soon your optimal focus time will automatically shorten, so make sure that the breaks you take are long and thorough enough: a nap is often a good idea.

CAREER
MOMENT

Another skill in your time management skill set – and one that it takes years to master perfectly – is to recognise, quickly and reliably, the difference between 'urgent' and 'important'. Busy people often have many urgent things to do, and can wear themselves out in the doing of all of those tasks. Smart people are those who recognise, from the mass of demands upon their time, what is actually important for them to achieve each day. This insight will help you at university, but even more so as a professional. We have all seen leaders and motivators who never seem to panic but, somehow, just do a good job and move on: they recognise that they face both important and urgent tasks, and are very clear about the difference.

15

Shaping your professional development

The first suggestion I want to make is that you go back to Chapter 8 (on graduate attributes), to consider again what graduate attributes you have acquired. When first you considered that chapter, you were introducing yourself to a new way of life; since then, you have developed your study skills and extended your reach into various aspects of study at university. You are now, as a more established undergraduate, in a good position to return to that chapter and reassess where you are. You will have developed a wider and more firmly rooted set of graduate attributes and, by working through the chapter again, you will be able to take stock of where you might go next in terms of making positive choices about how to hone them even more finely.

It may be that a clear career path is shaping up in your mind, or you may still be waiting to see how you feel about the many options open to you as a successful graduate. In either case, you will need to think about how you can shape your professional experience to fit the profile you need to present to the career marketplace.

This is not particularly about skills and knowledge: you are developing those, and the career moments in this guide, along with the guidance in Chapter 8, will help you to package them effectively. Rather, it is about showing that you have gone beyond study skills (however transferable they are) and gained some experience that is easily recognisable as professional and relevant.

In a way this can be slightly frustrating on the face of it. If you have already produced a presentation with excellent content and analysis, with an impressive set of slides, and have kept perfectly to time, as well as showing yourself adept at answering questions and leading a discussion, you will have gained a first class mark. Surely, you might ask, this should be enough to prove your worth? The answer is yes, and no. Any employer will be impressed with that achievement, of course, but what you have not proved is that you could present as brilliantly if you were handling less familiar, perhaps commercial material, in front of strangers, with an even tighter time frame and with critical questions designed to challenge you.

That being the case, you can see the need for enough professional experience to show your abilities in both camps – academic and professional – and also your commitment to the professional world. Although you will not want to damage your studies by taking too much time away from the classroom and lecture hall, an undergraduate with no professional experience at all does tend to be at a disadvantage. If nothing else, it can make your interview conversation rather stilted if you cannot refer to any experiences beyond school, college and university.

Where do I start?

Start from where you are, rather than where you want to go. If you have a clear career goal in mind, it might make it easier for you to identify types of experience that would be useful, but you need not wait until you are certain of your career goal. Indeed, some would argue that a career destination, if you stick to it too tightly, could impede your chance to gain some valuable experiences that do not fit strictly within the requirements of that career.

Your first task will be to analyse the experience you have already and recognise the skills you have acquired. This is not an overly difficult task, but it is easier to do with a friend or supporter who is able to prompt you as you go. Most of us underplay our achievements and overlook valuable material, so having a cheerleader beside you can be very useful.

There are many ways in which you might choose to record your professional experience, but you will always be looking to note the experience in detail, alongside the skills and attributes you developed as part of that experience and then, whenever it seems relevant, to note down any examples or anecdotes that you might introduce at interview. A brief example in Table 15.1 from one common type of student job will show you how this could work for you:

Table 15.1   Example professional experience chart

Job title: Bar work in a local pub		
Task	**Skill/attribute**	**Interview example**
Opening and setting up	Working within systems Teamwork Reliable	
Selling refreshments	Prioritising Working under pressure Cash handling Health and safety awareness	
Balancing the till	Basic financial skills Trustworthy	
Talking to customers	Dealing with members of the public Diplomacy Enthusiasm	Handling a customer complaint quickly and respectfully
Running the weekly quiz	Organisation Research Presenting skills	
Running the pub's social media sites	Marketing Social media skills Attention to detail	Increasing the weekly quiz attendance by 300 per cent

You will notice that there are only two interview stories to be told from this job, because they are both convincing and relevant to the types of job for which this student is hoping to apply. You might also recognise that a benefit to the employer is being highlighted in these interview examples: Chapter 8 (on graduate attributes) gave more detail on how this might work.

A job will not provide your only examples of skills and attributes at interview or on your CV. Your studies and other activities away from the classroom will offer you plenty more material to show your talents, but this chart does show how much proof you can acquire (as well as professional self-confidence) from just one everyday job.

You will not want to neglect your personal experience if you feel that it helps to demonstrate marketable skills. If, for example, you have children or other caring responsibilities, you could help visualise how this contributes to your skills inventory with a chart such as Table 15.2.

Table 15.2   Example personal/situational experience chart

Situation: Parent or carer		
Task	**Skill/attribute**	**Interview example**
Managing a household	Organisational skills Financial acumen Communication skills	
Dealing with outside agencies (school, care support)	Analysing situations Prioritising needs and actions Negotiation Dealing with a variety of people Understanding systems	When you succeeded in negotiating a good outcome for your dependant(s)
Meeting study deadlines alongside managing caring responsibilities	Flexibility Stamina Prioritisation Clarity of vision Determination	
Maintaining a positive relationship with a personal tutor and fellow students	Communication skills Respect for those in a situation different from your own Teamwork Reliability and trustworthiness	Being a team player is vital to success in so many careers that it makes sense to reinforce this with examples drawn from all areas of your life
Taking on major research projects such as a dissertation	Organisation Vision and oversight of a project Project management Ambition	The example of a dissertation would allow you to discuss your research and the skills and attributes you brought to the situation If the topic of your dissertation is not relevant to your career aims, it will not be wasted at interview because it still demonstrates these skills and qualities

Top tip

As you produce a table such as this, remember that your interviewer might have a similar early career experience to you. Talking about short-term contracts in modest jobs will be a point of connection, and will make the fact that you can relate that experience to your current career plans even more persuasive.

Can I use the experience I have already gained?

You certainly can, and it will save you time and effort if you acknowledge the value of what you already have 'in the career bank'. Any job you have ever done will have given you some skills and useful experience, even if it does not sound impressive to you at the moment. If you firmly focus on what you learned, and the experience you gained, rather than on the job title, you will find that even the most mundane job can suddenly shine as having offered you something of value.

When asked about their professional experience, students often tell me that they have 'only' had part-time jobs that did not really excite them. They can tell me all about their study skills, but they overlook the fact that their short-term, everyday jobs offer the only evidence they can provide of being trusted to handle cash, or working with the public, or organising an event. These students might need all or any of these skills, but do not appreciate that they have them already. The job titles might not have been especially impressive, but the experience was: eradicate the word 'only' from your mind as you examine the professional experience you already have.

Top tip

> If you have taken a whole series of low paid, reasonably unde-manding jobs, you need not list every single one of them, you can simply include a heading in your CV that can include them all by type, such as 'Part-time work' or 'Administrative experience' or 'Customer facing roles' and then you can list the range of skills and experience you gained in those posts.

So far in this chapter, I have been working on the assumption that you have had a job of some sort, but there is no reason why this would be the case. Plenty of students arrive at university never having had a job, and if you are in this category you might feel behind before you even start. You are not, and there is no need to worry about it.

First, gather up in your mind everything that you have done that might allow you to fill out the table above. The 'job title' in that table could be replaced by 'hobby/interest' or 'volunteer work' or 'travel experience' or 'home life'. You can then carry out exactly the same process to produce a table that reflects your life more accurately, and gives you a pleasing sense that you are not 'behind' at all. That last category, 'home life', can be an important one. If you have had caring

171

responsibilities in your family, or you have worked from home in a family business, never be tempted simply to discard such experiences. They are as valid as any other experience you could bring to your professional sense of self, and should not be underestimated; they often make for persuasive interview anecdotes.

How much experience do I need?

Probably not as much as you have been led to believe by your fellow students. You are about to be a well-educated, successful and ambitious graduate: professional experience is important, but you do not need to risk your academic success simply in order to gain experience, and you need social and/or restful time amongst all of this activity. Chapter 8 on graduate attributes will help you to decide what you need, either in generic professional skills and attributes or, if you have decided on a broad career area, on targeted skills and experience. The section above in this chapter will help you assess where you are. Now take a moment …

What do you need to achieve in terms of professional development? Does this mean that you need to gain more experience, or undertake training courses, or research activities, or various assessment tasks that will develop your skills? If you are not feeling confident about displaying your graduate attributes, how might your university opportunities, or professional experience, help with this? What does your paid work add to this?

Top tip

Avoid letting yourself be fooled into thinking that you need to take low paid work just because you are a student. You have valuable skills to offer, and you need to free up as much time as you can for your studying, so be bold and try for whichever part-time or short-term jobs are best paid in your area, even if they seem like a bit of a reach.

There is a case to be made for simply gaining as much experience as you can in your target career area, if you know that is what is demanded of a graduate hoping to enter that field (journalism, teaching and nursing would all come under this banner, for example). This can work well also for professional networking: gaining experience and contacts is just the sort of advantage that you will be seeking. However, always take that moment, from time to time, to work through your professional experience tables and radar charts to see whether there are any gaps to fill, or whether you can relax, knowing that you have enough experience to reach a successful interview and talk convincingly once you are there.

Top tip

> You will end up with several professional experience tables, one for each job, internship, voluntary position and so forth. This is all to the good, as it gives you a nice selection of examples and a good set of proofs that you have the skills and attributes to succeed in your chosen career. As you move through your time at university, though, let some of this fade into the background. If you find that your more recent experiences offer you similar proof of skills and attributes, it is fine to put the tables for your earlier jobs to one side. Focus on the best possible examples and anecdotes, wherever they come from.

What type of experience do I need?

Some of the experiences that will be useful to you have been mentioned throughout this chapter, but remember also that experience you see as 'just normal life at home' might be seen by employers as valuable. Working in a family firm is mentioned in the checklist below, but if your family undertakes other activities that could be seen to show you as capable and skilled (even if you have always just seen these as everyday 'chores') then make sure you include them in your profile.

This checklist might help you to think as widely as you can about what 'professional experience' could look like for you:

Checklist – types of professional experience

✓ Paid work.

✓ Voluntary activities.

✓ Running a club or society.

✓ Coaching a team.

(Continued)

(Continued)

✓ Volunteering for university roles such as student ambassador.

✓ Writing for your student newspaper or website.

✓ Creating and running a successful blog/website.

✓ Time spent working or studying abroad.

✓ A year in industry.

✓ A research project or placement in the professional world.

✓ Shadowing a professional.

✓ Running your own business.

✓ Working on a freelance basis.

✓ A role in your family's firm.

✓ Any award that involved training.

You will gather by now that experience is going to play a role in your journey towards early success in your career. Packaging your experience persuasively makes for a good CV, and being able to talk about it convincingly will underpin a good interview. However, there are advantages to not being perfect. If you notice (perhaps from your radar charts) that you do not excel in one area of your professional profile, and none of your professional experience tables help you to fill the gap, pause to consider how important it is. If it is not very important, and is something you can easily learn (such as being skilled in a particular software package) you might want to leave it, knowing that it will give a good (and genuine) question to raise at the end of an interview: 'Do you offer training in …?' (knowing that they do) is always a thoughtful way to round off a successful interview.

PART THREE

SUCCESSFUL ASSESSMENT

This part of the book reminds me of the layering that is part of university life: in fact, part of any learning experience. You will be using everything you have learnt so far from this guide as you approach assessment. So, for example, I can feel confident that you know how to make notes for an assignment (Chapter 10 on note taking), and you are clear about how to give an impressive presentation (Chapter 11 on presentations). All that is needed in this part is to give you some additional advice and information that will help you a little more as you face these challenges.

Given the amount of work we have already done together, these chapters can be brief, but I expect that you might return to them as easy reminders each time you face each form of assessment, until you feel completely confident about how you can succeed.

INSIDER HINT

Although the terms around assessment can change from university to university, you will usually hear the term 'formative' being used for any assignment where the grade or mark does not count towards the final mark for a module. This would include 'practice essays', for example, also sometimes called 'term essays' or, oddly, 'non-assessed essays'. Any assignment which has a mark or grade that counts towards the final mark of a module (that is, it gives you credit for the module) is usually called a 'summative' assignment.

16

Your first assessed essay/report

Essays and reports still provide a mainstay of assessment for many university courses, in all disciplines, so there is going to be a fair amount of variation between institutions, depending on how they are being used and whether they are formative or summative. The answers you are being given here must therefore be taken as broad guidelines rather than firm instructions. My intention is to give you a sense of what might be considered the norm, as far as such a thing exists, with an awareness that universities differ in their assessment practices.

When might my first assignment be set?

Probably earlier than you expect. It would not be unusual to be given a practice (formative) essay within the first four to six weeks of your time at university; you might be expected to submit a credit-bearing essay or report (summative) by the end of your first term or at the start of your second.

Top tip

> If you are working in a subject area for which essays and reports are the most common type of assessment, you might find that your essay/report deadlines all tend to fall in the same week of term. This is annoying, but it is not necessarily intentional: it is most likely the result of module convenors not conferring on deadlines. It is also sometimes thought to be good for students, because they will face simultaneous deadlines in their professional life.

How long would an assignment usually be?

A formative or practice assignment is sometimes a little shorter than the summative assignment for a module, and this is because it is designed to ensure that you are able to construct and write an assignment effectively, rather than expecting highly developed knowledge in the subject area. This might sound like good news, but it can be harder to produce a shorter assignment. You have very little room for manoeuvre and so you will need to plan thoroughly and write precisely.

In your summative assignment you will have more space to show off your knowledge and to stray into a few interesting tangential areas, although ideally not too many. The structure of an undergraduate assignment underpins everything that the student is trying to achieve; gaining a high mark is a real struggle if your structure is ineffectual. That is why planning is so important.

INSIDER
HINT

Students are usually told that the deadline for a formative assignment is an absolute cut off point. This is done to stop a group of students from submitting assignments over several weeks, making marking both difficult and unfair on the students who submitted on time. However, if you are unable to hand in a practice assignment you might ask if you could hand in a plan of the work you would have produced. This gives you the benefit of a mark, and also means that, if you were ill when several assignments were due in, you will not have to spend time on your return catching up on several full pieces of work.

Will I have a choice of questions?

Sometimes you will, for formative and summative essays, reports and other assignments, and students often express a strong preference for either a choice of questions or no choice at all. This is not something you need to worry about. If there is just one question, it is because the module convenor or lecturer has decided that there is one area that it is crucial for you to have understood thoroughly, so it is to your benefit to write on that topic and gain feedback.

What about making up my own title?

You might be required to make up your own assignment title even in your first few assignments, although this would be more usual later on in your course, once you have a good understanding of university assignments and your degree field.

178

Top tip

If there is a specific topic that is concerning you, perhaps you are unsure whether you have grasped the threshold concepts, you might ask to write a formative essay on that area, with a title being supplied for you by the module convenor or lecturer. That way, you get the feedback you need. This essay might be in addition to the standard formative essay, or it could replace it, or you might produce a plan and opening paragraph for each, to demonstrate where you are in your learning.

INSIDER
HINT

Students sometimes worry about making up their own titles for essays and reports because they see the quality and relevance of the title itself are some sort of test. If you are unsure of the title you have chosen, or if you simply cannot think of a good title, ask your seminar leader or module convenor for help. As long as you have a rough idea of the issue or concept about which you would like to write, the help is there to craft that into a suitable title.

Can I use images or my own format?

Usually, but always check. There are degrees of flexibility as to what students are permitted to do within a summative assignment, and you will not know how your department works until you ask. You will be given instructions (sometimes called an 'essay rubric' or 'assignment rubric') and you will know what is expected of you (usually from the module 'assessment outcomes', 'marking criteria' and, often, the 'marking/grading rubric') but you might still have some questions, which might be answered in person or by checking back to your instructions and the notes you made on your formative essay.

Checklist – questions to ask about summative essays/reports

✓ Can I choose to use either an essay or a report format?

✓ Can I make up my own title, as long as it is approved?

✓ What percentage of the module mark derives from this assignment?

(Continued)

(Continued)

✓ Can I include images?

✓ Can I include bullet points?

✓ Is it permissible to use 'I' (the first person) in the assignment, or should it be impersonal?

✓ What are my key areas for improvement after my formative assignment?

✓ Is there any leeway over the word count?

✓ Should it be double spaced, and what size font should I use?

✓ Do I need to hand in a hard copy, or is submission entirely online?

✓ If I am away, could someone else hand the essay in for me?

How much time will I get to prepare and write my assignment?

A week or two would make sense for a formative essay or report. For a summative assignment, you might be given four or five weeks, or even longer if the submission date is after a vacation. These timings would be for a standard assignment that makes up a percentage of the overall marks for a module. For a more significant piece of work, such as an extended report after a placement, or a dissertation or forty-credit research project, far more time would be given.

This is, perhaps, longer than is especially helpful to many students. There is a long lead time offered so that students can access all the material they need, even if some texts are on loan from the library already (although with online reading resources this is less of a problem than it once was). Academics are also keen to give you time to ponder, and plan, and carry out the thorough research that will be needed.

In reality, many students ignore the assignment until they really feel they can avoid it no longer, and then exhaust themselves trying to produce it by the deadline. This is not an unreasonable position to take. You are busy, with many competing demands on your time, and you are waiting to find a gap so that you have time to think properly about your essays. The problem is, that gap is unlikely to appear.

There is a far easier way to approach this. Produce a plan as soon as you can after you receive the title (no more than a few days) and then let it lie for a while. You will put slots in your task lists to work on the assignment, so you will not be panicking, but all the time you will have that initial plan in your mind, which means that all the time, inevitably, you will be shaping the essay mentally, ready to review (and perhaps rewrite) the plan once you think about the essay in detail. Of course, if you have an active learning sheet in play for each essay, you will be working on them as you go along, perhaps on a daily basis, and that will make the whole process easier: and produce a more mature essay (even if you have to battle to keep to the word count because you find you have so much to write on the topic).

Should I plan or jump straight in?

You may have studied your way right through the pre-university education system without ever having made an essay or report plan: students often do. However, university is too important to leave to chance and, more to the point, you are being asked to do something different as an undergraduate. No longer are you simply given a strict rubric and told to write into that mould. You are being asked to think and argue independent of any clear and easy instructions. Even if you are given detailed guidance, the expectation at university is that you are a creative and independent thinker, able to articulate an argument and express your findings in an impressive way.

Top tip

> Do not leave planning to chance. If you have not planned before, or if you tend just to write heading and subheadings in a list and go from there, or if you are familiar with only one planning method, ask for help with planning as early as you can. University study will place new demands on the way you think and organise your thoughts, so even the most able students will benefit from knowing how to plan effectively.

You will also be expected to be able to talk through your ideas with your seminar leader or academic tutor. These are also, probably, the people who will be marking your assignment, so they will not be able (especially in the case of a summative assignment) to work through your draft essay with you, but they will usually be happy to comment on a plan, even if the comment is deliberately wide and does not go into too much detail.

So, a plan is not just a way to organise your material as you are about to write an assignment. It is the method you will use to begin thinking about it, it is the structure that you will revise and develop as you carry out research and think more thoroughly on the topic, and it is the tool you might also use to gain some valuable early feedback on the direction you are taking.

Planning can also be a way to surprise yourself into writing, and I regularly use plans in this way myself. If you struggle to begin writing an essay or report because you are anxious about it (and this is commonplace among students) then a plan is a great way to ambush yourself. By the time you have added all the detail you need to the plan you will feel that the assignment is so clear in your mind that it is almost written. Your confidence in yourself and the assignment will have been building all this time, and now you are ready to write.

How can I avoid plagiarism?

Plagiarism (taking someone else's words or ideas and not citing your source) is a very complex problem and it is one that you might tussle with in your early days as a student. Although your university will give you guidelines, you might still be left confused from time to time. It is why universities talk of 'poor academic practice' or similar when a student first appears to have plagiarised, because it is so easy to do inadvertently.

There is only one rule here: if you are in any doubt at all, ask for help.

Academics are used to seeing sources cited throughout an assignment and will only be alerted to a problem if a citation and/or quotation marks are not somewhere they expect them to be. If an additional citation is put in that is not absolutely necessary, this will not especially concern them. You will want to get this right, of course, but if you are in any doubt in your early work then always err on the side of putting citations and quotation marks in rather than leaving them out.

What if I go over the word count?

It would be surprising if you managed to write exactly to the word count in an essay. It is usual to have to think about adding in a few paragraphs or editing your words down to the word count. An essay title will have been carefully considered, written out, probably then discussed with a marking or teaching team and then possibly revised. One of the points under discussion will be the length of the essay or report in relation to the title. If your essay is under-length, you might have missed a vital area that you were expected to cover; if you stray into a seriously over-length essay you may have misunderstood the essay requirements or you are struggling to express yourself clearly.

> **CAREER MOMENT**
>
> The ability to flex your language and argument so as to express your thoughts in more or fewer words is an important skill in many careers. If you are expected to write reports, where clients expect a certain length of report, you will need to develop the ability to control your word count in many different situations. Learning this now will ensure success in this area in future.

What is the best way to check my assignment before submission?

Probably not the way you were taught to do it earlier in your studies, mainly because this work might be longer and will be more individually crafted. Reading an essay or report through once or twice, from start to finish, is not the best way to find mistakes. Instead, try this method:

Checklist – checking an assignment

✓ Check all your headings and subheadings first, if you have any.

✓ Skim through the assignment at a fairly fast pace – fast enough so that you cannot read full sentences, but you can see the shape of what you have produced. Have a large highlighter pen in your hand.

✓ Whenever you come to a point that was not in your plan, put an 'I' in the margin – you might need to add this point into your introduction.

✓ If you come across material that you now believe would be better placed in the appendices or annexes of a report, put an 'A' in the margin.

✓ If you have included illustrations, graphs, charts or tables, are they all clearly labelled?

(Continued)

183

(Continued)

✓ If you are using a report format, have you included enough white space? That is, have you left plenty of space around graphs and illustrations; have you started each new section on a new page?

✓ Slow down a little towards the end of this first read through – does the style dip at this point, or have you made basic errors because you were getting tired as you wrote?

✓ Check your table of contents (if you have one) or the ordering of your paragraphs. Now that you have skimmed through the whole assignment, does the ordering seem logical to you? Has the order allowed you to make a strong argument, or to put your points in such a way that the process you are describing is clear?

✓ If you are producing a summary for the assignment, is it inclusive enough and to the point?

✓ Take a few minutes to look through your final section: are you being clear and strong in what you are trying to say?

✓ Are you writing just to one person – your seminar leader? Make sure that your assign-ment is clear enough for readers beyond that one person; it may be seen by a second marker and by external examiners.

✓ Only after all of this do you read through it slowly and carefully, just once, looking for typing errors or mistakes in your writing. You will have moved far enough away from the assignment by now to be able to see it objectively and proof read it effectively.

Top tip

> The easiest way to lose marks on an essay or report is not to check it thoroughly, or not to check it at all. Markers can deduct marks solely for poor use of English, and they do, but failing to check also has a deeper detrimental effect. If you have not checked an essay, you have no clear idea of whether your points hang together or whether your argument is clear and convincing. In a scientific report, any unchecked material brings with it the danger of you simply looking as if you do not know the facts. If you are short of time, spend the last bit of time before the deadline checking rather than writing.

If the submission goes wrong, what do I do?

If for any reason you cannot submit by the deadline, tell someone, as soon as you can. Remember that university administrators and academics see this happening regularly, so they expect some students to have problems. If you had a problem with online submission, it may have been the fault of the online system and administrators will be able to prove this with you. For hard copy submission you can usually find the person who was taking the work in easily enough, so that you can explain the problem and hand the work in late with a note explaining what happened.

Top tip

Late penalties on assignments can be harsh: a 10 per cent reduction of your mark per day (or part of a day) would not be unusual. This means that the very worst thing you can do is sit at home worrying that you have missed the deadline: you might be costing yourself marks that you did not need to lose. Take action fast to save those marks.

This chapter has been walking you through your first essays and reports, but many of the guidance points are going to be relevant to your other assignments as well, so make sure that you return to this chapter whenever you need to remind yourself of some of the practical aspects of assignments. Essays and reports might form a large proportion of your assessment at university, but there will also be the chance to excel in other forms of assessment, and we will turn to these later; first, I want to explore with you how to make the most of the marks and feedback you will receive.

17

Your first marks/grades

Before we begin, a note is needed about 'marks' and 'grades'. Although the terms are used by lecturers and students fairly interchangeably, and I will be alternating between them in this chapter, there is a difference. A mark is a number (or percentage) awarded for your work. So, six out of ten is a mark, as is 54 per cent. A grade is a band within which your piece of work has been judged to sit, such as A-, B++, C.

A note also on elements of assessment. It might be that a mark awarded for a piece of work comprises more than one element. If you give a presentation, for example, the preparation work and written output (a handout, slides, notes and so forth) may make up 70 per cent of the mark, whilst your performance on the day may only make up a small percentage of the mark (in this case, 30 per cent).

A reminder also about the difference between a 'formative' and 'summative' assignment. Any assignment that has a mark which counts towards the final mark of your module is usually called a 'summative' assignment; assignments that are for practice and do not count towards your final module mark are called 'formative'.

If you are given a rubric it might be offering you specific guidance (how many texts to include, how long the word count must be, how many formulae to include), alongside presentation rules (such as how to lay out your equations, what font size and line spacing to use). The marker will take these into account and it might affect your mark. However, the rubric might be used far more directly in the marking process and you might be awarded a mark specifically for your introduction, and then another for your use of sources, and then a third for you paragraphing and then another for the ordering of your argument and so on. Those marks would then be averaged to give your overall mark.

There are not necessarily advantages or disadvantages to you in any of these ways of marking, but universities and departments do tend to feel quite strongly about how they do these things, and they will be teaching you in such a way that you can perform well within their marking system, so it pays to be clear about just how your mark will be calculated.

INSIDER
HINT

Recognising that assignments are a form of challenge, and they offer a result that is sometimes elating and sometimes disappointing, it is worth giving a moment's thought to how a poor mark might feel. Even the best students can receive a rogue mark that is much lower than anyone would have expected, and it can be crushing if this happens to you. However, most universities will not allow students to appeal against an academic judgement of their work: the only type of appeal would be against the process by which a piece of work has been marked. So many students each year ask me if they can have their essay marked again, or if they can have a second try, that it seems worth reminding you to make sure that you know the rules of assessment at your university from the outset.

When and how will I receive my marks?

For formative work, you will most usually receive a mark written on your essay, handed back in a seminar or via the student mail system. You can usually expect this mark within a week or so. For summative assignments, your university might have a strict protocol around marking summative work, with a turnaround time that is expected of all markers for every piece of assessed work. When you receive your mark, never forget that it was given to your work by a real person, someone who has considered the assessment, and your response, in detail. Even a computer-marked multiple choice test will have been designed, carefully and methodically, by an academic. With this in mind, remember that the academic who marked your work is in the best possible position to reflect with you on your performance and should be consulted when you want to talk through your feedback.

INSIDER
HINT

Your university might publish, and make much of, an impressive turnaround time for summative work, but students are not always clear about exactly what this means, so it is worth checking. A stipulated number of days to return your essay seems so simple, but does that span of time include or exclude weekends? What about bank holidays, or vacation times, or university closure days (which will be different)? Finding out the exact due date for return is far easier than trying to calculate it for yourself for each assignment you submit.

If you do not receive a mark for your work at all, or if the return of your assignments is slower than you expected, there will be a simple explanation. The marker might have noted down your formative work mark but not written it on your essay; the strict turnaround time for marks only works if a severe case of flu does not hit half the academics in a department. It will feel worrying if things do not go as you had expected, but this can be a short-lived moment of anxiety: just ask.

Top tip

Try not to become anxious if the mark for your formative piece of work feels more public than you would have liked. The marked essay might be handed around a seminar group, but nobody will be interested in any but their own mark. You might find that your seminar leaders leave marked essays in a box in a corridor, or in a rack on their office doors, ready for you to collect. Again, this is such common practice that nobody will take any notice of your marked assignment.

Whilst summative work submitted in hard copy will usually be returned to you via a central collection point, work submitted online might be accessed in a variety of ways. Universities sometimes use their VLE to mark and return marks and feedback, and sometimes use a software package (such as Turnitin®) for some of their assignments. To some extent, the submission and feedback means that is used will depend on ease of use for the student and marker, whether or not the assignment is a group or individual piece of work, and how large the file size for submission is likely to be.

INSIDER HINT

I used to be astonished at how often bright and engaged students were missing the online feedback that I had spent time and effort producing for them. Then I realised it was not their

(Continued)

(Continued)

fault at all. Students are asked to look at different areas of the VLE or assignment software depending on what type of work has been handed in and how it has been marked. Yet students are often given no instructions on how to find their feedback, or are given instructions that are easy to overlook online.

I mark assessed presentations and lodge my handwritten feedback form online via a scan; I give written feedback in an online only version on our VLE for group screencasts; I use Turnitin® to give both audiofile and written feedback, as well using the other feedback features that the system offers. I had to learn how to do all of this, yet I seem to expect my students just to know how to do it! Make sure that your seminar leader or course convenor gives you (or sends you a link to) a set of clear and comprehensive instructions. Feedback is meant to be helpful, not a test of how well you can navigate a system.

What if I am disappointed with my mark?

Never trust your very first response to a mark. Complete elation, utter astonishment, bruised disappointment, complete despair: none of these are real; they are just reactions in the moment. You cannot stop them happening, but as soon as you can you need to work out why you received the mark you were awarded. To do this with as little damage as possible to your confidence you need to plan in advance.

Make sure you know exactly how to access your mark and *all* the feedback on offer. Online systems allow for at least three or four different types of feedback, and they are not all as easy to access in detail as you might

Top tip

> If you are upset by a mark, or outright shocked at how well you have done, give yourself space now to absorb what has happened. Taking time to take it in, thinking about it, perhaps talking to your family and friends, can be helpful if it means that you come to the feedback ready to take in what is being said.
>
> A word of caution, though: only talk to friends who you feel are truly sympathetic. Friends who might enjoy your disappointment or pick holes in your happiness are best avoided for the moment.

expect. Student support administrators can be useful in helping you to navigate any online system.

Know when you are to get your mark back, and give yourself enough time to think about it before you have to dash off to the next task of the day, if you possibly can. Take in your mark and let yourself react in any way you want – there is nothing you can do about that. Then, take the time to think about it for a moment or two before you look at any feedback. Is the mark, delightful or dreadful as it may be, a complete surprise to you, or had you convinced yourself in the nervousness leading up to the release of marks that you had done better or worse than you should realistically have expected?

After this reality check, work through the feedback, but with a pen and paper to make notes. If you are given feedback online, you might want to print it out if you think you will need to consider it in depth and refer to it again later. Read it through and make notes of questions you might want to ask of the marker but also, just as importantly, make a brief note of the types of comments you are getting. By brief note, I mean perhaps just one word. That way, if you see 'sentence' repeatedly in your notes, you know that sentence structure is causing you problems.

How can I understand my mark?

Once you have made notes you might see a pattern emerging, but you might just see a series of points, each one of which needs to be addressed. It does not much matter how many different points are made by way of areas for improvement: you have time to do all that you need to succeed. However, you will need to manage your expectations, and this is done by balancing the mark and the comments. If you have a lower mark than you would like and you have plenty of comments on why the mark was low, you can expect to be taking some time working yourself into different writing habits, whereas if you have a disappointing mark because you made one major error, there might be nothing fundamentally wrong with your writing at all, and your mark will improve significantly next time.

However unfair you feel a mark may be, do not let yourself be confused by any note on your work or on a printout of marks for a group that states 'provisional mark' or 'marks are provisional until ratification' or similar. This means that any piece of work, or set of module marks, might be scrutinised by an external examiner (a visiting academic who sees the marks and comments on them) later in the academic year, and that external examiner might choose to change some of the grades/marks awarded. It usually does not mean that the mark is provisional in any other sense. That is, you cannot appeal a mark because you are not happy with it on the basis that it is being called provisional within this context. Marks can be checked and agreed by three, or even more, markers within an institution. They will be provisional during this process, and still be provisional until an examination board meeting has taken place.

Funnily enough, feedback on a high mark can be the most difficult to negotiate so as to improve next time. A marker might have spent so much time and space giving you positive feedback that the feeding forward part of the process, so that you can keep up this level of recognition, might have been less full. This might just be the result of genuine enthusiasm for what you have written (or produced, or presented) or it may be an assumption that you know exactly why you were awarded such a high mark, and you do not really need much help. This might not be true: students with high marks need feedback as much as any other student, either because they have no real idea how they achieved the mark, or because they want to continue to climb even from an impressive starting point.

You might contact your family as soon as you receive a mark that either delights or disappoints you. Before you do this, recognise that your family may not be able to help you to understand your marks. Even if you come from a family of academics, it is very difficult to give an accurate assessment of a mark and feedback from a distance and out of context. However, your family could be the perfect people to call for some moral support, or to share your happiness in a grade you have received. If you do call your family to let them know how unhappy you are in a mark, remember to call them again the next day when you feel a little better, and again the following week once you have spoken to the marker and understand why you received the mark. Often families are left hanging with a weight of anxiety that need not be there, but they are hesitant about interfering and so just sit and worry about you instead.

A mark, whether it is higher than you expected or lower than you wanted, can feel like the end of something. You have produced a piece of work, it has been judged and a mark has been awarded. Yet it is only ever a milestone in your study journey. You will be taking that mark, and the comments of the marker, with you as you approach the next challenge.

It can help you to see assessments as a learning opportunity if you stick to the same routine of asking these questions for each assignment:

Checklist – making the most of marks and feedback

✓ Is the mark formative or summative? Find this out before you begin to work on the assignment.

✓ If the mark is summative, what percentage of the overall module grade relies on this assignment?

✓ Will you be given a percentage mark or a grade? How does this relate to a degree classification?

✓ Will your feedback be in the form of a rubric or grade chart, which will give detail on some pre-set aspects of your assignment, or should you expect more discursive feedback, or both?

✓ Will the feedback be offered electronically on a marking system or in a separate document, or by audio or video files?

✓ How long will you have to wait for the mark? Will you get the feedback at the same time?

✓ Do you have the opportunity to talk to someone about your mark and your feedback? Is this your personal tutor, the seminar leader, the module convenor or perhaps all of them?

✓ Have you taken enough time to think about your mark and the feedback? Reading through or listening to your feedback several times, making notes as you go, will help you to focus.

✓ Have you talked to supporters, friends or family, who will sympathise with any disappointment so that you can get it out of the way before you focus on the detail of the feedback?

✓ Have you made notes that highlight any comments you did not fully grasp, but also comments that seem to be helping you towards better grades?

✓ Are you ready to share the pleasing aspects of your feedback, so that you and your academic can talk about how well you are doing in some areas?

(Continued)

(Continued)

✓ Have you left enough time to talk through the points you want to discuss? Try not to have corridor conversations about your feedback: set aside thirty minutes with an academic if you want to peruse your feedback thoroughly. Even a couple of quick queries can easily become a more in-depth discussion.

✓ Once you have received your feedback and discussed it, have you made notes so that you can easily reflect on that feedback as you begin your next assignment?

Being able to see 'feedback' also as 'feed forward' is going to be crucial to your success. Degree courses are designed to offer building blocks to students. We expect greater things of them in their second year than we did in their first, and by their third or fourth year we mark against an expectation of knowledge, articulation and polished presentation. We are raising the bar at every stage, so you have to raise your game. That means understanding and internalising your feedback so that it is useful to you and genuinely becomes feed forward: a chance for you to reflect, make changes and then move ahead.

18

Your first marking tutorial

What is a tutorial?

This is another of those slightly confusing university terms. By a 'tutorial' in this guide I mean an 'assignment tutorial' or 'essay tutorial', rather than a general seminar. This is a chance to meet with a lecturer (the marker of your work, or the module convenor, or an academic or personal tutor) to talk through what you wrote or produced and the comments the marker made.

Tutorials might be offered to individuals, or you might be talking to the lecturer in a group. The lecturer will have decided on the most useful way to do this; a group that has made many similar errors or has done superbly well in the same elements might benefit from talking through the assignment together.

Some lecturers still put a note on their doors asking students to sign up to tutorials; others ask you to sign up to appointments online. Occasionally, a lecturer might set aside an afternoon and ask students on a module just to turn up if they want to talk through their marks, and others ask students who want a tutorial to email for a time slot, assuming that no email means no need for a tutorial for this assignment.

Top tip

If you have a query on an assignment that is guaranteed to take no more than two or three minutes, you might check the door of your lecturer's room to see if 'office hours' or 'consultation hours' are offered. Such a query might be, for example, 'Should I underline headings?', or 'Was the grade for the presentation a group or individual mark?'. Anything much more complex than that would need a meeting, but very brief queries can save you and the lecturer from committing to a longer meeting that you do not need at the moment.

How do I talk to the lecturer?

Honestly, but also positively. It is a waste of your time together if you never get past the stage of bemoaning a mark that crushed you, but your lecturer would want to know that you were upset and that it has taken you a moment but you are now ready to move forward. Lecturers get excited by giving excellent marks, so do not let your modesty get the better of you. If you are delighted, say so, then you can share a moment of congratulation before you get down to the work of making sure you can achieve similarly high marks in future.

This time has been put aside just for you, so you can react to it as a positive opportunity for improvement and talk to the lecturer in that spirit. The most productive tutorials are those where the student has accepted the mark, worked through the feedback and is ready to ask questions about how to get a better grade next time.

INSIDER
HINT

From the academic's point of view, this is a chance to help you improve in future, not a meeting in which they are especially concerned about the exact mark you were awarded. Although the mark might be at the forefront of your mind as you walk in, the academic will probably only be thinking in terms of a 'low 2:2' or a 'high 2:1', so there is little point in asking for the exact mark to be explained or justified. It is a much better use of your time to think forward, and focus on how to maintain and/or improve your grades.

How can I take some control of a tutorial?

You are in control of the tutorial, as long as you have prepared. You might spend the entire time talking about one aspect of essay writing that you have never grasped, or one threshold concept or scientific principle that has always eluded you. If half an hour has been set aside for your tutorial and you only need to spend ten minutes talking through this one point, that is fine. You need not worry about 'filling the time': the lecturer will have no problem using that spare twenty minutes for other tasks until the next student arrives.

You might be much more general in your approach, and want to work through the feedback point by point. This works well, but make sure that you are only talking about the points that will make the most difference to your future marks, in those areas where you need most help. If you have made notes it helps if you arrange and order them in advance, with your most pressing queries first. If the feedback is handwritten and you cannot read it, there is no need to be embarrassed: academics with poor handwriting know it and are not offended by being asked to read a comment to you.

If you are concerned about what you need to say, if, perhaps, you get tongue tied in meetings with lecturers or you struggle to make your points clearly, you could email in advance with a note of the top areas you would like to cover. Be aware of time, though. If you send fifty queries for a half hour tutorial, the lecturer will feel the pressure of time and might dash through too fast for you. Make sure that you have checked there is no other route to finding the answer to your questions before the tutorial, so that you present a reasonable number of queries for the time allowed.

Top tip

This is where study groups can come in handy. You need not share your mark with a group, but if you have all been working together on a module you might like to meet up once after the release of the marks. You might collectively be able to answer some of the queries that you had on your list, which would save you time in your tutorial as you would need to do no more than confirm the information before moving on to your next point.

The notes you made might be enough to guarantee a detailed conversation, but you might also want to print out your essay and the feedback comments made on it, with a copy for each of you. That way you can highlight sections that you would like to talk about and the lecturer is reminded of exactly what comments were made.

How detailed your preparation becomes will depend on how you work and how much detailed feedback you need. Lecturers are used to seeing students prepare for these meetings in many different ways, and so your tutorial should run smoothly from the lecturer's point of view whatever you have done to get ready for it.

Moving forward from your first marking tutorials

Your tutorial time can be made more productive by using the notes you prepared beforehand, but try to avoid the temptation to keep talking and make no notes during the meeting. This might leave you inspired and well informed for a few hours, but much of the detail will soon fade from your mind. Ask at the beginning of the meeting if the lecturer would mind you making notes. This is not because a lecturer would ever object to a student taking notes in a meeting, but because it acts as a reminder to you both to keep a record.

Once you have had time to digest the notes you made at the meeting you might not need to do anything else, except keep those notes to hand ready to check them when you are working on your next assignment. Some students take a slightly different approach. They will make a very brief set of bullet pointed notes reiterating what was said in the meeting and also confirming the details of any additional resources that were recommended. They then email the lecturer to ask for confirmation that these notes are correct. This can be a good way to make sure that you move forward on solid ground, having made the most of the chance to discuss your work in such detail.

One final thought on tutorials: if you do not want a tutorial right now, you do not need to have one. Email your lecturer to explain that you need some more time to work through the comments, and ask if you could arrange a tutorial for a later date. This will not create any difficulties and it will put you in the best possible position to turn your 'feedback' into 'feed forward'.

CAREER
MOMENT

The techniques you will use for a tutorial, and the approach you take to it, will affect your future professional development, because the attitude that you bring to this experience will be replicated in every appraisal that you undergo as a professional. Learning how to take criticism productively will be an important stepping stone to your future success.

19

Your first research project

A research project can take many forms at university. For some degree programmes it is a regular part of your studying; for others, it only comes into play towards the end of a course, with a dissertation or an extended research project. Before we move on, we could look at what might be meant in your university by a research project.

Checklist – research projects

✓ An essay for which you make up your title.

✓ A presentation reporting on a desk-based research project.

✓ A project that took place during a year abroad.

✓ A lab-based project for which you set your own research questions.

✓ A placement away from university on which you report on your return.

✓ A credit-bearing, independent project based on original material you found.

✓ A dissertation or long essay.

How do I decide on a topic?

You might decide on your own topic for a research project, although you could be given suggestions of areas you could cover. Although this will feel like an independent part of your studying, and this can be daunting, time will always have been set aside by your tutors to help you with your project, and that includes settling on a topic. Telling the tutor that you have absolutely no ideas for a research project will only get you so far; you are likely to be given a topic idea that is fairly standard and not really what you want. Far better to offer some thoughts on research topics that appeal to you and then work together on the best project title.

> **CAREER MOMENT**

Your research project is likely to be the most popular topic of conversation at interview. This is because it is unique to you, which makes the interview more interesting. The interviewer or interview panel will assume that you are keen on the topic and so will talk with enthusiasm about it. Although you will want to undertake a research project that appeals to you and that you think you can handle, keep an eye on your career plans at this stage. If you can decide on a project that showcases skills that you will need in your chosen career path, or that you feel are lacking on your radar chart, that is all to the good. If you can undertake a project that relates directly to your career area of choice, and the project appeals to you, that would be even better.

How do I find my research questions?

The fundamental difference between a standard assignment, in which you answer a question with the material you have been given in lectures and seminars, alongside your own independent study material, and a research project, is that the latter asks you to think of research questions. This is perhaps the most challenging aspect of a research project for most students, not because you have not asked yourself many questions as you study, but because your other assignments will have asked you to focus on answers, not questions.

You will need to set out some fundamental research questions (perhaps just two or three) at the outset of your project, and the entire project might hang on these, so this is the point when you need the most help and support from your research supervisor (who might be the module convenor, a lecturer assigned to your project or your academic tutor). You are likely to come up with some thoughts ('I think it is interesting that this factor affects that outcome ...' or 'I have often noticed that this text has influenced that sphere of life ...') and it will be the task of your supervisor to work with you to convert these thoughts into research questions.

This is not an easy idea to come to terms with, so Table 19.1 gives some very easy examples to show you how to flip a thought, or an answer, into research questions.

Table 19.1 Finding research questions

Answer to a question	Possible research question
Plant leaves are green because they contain chlorophyll.	• How much chlorophyll would produce optimum results in a low light polytunnel? • How does variegation in leaves affect their need for sunlight? • Does a drop in chlorophyll levels in tomato plant leaves signal the beginnings of blight?
Shakespeare's play *Romeo and Juliet* is a tragedy, showing families at war.	• Has the play ever been banned in countries where royal families are at war? • In what ways did family tragedies on stage affect the eighteenth-century novel? • Why are modern adaptations of *Romeo and Juliet* popular in the twenty-first century?
An international war can bring a nation together with a firm sense of camaraderie and nationhood.	• How does the culture of the warring nation affect its sense of nationhood? • During the Second World War, was Lancashire more or less integrated into the sense of nationhood that is described in the history texts? • What part did the British royal family play in creating a sense of nation during the Second World War?
A global financial crisis can lead to recession, and sometimes depression, across the world.	• How much do private holders of wealth affect our global financial health? • At which point, and why, is 'recession' redefined as 'depression'? • What factors might lead financial analysts to underestimate the impact of a financial crisis?

There are several aspects of these research questions that you might have noticed:

- They tend to be more specific than the answers that were given in the left-hand column: essay answers aim to come to conclusions; research questions open up your mind.
- They are still all too broad for the purpose: the student would have to narrow them down significantly in order to produce a working plan for a research project that is feasible.
- They are all too vague: specifics will be needed even for those that, on the surface, seem quite focused.
- They all lead naturally to more questions: this is always the case with research questions.
- They cannot be answered fully: and that is to be expected.

This last point is important to you as you prepare for a research project: you are not expected to come up with the 'final word' on your topic. You will reach some conclusions, but they are in themselves likely to lead to more questions; some of the best research projects I have seen are those that conclude with a neat set of intriguing research questions that have yet to be answered.

Although you might only have a couple of research questions at the outset, more will bubble up as you explore your research area, so keep a note of them as they arise. They may be discarded or mentioned only as food for thought at the end of your project, but they are also potential clues as to where you go next.

Whatever your topic, you can be fairly sure that your research project, as you conceive of it at the outset, will be too big: they invariably are. This is not a bad problem to have, but you do have to recognise that it is a problem. You will not be able to go over the word count, and you have been given a limited amount of time in which to produce your result and draw your conclusions, so you will need to be asking yourself all the time how and where you can narrow down your topic.

Research questions are the solution. Narrowing down can be straightforward if you are clear about your questions: when the project looks to be growing too big, you can simply lop off a research question and put it to one side. This is much quicker than trying to edit down to a word count later, and the question is still nearby if you decide later that you can include it.

> CAREER
> MOMENT

Although a research project sounds academic, and so firmly part of your studying life, you are likely to be carrying out research projects throughout your professional life. Whenever there is a need for an answer, somebody will be carrying out a research project. They might be called 'tender bids' or 'scoping projects', they might not be called anything in particular, but they will be an important part of your life. That is why it is so important to master research techniques whilst you are at university: they could form a large part of your sales pitch in the career marketplace.

What is the right format to present my findings?

If you are given a choice, opt for a report format. It is usually the best way to make your research findings clear and its structure lends itself to a logical flow of findings and conclusions. It also has the advantage of allowing you to write in a format that is commonplace in the professional world.

How should I organise my research project time?

You will be using all of the time management techniques we explored in Chapter 14 (on managing your time), but there are a few additional points to bear in mind for a research project. You will need to divide your time in a way that could seem unfamiliar to you. You might be used to carrying out some research for an assignment, collating together and thinking through your lecture, seminar and reading notes, then making a plan so that you can get on with the writing. For a research project you should think about a plan at the outset.

INSIDER HINT

Your research supervisor might be barred from commenting on more than a limited amount of your detailed writing. Planning your time effectively can ensure that you gain the level of supervision you need despite this restriction. If you make plans early on in the project, even if they change later, your supervisor will feel free to comment on them in as much detail as you need. This will give you precise, relevant supervision at the point where you need it most.

If you make a plan at the beginning, even just a sheet showing the research questions that you have, you will be able to keep a clear overview of your project. As you carry out research, you will adapt and develop the plan, perhaps making a separate plan for each section of your project. The plan guides you through and so you can carry out research with confidence, knowing that you are not losing your way. If the project starts to feel too cumbersome, consider whether to jettison a research question, or to replace a question with another, more interesting question.

Several benefits arise from working only with a plan and your research material for as long as you can:

Checklist – benefits of research plans

✓ Your plan is an easier way to see where you are heading than paragraphs of writing that you have to wade through each time you want to remind yourself of where to go next.

(Continued)

(Continued)

✓ You are more likely to avoid the problem of too many words: it can be time consuming to have to halve your word count at the edit stage, and the final product might be compromised.

✓ You are less likely to lose your way and go off point if you can see your plan clearly in front of you, rather than pages of written up research.

✓ If you decide that you have to abandon a research question, you will more easily be able to see how this affects the shape of your project if you have a plan in place.

✓ It can be painful to delete your words: a plan tends to feel more flexible.

Only when you feel secure in what you want to say will you write, which means that you might be writing later in the assignment process than usual. For some students this can feel awkward, because they are used to writing in order to organise their thoughts. I would suggest that you try an early plan first, bearing in mind the benefits above, and then, if you find it too stressful, revert to your more usual way of working.

Top tip

This planning process is also productive for your other assignments, so if you practise it early on in your time at university you will gain the advantage of this way of working, as well as preparing for the larger projects that will be expected of you later in your studies.

In terms of timing, developing your project through extensive planning will result in far more time spent on research and planning than on writing. For a dissertation, for example, you might be required to choose your subject, and be allocated a supervisor, a year before it is due to be submitted. You will be planning within the first couple of weeks, identifying your research questions and making a sketchy, flexible plan around these. You might then be carrying out research for six months, not writing but adjusting your plan or plans as needed. You might then write a portion of the dissertation, to make sure that you are on the right track, and so that your supervisor can check that your writing style is working well for what you are trying to achieve. You will simultaneously be researching, and adjusting your plan, at this stage.

It is only in the last three months or so that you will really concentrate on your writing, secure in the knowledge that you have carried out enough research to be firm in the argument you are making. Whilst you write, you might break off from time to time to check some facts or to carry out some minor piece of investigation, but you will not need to do this very much. You will be writing from your final, probably very full, plan. You will be adjusting your thoughts a little as you write, but not very much, and then you will have given yourself plenty of time to polish your work to the point where you are content to submit.

CAREER
MOMENT

Professional research projects require a level of flexibility. Global circumstances might alter, the client may change course, the budget could increase; all of these factors will change the way your project develops. Being able to plan in a way that allows flexibility for the longest possible time is often an advantage, and is something that you could talk about at interview in relation to your research project.

Each university, and every department, will have their own way of working around research projects, so you will be given guidance as you progress. Your department's system will be designed to support whichever way of working you are asked to follow. You can expect a high level of support and some interesting conversations along the way. Your research project might well be the work you are most proud of when you graduate.

20

Group projects

The amount of studying you will be undertaking as part of a group will depend on your subject area and the way in which teaching methods have developed in your university. Even for those universities and departments in which group work has not been deliberately cultivated as a teaching and learning technique, group work will arise from time to time.

If the group work involves producing work that is not part of summative assessment, you will probably feel positively towards it and make a greater or lesser effort depending on the task in hand and your other commitments.

Checklist – types of formative group work

✓ Giving an unassessed seminar presentation as a group.

✓ A pair of students preparing material for discussion in a seminar.

✓ Laboratory sessions that are not assessed.

✓ Workshops in which you complete tasks as groups.

✓ Flipped learning, in which a group views material online and then prepares questions for discussion.

✓ A study, reading or revision group.

✓ Talking to visitors to the university as a group.

✓ Producing a group wiki, blog, website or learning journal that is not formally assessed.

Any of these might inform your learning as you progress through university. In this chapter the focus will be on summative group work that is assessed as part of a credit-bearing module, although much of the advice will apply to both types of situation.

How do I get started on a group project?

By knowing exactly what you are expected to do, and how the project is going to be assessed:

Checklist – key questions around group work

✓   How large is the group to be?

✓   Will I be choosing my own group members?

✓   What is the deadline for the assignment?

✓   What exactly are we to produce (perhaps a presentation, or a wiki and a demonstration, or a report on a project, or a screencast with commentary)?

✓   Is the mark divided between different elements of the assignment?

✓   Will we be awarded a group mark, or an individual mark, or a combination of the two?

✓   Is any peer assessment involved (that is, will group members have any say in an individual's mark)?

What role should I take in the group?

Groups work well if everyone plays to their strengths. That means knowing how you work best in a group, and asking everyone else what role they would like to take on. There are well understood and clearly defined roles within groups (such as being the person who likes to organise the project, and those who are more creative thinkers, and those who like to solve problems, and those who are good at chairing meetings, and those who prefer to finish things off neatly). You can find tests online that will show you the type of person you are, and your Careers Service should also be able to offer you these tests (they are good fun as well as being useful).

Your Careers Service may have access to these tests because they are used extensively in professional selection processes. That tells you everything you need to know about how important group work could be to your future success: employers *like* you to have skills and qualifications, but they *need* you to be the right fit for their team.

Once you know where your strengths lie as a group you will also be aware of any gaps in the group dynamic. For example, you might be alerted to the fact that, if there is no organiser in your group and plenty of creative types, you will all have to work extra hard to make sure that you meet the deadline.

You might also spend time thinking of the skills you have in your group. This can be a revelation, and it will make everyone in the group feel positive about what they have to offer. It takes only a few minutes to give everyone a piece of paper and ask them to write down what skills they think they are bringing to the activity and also, perhaps, those areas in which they are less strong.

Task: Carrying out a research project and giving a presentation on the outcome	
Name: (each person would produce a sheet)	
Skill to be used	Task to be done
Posting to a blog	Updating the project blog on the VLE
Working with online presentations	Putting material we produce into the presentation
Less strong area	
Speaking in front of an audience	Will do the tech during the presentation (setting up the slides and moving them forward, setting the lights)

Figure 20.1   Example worksheet: using skills and experience within the group

There are a few details to notice in the example in Figure 20.1. Each person does not need to bring more than a few skills to the group (although there would usually be more than is listed here) and so everyone can pick and choose where they can contribute best. Each person can be honest at the outset about what they would prefer not to do, and in these early planning stages nobody is likely to object if there is something you would rather not do. By being clear between you early on, there is less pressure and far less chance of discord in the group.

By producing these sheets, you are likely to find unexpected talents within the group and this might change the way you approach the task, or perhaps the parameters of the task. You will also find people working together based on skills rather than who they know already; in the example above, the student may be working with one person on the blog and another on the presentation slides. This tends to lead to a more efficient way of working.

If you do not know each other well you might like to carry out this exercise by email, but if you are brave enough to give it a go together, it usually makes for an even more positive start to your teamwork.

INSIDER HINT

Although you might be told that the composition of the groups is final and that you just have to get on with it, no tutor will want you to suffer in a group that will upset you. If you have arguments during the task, your tutor will be reluctant to get involved: overcoming arguments is part of life. However, if you have a genuine and good reason to want to change groups, take this to your tutor and ask to be moved at the beginning of the task.

Keeping in touch

One of the most troublesome aspects of group work at university is keeping in touch, either online or in person. Some students really enjoy face-to-face meetings in which they can share ideas; others hate this, and would much prefer to exchange emails. Some students will be at a point in the term where they have time on their hands, whilst others are snowed under with work and deadlines.

For a longer project, much of this works itself out because people contribute in their own best way at different points, and everyone's workload changes as the project takes shape. Whatever the length of the project, though, it is a good idea to decide early on how you are going to keep in touch. Ideally, one way for the formal, completed parts of the project (such as some shared cloud space) so that you can work on the assignment together, and another way to arrange meetings (making one person in charge of that) and then any other ways you like (social media, Skype, chats between lectures) to keep ideas flowing well.

Making the time count

A timeline of your planned activity as a group is vital, not because you want to tie everyone down, but because you do not all want to feel guilty, all the time. If everyone vaguely feels that they really should be doing something, and that perhaps they are letting the group down, or perhaps someone feels that they are working on the project each day, and nobody else is doing much, you end up with bad feeling for no reason.

> CAREER
> MOMENT

If this is starting to sound a bit like project management, that is because it is. Project management is a discipline in itself, with high level qualifications attached to it, but students struggle to demonstrate experience of project management at any level. Be bold about this. If your project is a success and you can see how your contribution helped to make that happen, it needs to be on your CV and a key talking point at interview.

Clearly understood roles in your group are valuable: clearly defined tasks, within a timeframe that is shared, are essential to your smooth success. Although it may be a more formal way to start a group project than you are used to, you might consider asking each person what role they would like to take, based on their personality type in a group, but also on their other commitments and their skills. For example, someone whose disposition suits being a chairperson might be happy to chair meetings, but only after an assignment has been handed in.

Timing	Tasks	Members
Week One	First meeting	Date/time decided in class by whole group
Week One	Carry out the skills inventories for each member of the group	This is probably you, as you have read this book!
Week One	Check on the brief and circulate all the details	Names
Week One	Produce a timeline for the project	Names
Week One	Decide on the presentation software	Names

(Continued)

211

Figure 20.2   (Continued)

Timing	Tasks	Members
Week One	Set up the blog and post to it	Names
Week One	Produce a schedule of blog posts for the duration of the project	Names
Week Two		
Week Two...		

Figure 20.2   Example task allocation for a project leading to a presentation

You will notice straight away that there are several different types of task in the first week, and there are likely to be even more than this, for every week of a project. This is a good thing, especially if you are all busy. Dividing tasks up and working to a realistic but firm timescale will make your project far easier to handle. Figure 20.2 suggests that more than one name would be placed beside some of the tasks: this allows people to work together across the group and so help to keep a sense of positive teamwork. This may be more planning than you are used to seeing, but time spent planning is rarely wasted in group activities, so it is worth the effort.

What if someone is not contributing?

You can fend off this problem before the project gets underway. By deciding on ways to communicate you have already helped everyone to contribute; now make sure that your timeline shows not just a series of tasks, but a row of deadlines for outcomes. You might begin your timeline with, for example, 'Week Five – all team members to work on research around gender in higher education', but already you have given yourself a problem. This is a huge topic, not amenable to quick and easy research, so you risk too much time being spent on it without much result. You need to add an outcome and a deadline: 'Week Five – all team members to work on research around gender in higher education. Each team member to pro-duce two bullet points, with statistics if needed, and one possible illustration for the first presentation slide by midday on Friday'.

Top tip

Using cloud services to work on your materials can save you time and make it far easier to work in a genuinely collaborative way. It also gives you the advantage of being able to show who has contributed to the task. Make sure that you use one of the many free cloud-based drives, and if you wish to keep your material private (or you are required to keep it confidential) ask about cloud space for students within your university's VLE.

By making specific and time sensitive demands on the team, you are making it easy on yourselves. Everyone agrees to and is sharing one timeline, with deadlines for multiple, manageable tasks, so everyone sees that the project is achievable in the time available.

Another advantage to working in this way is that if someone is not attending meetings, or seems quiet, you have no need to worry unduly. Either that person is just shy or busy and preoccupied, and will produce the results you need despite not being very involved in meetings, or the person will fail to deliver. Rather than the organiser of meetings nagging at that team member, or everyone getting cross with an apparent lack of participation, everyone can just focus on what they need to do. If the team member fails to deliver, you will have solid grounds to approach your tutor and you can demonstrate that the student has simply failed to engage adequately.

INSIDER
HINT

So often, I have seen hard-working groups wasting hour upon hour of their time worrying about one member who is not participating well in a group task. They sometimes have a genuine concern for that student's wellbeing; sometimes they are outraged and feel cheated of the time that might have been spent contributing; surprisingly, they often come to enjoy the situation: a missing member can be useful for team bonding. None of this is of any real help to the group at all, and is a temptation you might want to resist.

The future of the group

A group at university is usually formed to serve just one purpose, but it need not fold once that task is complete. If you have enjoyed working in a group, and you all seem to help each other perform better, you might think about whether you could carry out some further projects together. If you are in a module again, you could get together for any group tasks that are part of that module's activity. If you are not given that opportunity, you might form a productive lab group or revision group. Groups working really well together are not as common as you might think: if you have had a good experience, try to prolong it if you can.

CAREER
MOMENT

Connecting your university experience with your career ambitions is not always as obvious as you might like, but groups in which you have worked well do more than provide a compelling section to your CV. These are fellow students who, like you, might have some professional contacts and experience, some knowledge of career areas, who, at the very least, might enjoy researching career options with you. Later on, they might be the people with whom you practise your interview questions, or in front of whom you rehearse your interview presentation. A good group is valuable to each of its members both in the short-term task and in long-term support.

21

Your first placement

Placement opportunities, like group work projects, vary greatly from university to university, so the advice offered here will help you make the most of the opportunity in whatever form it takes for you. The aim is to ensure that you can succeed without encountering problems that could be avoided with some advanced insight.

What are placements?

Placements give you the chance to carry out a project away from the lecture theatre and seminar room. They allow you to apply your learning to the world away from university, at the same time deepening your understanding of your subject. They are a fantastic way to notch up some experience in the professional world; they also help you develop your skills as well as your subject understanding. They are, however, hard work, requiring dedication and motivation from those students who undertake them. There are several types of placement opportunities you might be offered at university.

Checklist – types of placement

✓ An independent research project that takes place away from the classroom (these might still be undertaken on campus, if your university has archives or departments needing research activity to be undertaken).

✓ A career placement (this might be work experience, or a professional internship, the report from which might count towards the grade on a career or vocational module).

(Continued)

(Continued)

✓ Studying or working abroad.

✓ An industrial placement of up to a year.

If a placement is a compulsory part of a module, you will be made aware of this when you are making your module choices. If a placement is a compulsory part of your degree, this will have fed into your decision making when you chose your degree course.

INSIDER
HINT

If you have chosen a degree with a compulsory placement element (a year abroad, say, or a term in industry) you are obviously keen to grasp this opportunity. However, if your circumstances change (you need to take on carer responsibilities, or you become overly anxious about this aspect of your degree for some reason) you need not fear that you will be jeopardising your entire degree outcome if you are not able to proceed with a placement. Although it is not guaranteed, there will be contingency plans in place to cover most circumstances that students can encounter, including not being able to start, or complete, a placement. Seek help and advice early if you start to feel you might need it.

Why would I be interested in a placement?

There are many reasons why students opt for placements. As soon as you begin to think about it, you are likely to get a fairly immediate sense of whether a placement would suit you.

Checklist – why undertake a placement?

✓ You want to try out a career area.

✓ You want to expand your professional network.

✓ You need some professional experience on your CV.

✓ You will enjoy spending some time in the world away from university.

✓ You enjoy working independently on a research project.

✓ Travel (in your own country or abroad) appeals to you.

✓ You feel passionately about your subject.

✓ You relish the chance to apply your knowledge in a new setting.

✓ Expanding your skills set is important to you.

✓ You believe you will achieve a better grade if you work on an independent project.

For some students, every one of these reasons is relevant; for others, just one reason is enough to tempt them into exploring the idea of a placement. However, if the thought of a placement does not appeal to you at all, you are probably best to ignore it at this stage. Later on you can return to the idea again to think about whether it could work for you, but undertaking a placement reluctantly, on the basis that you think you should do it, but with no real enthusiasm, is usually a mistake.

CAREER
MOMENT

Placements (either linked to your academic studies or as stand-alone professional internships or work experience) are clearly going to be an important part of a career strategy for many students. However, they are often unpaid and can cost you in travel and other expenses. If you are not in a position to think about a placement that is unpaid, do not give up. Ask your Careers Service to help you find paid work that will boost your CV and professional network.

Preparing for the experience

Your department will make clear to you the practicalities and administration around placements. Sometimes placements are organised by a department and students apply internally for them; in other areas students are expected to source their own placements. Although the former option might sound more appealing, students can find that being given a prearranged placement does not offer them enough choice and autonomy. They would rather work closely with a tutor to think about the perfect placement for them, and then secure it themselves.

Top tip

> You do not need to assume that a placement will cost you money. If you are carrying out a research project or professional activity that will be of benefit to the organisation within which you are undertaking your placement, that organisation may be happy to pay you for your time, or to pay you for your travel costs. If you are expected to meet the costs of the placement, you might be able to negotiate working from home for some of the time to reduce the travel costs, or working outside peak travel hours.

Even the most well-established placement systems will leave students with a moment when they realise they have taken the plunge. They are on placement, perhaps many miles from home and/or their university, and they must manage situations as they arise. Do as much as you can before your placement begins to make sure that this is not a difficult time for you.

Checklist – preparing for a placement

✓ Make sure you know about assessment: are you judged on your performance on placement, or only on the report you complete as a result of it?

✓ Do you know the phone number of your placement contact, and a backup contact in case you are held up on your first day's journey?

✓ What hours are you expected to be there? Every day?

✓ Is there a dress code?

✓ Are you working only on your research project, or might you be carrying out some routine business tasks as well?

✓ Will you have to pay your own travel costs?

✓ Have you sent your contact a clear outline of what you will do, or have you left it more open, so that you can decide on the detail of your activities once you get there?

✓ Are you sure you (and the organisation) have completed any paperwork, such as confidentiality agreements, legal contracts, health and safety and insurance guarantees?

✓ Have you made one final check with the module convenor or your tutor as to any academic outcomes that are expected from the placement?

✓ How will you report on your findings? What is the submission date? Will you have time to discuss your assignment with a tutor before you submit?

✓ Are you expected to keep a learning log or journal during your time on placement? Will this be assessed, and is it in hard copy or online?

✓ Is there anywhere you can go online to talk to your fellow students on placement?

✓ Do you have an emergency contact at university if you are on placement over a vacation period, or when your placement tutor is on research leave or similar?

✓ If you are studying abroad, is there a general induction event you should attend? When and where is it?

Although there might be a plethora of other queries that come to mind as you prepare, if you are clear on these basic aspects of your placement you will feel far more ready to enjoy the experience.

Reporting on a placement

It would be logical to assume that you would report on a placement in a report format, and this is often the case. Sometimes you will be writing a fairly brief report; sometimes it acts as a dissertation in your degree programme and so is lengthy – maybe 10,000 words or so. If you are given the choice between an essay format and a report, it is worth giving serious consideration to a report. It has many advantages:

Checklist – advantages of reports

✓ It might be the only time you have the opportunity to try out a report.

✓ You will be given instruction in how to produce a report, which is useful in itself.

✓ The report format lends itself well to placements and their outcomes.

✓ You will be able to attach additional material to a report (in the form of appendices and annexes) so the word count will be less restricting. A report would include images, and perhaps charts and tables, so you will have a creative range of options.

✓ This is a document you could share at interview; it will be something to view with pride.

In addition to a report, essay, learning journal or dissertation, you might also be expected to give a presentation on your placement. In some cases, students are asked to give two presentations: one before they leave to outline their plans and one on their return. You will want to know whether this presentation, or presentations, form part of the summative assessment for the placement.

You will probably be used to receiving marks for your assignments, a percentage figure that falls into a band (a 65 per cent being called a 'solid 2:1', for example). If your placement activity is to be assessed as summative (that is, it counts towards your degree) you would quite reasonably expect the same marking system to be used. However, the results offered for your placement or year abroad might be 'pass' or 'fail', or you might find that a mark given on placement will be 'converted' in some way to a mark that relates to your degree marking system. Make sure that you know how your placement work is being assessed, and how this relates to your overall degree mark: it might not be as simple as you expect.

A written or oral report to your lecturers on your placement is what you would expect; what is often not expected is that your placement provider might also want a formal report. If it is just a case of sending a copy of your academic report to your contact, that would be simple enough, but placement providers can also ask you to give a presentation to a department on your findings, or prepare a board-level report. Neither of these will necessarily be replications of your university work, so be ready to produce an additional report and a presentation if you are asked, even if you have to produce a different report for commercial consumption than you would do for academic credit.

Top tip

You will have permission from your placement provider to produce a report for academic purposes, but perhaps not beyond that. If you are thinking of talking about your project at interview and want to show your report, you could work with your placement provider to produce a revised or redacted version of the report that can be used in a different setting.

There might be a commercial aspect to your placement, even if it is not labelled as work experience or a professional internship. If you are undertaking an academic placement, perhaps based on an independent research project, this might have commercial implications for your placement organisation. This can be a good thing (some of my students have unexpectedly been paid for their work because it was so useful to their placement organisation) but you need to make sure that you have permission to release your report to academics for the purposes of marking it. This should be confirmed before you finalise your placement arrangements.

Top tip

Whilst you are on placement, gather up (with the organisation's permission) every scrap of material you might need. If you think it would look impressive to produce your placement report on headed paper, ask to take some away with you. If there are emails, documents or webpages relevant to your research, print them off before you leave. If you come across any material they are happy for you to have (company brochures, archive catalogues, website drafts), take them away with you even if you are not quite sure whether or not you will use them. You can always shred them later if they are irrelevant to your final report.

When thinking about reporting on your placement you will find yourself in a contrary position. On the one hand, you want to make a note of everything you do and then reflect upon what is happening so that you do not miss anything. On the other hand, some of what you do will be irrelevant to your overall outcome. This position repeatedly causes problems for students, but there is a practical solution. Keep a log book of what you do, and add to this from time to time your reflections on what you are learning or how you are applying your knowledge and skills (sometimes students prefer to keep two separate sets of notes, one to record activity and one to record their thoughts). That way, nothing of the experience is lost.

As your placement progresses it will become clear to you that you cannot report on all of your thoughts and experiences. Even if you decided in advance on a very narrow research project, the experience of working in a dynamic professional environment will lead you into interesting avenues and trains of thought, and you will not have a word count sufficient to record everything.

Although this can feel frustrating, it is a favourable place to be sitting. You know that you have a mass of material, but you will also come to see (as you may already have done in essays) that the secret of a successful piece of academic work can sometimes be its tight focus. As you enjoy your placement, let your mind wander from time to time. Is a pattern emerging that would make an interesting report? Have you done one or two activities that really stand out for you? Did one of your findings encapsulate all that you want to say about this area? Your log/diary and your pieces of reflection can all be included in an appendix added to your report, but you can focus in detail on whatever you choose, knowing that it will allow you to show off your expertise in the best way possible.

CAREER
MOMENT

Graduates often report that the most difficult transition they make when moving from university to the professional world is learning how to write and say only what is needed, not everything they know on a topic. This switch, from proving to a marker that you have mastered an area, to working with colleagues and clients who only need a small slice of your knowledge, well applied, can start with your placement. Learning how to nuance your knowledge and apply it to good effect is a professional talent that any employer or client will value.

A placement demands commitment and effort from you, so you will want to make it count in your grade. Work with your placement tutor, or seminar convenor, or any other academic who is involved in your placement, discussing your ideas for the report and how well they might fit the marking criteria. If you have arranged your placement you will, to some extent, have set your own assessment criteria, so an email or two whilst on placement, asking for advice on what you hope to include in your final report, would not be unexpected or out of place.

Some placement adventures

To help you think through how a placement might be narrowed down at the reporting stage, here are some examples from my own students over the years, all of whom chose to focus on just one aspect of their two-week placement linked to a module:

- A museum of an author's life and work: focusing not on the author's manuscripts, as intended, but on his sister's writing process, having found some of her travel writing in a box in the attic; this was found three days before the end of the placement.
- A radio station: deciding to look at how the gender of a speaker might dictate the words used in a radio charity appeal; this was one afternoon's activity.
- The head office of a supermarket chain: deciding to analyse the poetic techniques used in encouraging customers to recycle, having noticed alliteration on a poster in the office.

- A television station: looking at just three pages of a website linked to a programme based on the novel a student was studying.

Making the most of the opportunity

Your goal will be to gain the best grade for your placement assessment, but there is much more that you can achieve through this experience. You now have a solid professional network – perhaps the first that you have deliberately cultivated. These are people to whom you might return for a reference or to hear about career opportunities in the future.

Top tip

Take time to check out every noticeboard and weblink where you are carrying out your placement. Are part-time vacation jobs being offered, or perhaps there is a website where vacancies are posted? Are there any free training opportunities that you could pursue? Perhaps there is a staff Facebook site that you could join to find out more about the wider organisation and possible future openings?

Once you have recognised that you now have a professional network, it can be easier to start to identify others. Keep in touch with your fellow students on placement. Did their placement provider sound like a good fit for your career ambitions? Could they put you in touch with anyone who might be a useful contact in future?

INSIDER HINT

Over the years I have had students confide in me, often some time after a placement, that they felt uncomfortable with some of the activity that they witnessed whilst on placement. They did not want to be seen as trouble makers and so they ignored it, but later wished that they had spoken out. You need not be in this situation: if anything at all happens on your placement that concerns or worries you, talk to your placement supervisor (either in the placement organisation or your academic supervisor) and share your concerns. Matters such as this are properly dealt with by those who are supporting your work: they should never be allowed to come between you and the excellent placement experience you deserve.

You might form friendships whilst you are on placement, and this can be a long-term bonus in your studying life without you having to make any effort except keeping in contact. Students often tell me that staying in touch with recent graduates they met on placement has helped to keep them focused on their career goals, which has motivated them in their studying and also inspired them to take up every relevant opportunity they can before they graduate.

CAREER
MOMENT

It is such a bonus if you are offered additional work – paid or unpaid – with your placement provider in the future, and the career insights and networks you gain are also a great benefit. It is also worth remembering, however, that knowing what you *do not* want to do in future is equally useful. I have known students who have cherished a career ambition since childhood, who then go on placement to an organisation and find that they would hate to do the job. They have saved themselves huge amounts of time and heartache by discovering that during their degree course.

Would a placement suit the type of person I am?

Although placements suits students who are happy to work away from university and are self-motivated, hardworking and imbued with a reasonable level of confidence, this stereotypical idea of a placement student is not the whole story. I have worked with hundreds of placement students and so I know that they come from all walks of life, with many and varied approaches to their studies and their sense of self. Some are confident; some are shy but passionate about their field. Some are highly organised, some need far more help to keep them on track, and support to keep them motivated. What unites them is not what they bring to the placement, but what they take from it. I have never heard a student regret undertaking a placement, even if it did not turn out perfectly. This is, I think, partly because those students who know it is not for them do not select the option, but also partly because, with the right support, each student finds something to learn and a benefit to be gained from a placement. That is what students are like.

22

Your first exams

You might already have an idea of the preparation and timing that works for you when it comes to exams, and if exams are not a method of assessment that works well for you, you might have chosen modules that are not assessed in this way. It is unlikely that you can undertake an entire degree programme with no exams, and they feel more challenging at university than at school or college. There are several reasons for this:

- Nobody is telling you when to start revising.
- Extensive revision is not usually factored into the term's teaching schedule.
- Module convenors will probably not concern themselves with all of the demands on your time when they are setting up exams for their modules.
- You might not have needed to revise very much for previous exams, so this could be fairly new to you, but university exams will require revision if you are to do well.
- If you have had an unpleasant exam experience during your pre-university exams, you might be anxious about facing more exams.

INSIDER HINT

Some of the most nervous students I meet are those who have done well in previous exams, but who suddenly find themselves very anxious about university exams. Not having had previous exam anxiety, this comes as a nasty surprise. The shock of feeling so worried in itself seems to make matters much worse: this is not how they are used to seeing themselves. If you start to feel anxious about exams, to a level you were not expecting, talk to your personal tutor as soon as you can. Early support is the best way forward.

What type of exams might I face?

It would be unusual for a student to come across all of the different types of exam listed here, but it is a good idea to be aware of the types of exam that you might face during your time at university:

1. **Essay exams**: you will be asked to write essays in response to a series of questions, usually allowing you to choose between several questions and normally with two or three essays per paper.
2. **Short answer exams**: you will be required to write prose (like an essay exam) but your answers will be short and to the point and there will be more of them on the paper than in an essay exam (eight to ten, perhaps).
3. **Multiple choice exams**: either online or in hard copy, you will be asked a question and given a choice of (usually) three or four answers, from which you can choose one. You might be given the outline of a situation and asked to choose which state-ment best describes the situation in detail or a solution to the problems described in the outline.
4. **Open-book exams**: you will be allowed to take some books, and perhaps some notes, into the exam with you. This is especially the case if there are long quotations to remember, or formulae and equations that are essential to your answers.
5. **Take home exams**: you will be given the exam paper and allowed to take it home to produce your answer before a deadline.
6. **Seen exams**: you will be given the exam paper in advance, but you write your answers in an exam room some time later.
7. **Problem or case-based exams**: a scenario is set out for you and you are required to comment on it (in the case of a legal exam, for example) or to solve the problem that is posed.
8. **Oral exams**: within language learning, oral exams are commonplace, but they need not be face to face; they might be recorded on audio or video. Oral exams after written exams have taken place are sometimes used to determine grades for students whose exam performance is borderline or about whose work examiners are divided. These are called viva voce exams (usually known as a 'viva') and are not as common as they once were.
9. **Computational papers**: you would be required to work through computations under exam conditions; you would usually have plenty of experience of similar computations from your class-based activities.
10. **Mixed exams**: any of the exam formats listed here might be mixed in one exam sitting, or in one exam paper. You might, for example, be asked to complete a multiple choice paper before moving on to a computational paper, or one exam paper might offer you three short-answer questions followed by one or more longer essay questions.

When should I begin to prepare for exams?

Although the answer to this will depend on how you like to work, the timing of your final stretch of revision may depend upon other commitments. If you are preparing for a class test or online exam, you will probably be expected to prepare for it during your usual study hours; if there is a set of exams straight after a vacation, the assumption will be that you will be revising over that vacation.

INSIDER HINT

Universities put thought and effort into supporting students if they need help, and this includes making provision if a student needs to hand in a coursework assignment later than the original submission date. With automated systems, students can sometimes do this without even speaking to a tutor or module convenor. This automation is designed to make things easier for students and less time consuming for academics, but it does mean that students are not always given advice about the knock-on effect of late submission. If you are going to ask for an extension on your coursework deadline, always think about how this will affect your exam performance.

If you need an extension, you will of course apply for one, but you might be in two minds. Perhaps you were unwell but you had already completed most of an essay; it would be tempting to ask for extra time, but if this removes a couple of days of your time when you would have been revising, this extension could be counterproductive. Just because there are online systems, this does not mean that academics do not want to talk to you; if you are unsure, ask for advice. If you cannot see someone quickly enough, you can always put your case for an extension through the system and then hand in on time regardless.

How can I revise most effectively?

The very best way to revise is to avoid 'revision' in the traditional sense, as much as you possibly can. That is, minimise the amount of time you spend poring over flash cards, or reading through reams of notes, in the hope that you will remember enough for the exam. Instead, you can prepare for exams from the very beginning of each course, so that you are simply refreshing your memory before the exam: this leads to deeper learning, better understanding and far less anxiety. In effect, you are ambushing yourself, by continually revising, in one way or another and as part of your everyday routine, every now and then throughout the year.

CAREER
MOMENT

This guide is, I hope, encouraging you to take exactly this approach to your career planning and professional development. Rather than bombarding you with careers advice right at the end of your time at university, I hope that you have been able to take moments throughout this book to think about your career options and to prepare for success, little by little. It is a far more effective way of working than a huge panic in the weeks leading up to graduation.

There are many ways in which you can revise during the academic year as outlined in the checklist below, some of which have already been suggested in earlier chapters:

Checklist – ambushing yourself into revising

✓ Rework your lecture notes regularly by reducing them to a set of shorter notes.

✓ When you feel confident in an area, lecture/seminar notes can be reduced again to a bullet pointed list of key ideas/material.

✓ Use seminar time to ask questions that lead directly towards assessment, if there is an area that is likely to come up in exams and is worrying you.

✓ Use active learning sheets if you are in a learning event where brief but well-structured notes would work well.

✓ Connections sheets that you add to regularly can be a good way to draw material together for assessment.

✓ When you have a lull in study time, try out a few exam answer plans, to see how well you have grasped the material, but also to use later for revision.

✓ If you are a member of a study group, try to give yourself a few minutes at the end of each session to think forward to exams: have you helped yourself to succeed?

✓ Your study/reading group might become a revision group in the weeks leading up to the end of term.

✓ Your study advisors and/or personal tutor, along with your module convenors, are there to help you with exam technique: work on this early, before you get nervous. It will inform the way you revise.

✓ Going home for a day or two with the sole purpose of reviewing and reworking your module material, with exams in mind, can be time very well spent, as long as your friends and family are aware of the plan and let you work to it.

If you have been able to ambush yourself during the year, you will come to your final stint of revision feeling rather pleased with yourself, knowing that most of the work has been done already. This is just a time for you to refresh your memory and polish your understanding so that you achieve the best possible marks.

How do I keep going with my revision?

The secret to revision stamina is to make sure that you look after yourself. However intelligent and determined you are, if you are overtired, hungry or thirsty, feeling anxious or doubting your abilities, you will struggle to stay motivated and productive. Here are some ideas to keep you on track:

Checklist – revision stamina

✓   Keep to regular patterns of eating if you can, so that your energy does not spike and ebb.

✓   Hydration is essential, so make sure that you keep a drink nearby.

✓   Make sure that your revision is planned well enough to give yourself some time off.

✓   If you are not an organised person, pair up with a more organised student to help keep each other on track.

✓   Keep a notebook nearby so that you can jot down any queries or worries you have (or sudden bright ideas). That way you will not be lured back to your revision when you are trying to relax.

✓   If you feel more anxious than you had expected, ask your university support services (such as wellbeing, study advice and similar services) to help you cope.

✓   Vary your tasks during revision to keep boredom at bay.

✓   Reflect each day on how much you are achieving, setting aside time for brief tests if you know they will help.

✓   If you enjoy working with others, join a revision group early on (or set up a group if that would suit you better).

✓   If you are used to special exam arrangements, your university will be able to put these in place for you, but only if you contact the exams office or support services early enough. Worrying needlessly about practical arrangements will sap your stamina.

✓   If you feel that you are sinking at any point, and just cannot seem to stay ahead, or if you feel very anxious, panicked or overly fatigued, get the help you need straight away. Nobody will judge you for asking for help, except to think that you are taking sensible steps to look after yourself.

What about the practicalities of exams?

What you will not want to do in this final stage is panic, even subconsciously, about the practicalities of exams. It is a distraction that need not be there, and it will build as exam time approaches, which will hamper your efforts. You might encounter several 'final stages', with class tests to prepare for during the term, followed by some online tests (perhaps alongside an assessed piece of coursework or a lab practical for which you are preparing at the same time), with a final exam, maybe some weeks or months after the completion of the module. Regardless of how many different forms of assessment you encounter, the final stage of exam preparation can be similar. Indeed, a process you repeat to help you prepare will reinforce your sense of purpose and also become a comforting routine before each exam or set of exams.

CAREER
MOMENT

You will find it reassuring to repeat this preparation process when you are invited to an interview. Noting down where it is to be held (not always the office you might expect), knowing how long it will be and whether a presentation, team activity or lunch is included, thinking about the type of areas that might be covered in interview and making a note to work on these: all of this will feel familiar from your exam preparation and will help you feel more confident, because you have done it all before.

As soon as you can, and ideally before you really settle into your final revision push, check all the practical details that might be relevant, for each exam:

Checklist – the practicalities of exams

✓ When is the exam?

✓ Is it in the usual place you study, or somewhere else (and do you need to go there now to make sure you know exactly where you are going on the day)?

✓ How long is the exam, and how is that timing divided between different tasks on the paper (essay, short answer, multiple choice questions, lab analysis and so on)?

✓ If the module has run before, are there past papers you could print off for reference?

✓ If the module is running for the first time, is the convenor going to give you example papers?

✓ Have there been changes to the module this year, and will this affect the types of questions being asked on the exam paper?

✓ What percentage of the overall module mark is accounted for by the exam?

✓ On the exam paper, are marks divided equally between questions, or do you need to think strategically about how you divide your time in the exam?

✓ Is there going to be a viva (that is, a meeting to talk about your knowledge) following the exam?

✓ If you are asked to demonstrate under exam conditions, or you have an oral exam, how much of the mark relies on written evidence you produce alongside the live event?

If you are nervous about exams, write all of this information down and keep it somewhere, out of sight but easily accessible. That way, you can remind yourself of the practicalities whenever you become concerned about them. Not all of the information will be ready at the same time, so a written list will allow you to add details as you get them. This list could usefully be started whilst you are still studying on the module – the past papers might be on the VLE and could form a good basis for a study group discussion. Organising yourself early on like this can be the most effective way to reduce your nerves as well as prepare.

INSIDER HINT

Every year, some students will come to me to say that they have been given the most horrendous timetable. They have a huge gap between their first and second exam, and then three exams over three days. They are convinced that disaster has befallen them and certain that this will have a detrimental effect on their exam performance. It never does. It might make you feel more stressed if you have a challenging exam timetable, and you might find that you are more tired than you would have liked, but that will not stop you doing well. The only factor that might affect your performance is allowing yourself to become so upset about your exam timetable that you start to lose confidence and believe that you will not perform at your best. An exam timetable is irrelevant: your performance will reflect your level regardless of when you are tested.

You will be offered exam help and support from university advisors if you need it, and you might find a revision group helpful (but remember my words of caution in Chapter 12 where study groups were discussed). However, much of any student's final stage revision relies on you being able to identify revision methods that work for you, and your subject, and then just getting on with it, bearing in mind that, if you follow the advice in this guide, you will have done most of the work before you reach this stage.

Given that you have faced exams before, you might have your own preferred methods of revising, but you might like to take a few minutes to think about what might work better for you, especially if you have not revised in much detail for previous exams, or you have not found a method that helps you enough.

What revision methods should I use?

The revision method that works best for you will probably relate to your learning style, so here is some guidance based on those preferences:

Checklist – revision ideas for different learning preferences

For the aural preference student:

✓ Ask family and friends to test you on your notes to help you engage.

✓ Record yourself on your phone, outlining some salient point, and play it back, to reinforce your recall.

✓ Attend every revision seminar or lecture you can, so that you can hear the facts and ideas being explained to you again.

✓ Listen to podcasts that explore your subject area. If you are struggling in an area and can spare the time, see if your university offers lecture capture with a recording of some of your lectures.

For the kinaesthetic preference student:

✓ Walk around as you repeat back information: the movement will underpin your recall.

✓ Try using the 'memory palace' revision tool (also called the method of loci): visualise each fact as sitting in your study room or bedroom, then walk around the room as you try to imagine each fact sitting there, so that in the exam you can 'walk' in your imagination.

✓ In a study group, you could all demonstrate what you mean as you explain to each other the theories or processes that you are trying to master: sometimes this might be a 'physical diagram' that you make together by standing in a particular pattern.

✓ If you rely on timelines, flowcharts or other diagrams, make them enormous, so that you physically have to move around to see all the detail.

For the visual preference student:

✓ Flash cards could be your best friend in revision, and you probably use them already.

✓ Using a mind map could appeal to you, and learning how to produce a mind map early on will help you with much of your studying.

✓ Videoclips online will help to deepen your understanding.

✓ If you feel that your grasp on a topic is slipping, rather than going straight back to your notes, see if there are presentation slides, ideally with images, lodged on your module VLE.

For the verbal preference student:

✓ If spoken words are your favourite way to learn, you will benefit from revision groups, as long as you enjoy revising alongside others.

✓ Your notes will already be your most important learning tool, and reworking them down to brief notes, perhaps on revision cards that you can hold in your hand, will offer you the best way to feel confident about your learning and recall.

✓ Reading through lecture handouts, perhaps highlighting important sections in them and returning to them later in your final revision push, would help you with instant exam recall.

These suggestions will only take you so far. Learning, and revision in particular, is to some extent about a habit in your way of working. If you have been using flash cards since you were five, and have never tried using anything else, you might want to experiment with a different method because it relates more to your learning preferences, but flash cards might always be the mainstay of your revision, because that is how you have been trained to recall information.

You will also need to be guided by whether you are a solitary or a social learner. If you are a verbal and a social learner, for example, you might enjoy revision groups where you all talk through what you know. If you are a verbal and a solitary learner, you might prefer to write down your thoughts in order to process them and recall the material. Again, by ambushing yourself throughout the year you will be able to work out exactly what suits you best.

Top tip

Variety will help keep your mind bright and engaged throughout your revision, so you will benefit from varying your revision tasks, using several different methods. Even if one particular technique is your favourite way to learn and recall, some movement from one technique to another, however brief, will help keep you going.

Should I do mock/practice exams?

Yes, for two reasons: they help you to remember and they help you to deepen your understanding. During your final push on revision, you are bound to be concerned, aware that your exam performance relies on you retaining the facts you need to give your answers. However, earlier revision and consolidation, as I am advocating in this guide, will give you the chance to work towards a long-term positive effect.

By writing practice essays or short answers, or producing brief plans for exam answers, or working through a series of practice multiple choice questions or demonstration rehearsals, you are repurposing the information you have, forcing yourself to use that information as a tool to allow you to create an argument or demonstrate the breadth of your understanding. This recall, linked to your understanding, becomes part of your deep subject knowledge, which is then extended and reinforced each time you use it for the next mock exam or practice test.

This process has another result, beyond aiding your understanding in the moment: it helps you to think forward, to prepare yourself (even though this is not your principal aim) for the next module and the next intellectual challenges. So by revising actively with practice tests, rehearsals for an oral exam or a lab practical, mock exam answers or plans for those answers, you are accomplishing two things at the same time: revising effectively and preparing for your next steps. Revision time stops being a case of looking back and 'wasting' learning time and becomes a way to learn more, faster, with your gaze on the next stage.

CAREER
MOMENT

Being able to flex and repurpose your specialist knowledge is always going to be a valuable professional skill, so finessing it now will mean that you are preparing not just for exams, but also for your future career success. This skill and how you have applied it, in exams and other contexts, can make for an engaging interview conversation. If you find tools that help you achieve this reworking of material, you will not want to discard them; they will be helpful to you after you graduate.

How can I calm my nerves?

Nerves are always good news when it comes to exams. They might not feel very comfortable, but imagine an exam for which you do not feel nervous. You stroll in, perhaps a few minutes late because you saw no need to check all the practical details in advance. You look at the paper but you are a bit tired from a late night, so you waste a few more minutes trying to concentrate. You start to produce an answer (you fail to write a plan before you plunge straight into the answer because you have not developed your exam technique) and then you work, really, really hard. Undertaking an exam without nervousness (as any student who has taken an exam under nerve calming medication would tell you) is very hard work.

INSIDER
HINT

It is tempting to calm your nerves by talking to fellow students, hoping for reassurance. This can work very well, and you will seek these people out, but remember also to avoid long conversations about exams and revision with anyone who makes you anxious.

The point of nervousness is that it prompts adrenaline to flow, which means that you are alert, ready to excel. Your mind is firing well and you make connections you would never have made outside the exam room. You write or type faster than you would ever have expected and you feel the weight of the exam, but in a good way. This is important, it matters to you (as is proved by your nerves) and you are determined to use everything you have to succeed.

Top tip

One irritating effect of being nervous is that it makes your mouth dry. This was fine for prehistoric man: it meant that your 'fight or flight' mechanism has kicked in and you were ready to run from the woolly mammoth. It is far less useful in a modern exam room: always have a bottle of water with you in an exam.

Being nervous about an exam is only a good state if you are able to use your nerves, rather than letting them overwhelm you. Learning some basic relaxation techniques is also helpful in other aspects of life, so you will be using your time wisely if you master these now. Most relaxation techniques rely on calming breaths, consciously relaxing your muscles, relieving areas of tension and focusing on your inner calm. Luckily, there are relaxation routines that take no more than a few minutes, so they are perfect in those minutes before you are allowed into the exam room and, if you find your nervousness rising worryingly when you are in the exam, you can return to your routine knowing that it is not going to take too long to get back to a better level of nerves.

INSIDER
HINT

I have noticed that, whatever relaxation techniques my students employ, they seem to gain some benefit from forming these techniques into a routine. Each time they need help with nerves, they return to exactly the same routine, and this in itself is calming, because it reassures them that they will get through this successfully, as they have done all the other challenges that they have faced. You can see this in sportspeople too, with a routine for serving in tennis, for example, or precisely the same warm-up routine for a player before every football match.

What should I do when I get into the exam room?

As with the relaxation routine, it helps if you can follow the same method each time. You will find what works for you, but here is a suggested routine that I find works well for many students:

Checklist – the first few minutes in an exam

✓ In the time when you are sitting down waiting to be told to start the exam, remind yourself of your mock exams and how they felt. This should feel different, but not so different that you cannot take comfort from the fact that you have practised for this moment.

✓ If you have established a relaxation routine, use it now if you feel your nerves are about to get the better of you: you need to be able to think sharply and write quickly, but not be so nervous that you cannot think straight.

✓ You do not want to spend the whole exam writing: usually you will be planning for ten minutes of each hour and checking for five minutes, leaving you forty-five minutes per hour of writing. Remind yourself of this before you begin to write, and do not be put off if other students are writing all around you; they have forgotten their exam technique and are writing too soon.

✓ For an essay or short answer exam, read all of the questions twice. For a multiple choice exam, skim through the questions, without trying to answer any of them, so as to give yourself a sense of the pattern and scope of questions.

✓ For any type of exam, jot down all of the stray material that you have been worried about forgetting in the exam as soon as you can. If you make a note of names, dates, authors, processes, formulae and similar at this stage, you will be more relaxed and ready to focus on answering the questions.

✓ For an essay or short answer exam, read the questions again and confirm your choice as to which you will answer.

✓ Remind yourself of your thinking before an essay or short answer exam: are you better off planning all of your answers first, and then writing all the answers, or do you prefer to plan and write each answer before moving on to the next?

✓ You will also have decided in advance whether you would be better to write an essay on your strongest area first, or whether to start with an answer in your least developed area whilst your mind is fresh. Either approach will work, so you can follow your personal preference on this.

✓ For a multiple choice exam, you will be able to answer some questions easily, so you can do these first (you do not need to answer in the order in which they are set) and then move on to the slightly more challenging questions, finishing with those for which you are really going to have to think hard.

✓ For an essay or short answer exam, aim to make two plans per answer: a brief plan (maybe just a handful of points that link together) and then a fuller plan (using your preferred planning method) to show in more detail how your argument will develop. This fuller plan will also include material such as quotes, facts, theories and examples you want to include.

✓ Check back to the material you jotted down at the beginning: is there anything there that you would want to add to your plan before you start to write?

This checklist can be remembered more easily as:

T = think back to your mock exams

R = use your relaxation techniques

T = recall how you plan to use your time wisely

Q = read all the questions first

S = jot down your stray material

O = in which order will you answer the questions?

P = plan

W = write

Which, as mnemonic, can be recalled as:

This **r**eally **t**imely **q**uestion **s**eems **o**bvious so **I** **w**ill **p**lay and **w**in.

The checklist of actions above might seem to be a longer or more complicated routine than you had expected, but it is easy once you have become used to this way of approaching an exam.

INSIDER HINT

I realise that you might feel anxious about being advised to spend so much of your time in the exam planning your answers, particularly as your lecturers will probably have told you that they only mark your essay answer, not the plans that you might produce. I have yet to meet an academic who can resist looking at a plan. If you run out of time, or you forget to include some brilliant material that you had hoped to showcase, your detailed and impressive plan will become your insurance policy. It shows the marker exactly where you had intended to go, even if pressure of time meant that you could not finish the paper, or the weight of the exam blew your answer off course from time to time.

Once you start to write, you can feel under a bit less pressure. You have made a good plan (or set of plans) and you can feel confident that you are heading in the right direction. For a multiple choice exam you can also remain confident as you go, because each question you think you have answered correctly will boost your confidence.

Top tip

> There is a strange tendency to speed up in multiple choice exams, as if you are so caught up in the excitement of knowing the answers, and so keen for it all to be over, that you naturally accelerate. Force yourself to slow down. An effective way to do this is to use practice multiple choice tests and time yourself so that you stop every four minutes and take a breath, look out of the window, or take a small sip of water. Those few seconds will halt the acceleration and help keep your performance steady and accurate.

Although you will hope to feel a reduction in nerves and a rise in confidence as you work through an exam paper, you can still suffer from an unexpected and inexplicable moment of confusion. What you have just written seems to be non-sensical, or you are convinced that the last six multiple choice answers you chose were all wrong. If this happens to you, it is not very likely to be real: it is just the effect of your nerves resurfacing for a moment.

This is inconvenient, but no more than that. Stop writing and take a moment or two to relax as best you can and clear your mind of your anxiety. When you look back you will see that there was no real problem. However, if you judge that those few minutes of anxiety impaired your writing style, or made your argument less clear, leave a line or two and move firmly on to your next point. In the time you have allowed for checking you will be able to come back and will find it easy to rewrite that small section if you need to.

The same technique applies if you are worried that you are going over time. Pause for a few minutes and consider: do you think you can keep writing now and then write less in other sections of the exam? Would this be detrimental, or could it work? If, having thought about it, you have simply spent too long on one section of the paper (whether it is a section of multiple choice answers, or an essay, or the short answer part of a mixed exam), move firmly on to the next paragraph, or section of answers, or next short answer question. In an essay or short answer exam, it is a good idea to leave a couple of lines clear when you do this, in case you have time to return later.

INSIDER HINT

Never worry about how messy your exam paper is by the end – you might have a plan, then a fuller plan, both with ticks all over them as you used the material. You might have put a scrawled line through them both as you finished your answer. Your answer will be neat for the most part, except when your pen ran out (if it is a handwritten exam). You might have left some gaps in which you did not judge it necessary to add anything at the end. Other gaps will have stars or numbers in them, directing the marker towards added paragraphs or sentences at the end that you would like to have inserted into your answer. None of this matters: academics are used to it all and will quite happily mark whatever they are given.

What should I do in the last few minutes of an exam?

This might depend on how you have structured your time. If you have planned, written and checked each answer as you go, you will only have a few minutes at the end of the exam in which to check your final answers. In a multiple choice test you are most likely to leave all of your checking to the end of the paper. Most of my students seem to feel better about writing their way through a whole exam paper and then making one final run-through check at the end. I can see why this would be the case: you want to unburden your mind of all of the material that you have been storing ready for this exam. Once it is safely on paper, you can take the time to check in a more thoughtful and thorough way.

Whichever way you approach checking (and neither way seems to affect the overall results that students gain) you will run the same risk: running out of time. It seems logical to spend every moment in the exam room frantically writing down as much as you possibly can, but this is never the best way to perform. If you give yourself planning time at the start, and then some thinking time during the exam, and then time to check at the end, rather than displaying just how much you know, you are proving what you can do with what you know. Your work will be judged not just on the knowledge you have demonstrated, but on how you have applied this knowledge.

Once you have accepted the need for planning and checking in an exam, you can still find that you have unintentionally run over time and have only a few minutes left to check all of your answers. In a multiple choice exam, your best course of action if this happens is to check the questions in the order in which you answered them. For the first, easy questions that you got out of the way, you run the greatest risk of having dashed through so quickly that you misread a question or mistakenly made the wrong selection. For the slightly harder questions, you are less at risk of making a minor mistake, but more open to having misunderstood exactly what was being asked of you, especially if two possible answers were very similar. For the hardest questions, about which you had to think the longest, you are less likely to have made a mistake and so if you run out of time before you have checked all your answers, you have left yourself in the safest position.

For short answer and essay exams, you might not have time to look through your entire exam script in as much detail as you would have liked, as slowly as you would have planned, but there are key mistakes that tend to crop up in exams that you should look out for:

Checklist – last minute exam checking

✓   Does the first paragraph of each essay set out clearly enough what you are hoping to achieve in the essay, especially if you strayed slightly from your plan when you were writing?

- ✓ Are all the factual details correct (dates, names, titles of texts, technical terms and so on)?

- ✓ If you left blanks because your writing seemed to be slipping and you lost your way in the argument you were trying to make, could you add in a small correction now that would help clear it up?

- ✓ If you left gaps because you were hoping to come back later and add something else, might just a few key words added now show where you were hoping to take your argument, given more time?

- ✓ Slow down about three quarters of the way through each answer: this is where you are most likely to have made mistakes that are so obvious they would make you cringe. Luckily, they will not make the marker cringe: academics understand that under exam pressure you do not always mean exactly what you wrote.

What should I do when I leave the exam room?

Do whatever you planned to do when you prepared for the exam. You need to have made a plan for this moment, because what you cannot risk doing is drifting to the nearest café or bar and spending three hours engaged in a detailed discussion of what you all wrote for every answer. However well you did, you will fixate on the one fact that you now believe you got wrong, or you will convince yourself that, because you answered an unpopular question, you must have answered the wrong question. Try not to do this to yourself. A brief chat with a friend or your revision group is all you need, and it gives you the chance to ask about the one point that has been niggling at you, then move on to the rest of your well-planned day.

The reason you need a well-planned day is that you knew before the exam whether you had to do any more revision today to get ready for the next exam, or whether you had planned to go home for a couple of days, or go out with a friend who is not on your course and so will not be able to analyse the exam. Having finished the exam your emotions will be running high and you could make the wrong choice about what to do next. Following your plan will be the best option, especially if it includes a treat to reward yourself for your hard work!

PART FOUR

MAKING IT COUNT

We are nearing the end of our journey together. If you are skimming through this book as you first come to look at it, there may be a temptation to decide to leave even glancing at this final part until the very last few weeks of your time at university, especially if you are not yet sure of your likely career trajectory. I can see why you might do this. The career moments throughout the guide will help you think about your career as you work through your degree, and so they, and the rest of the advice in the book, will lead you naturally to this point.

However, I would urge you to take a look through this section early on, just for reassurance. You will see that there is no need to feel guilty or anxious if you do not have your perfect career in place in the last stages of your degree. It will also convince you that there is much you can do to make a real difference to your career prospects even in the days and weeks before you graduate. Reassurance received, you can then happily return to the earlier parts until you come back to this part with far more experience, an abundance of skills and a firm sense of who you are.

It may not be perfectly clear to you whether you have chosen a career path or not. Maybe you are seriously considering several different options, or think you have decided on one path but are open to other opportunities as they arise. The chapters in this part of the book are deliberately short and designed to direct you to action for just this type of situation. It allows you to read through Chapters 23 and 24 relatively quickly and take from them what you need if you are in this 'in-between' situation that is common to many graduates. You might also like to go back to Chapter 15, which covers the shaping of your professional development. There may be a little more work you would like to do from that chapter before you move forward.

Top tip

Whether or not you have a clear career path in your mind, you must ensure, before you graduate and enter the job market, that your online presence is scrupulously clean. You might want to change the name you use on your Facebook page or similar sites for a while, just so that potential employers do not see a profile that is not showing the professional persona you are working to create. You need to search for yourself online regularly to make sure that nothing strange is popping up, and you need to make sure that any professional profile site such as LinkedIn is the absolute best you can make it.

This is not about lying to a potential employer or client. If you can be found online, you are offering that version of yourself to anyone who wants to browse. We all have different aspects of our lives and you, naturally, want to show the professional side of your life as well as possible at this stage in your career.

23

If you have not chosen a career by your final term

There is no reason to suppose that you will have made a firm career decision and full professional plan by the time you are heading towards graduation. This can suddenly feel quite worrying, but it need not concern you overly; it is part of a process and you are already on the path to career success.

Have I done something wrong?

Not at all. In fact, you may have done something that is just right for you. If you have followed the guidance in this book, analysing your graduate attributes and building on them, preparing for the professional world in all the ways that have been suggested, and creating a valuable career network, maybe, for you, that is enough for now.

It is not unusual to find students who work so hard in their final year at university that they simply do not have the head space to consider their career in as much detail as they might have hoped. For other students, their university experience and professional preparation has shown them that they do not want to enter the career they had dreamed of since childhood; that takes some adjustment and rethinking that cannot be undertaken lightly.

If you are facing the prospect of a few months, even a year or so, trying out different career areas, or simply earning some cash whilst you think, or if you plan to travel for a time, this is not a problem. It is perhaps something to be celebrated: you are using your time to best effect whilst you decide on the shape of the rest of your life.

Just because this is not time spent travelling firmly on a decisive career path does not mean that you should see yourself as worth less money than anyone else. Try to avoid falling into the trap of selling yourself short in the marketplace. The work you have carried out as a result of this guide puts you in a great position to market yourself so that you land a well-paid role, even if it is not in a career area that you will stay in for long. Being undecided on your career does not make you a failure: it just means that an employer will be lucky enough to benefit from your skills and attributes whilst you think about your options and develop appropriate professional networks.

Will I be behind in my career?

No, but you can make this a problem for yourself if you are not confident about what you are doing, at least in terms of your CV. During the time you are thinking through what to do, and working in a field that is not your perfect, targeted career, keep a note of the tasks you are undertaking and the skills and experience you are acquiring. Several jobs over the first couple of years after graduation can look like a plan if you are happy to collate them on your CV under headings.

This is sometimes called a functional CV, and it allows you to identify the skills and attributes an employer is looking for and then packaging your CV according to the functions you have fulfilled. In this way, tasks within several jobs, each of which gave you the chance to work with the public, are collated under one heading 'Public facing experience'. You can then list your tasks and achievements under that heading, thus showing the employer that you are the right person for the job. This type of CV is far easier for an employer to follow if your relevant skills are drawn from several jobs; they are just as relevant as anyone else's skills, but you might need to make this explicit in your CV.

How do I move forward?

Funnily enough, the best way to look forward at this point is to look back first. Make sure that you are confident in the work you have done on career preparation during your degree. With the little by little approach advocated in this guide you will have done far more work than you realised in understanding how your studying life will relate to your professional life. If you take time now to reflect on this, and to make a record of where you are in terms of your professional journey, you can feel that you are on solid ground as you contemplate your next steps. Your Careers Service is in the best position to help you with this reflection, so make use of the service now, even if you have not engaged before.

There are positive steps that you can take to move forward without committing yourself to one career and, as you have yet to decide on a career path, taking action that does not commit you firmly makes sense.

Checklist – action to move forward in your career journey

✓ Arrange to shadow professionals in a range of different roles. It does not matter if you end up ruling career options out in this way: this is useful in helping you make good choices.

✓ If your university town or city is a good location for employment, find out if the university itself is recruiting. That would offer you the chance to stay put whilst you explore.

✓ If a group of your friends are in the same position, you could consider taking a house together for at least a short-term let, so that you can support each other as you decide on career paths. This can sometimes be less disruptive than returning home and potentially losing contact with your university support network.

✓ Consider training, but not if it is very expensive and you are not yet sure of how helpful it will be. Local colleges usually offer good courses at reasonable prices.

✓ Think of skills rather than job titles: take on work (voluntary or paid) that gives you the chance to improve a skill you would like to use more in a future career.

✓ Internships (that is, work experience for a limited time) will give you the chance to network, learn more about a career area and develop relevant skills and experience. You might want to organise a series of relatively short internships so that you gain a good sense of what you like and what you would prefer not to do.

✓ Produce a brilliant online presence. This might mean creating a website that showcases you in some way, or a blog that has relevance to your professional aspirations, even if you have not decided on an exact career role. Remember the warning in the 'top tip' above and be vigilant about keeping your online presence positive and professional.

(Continued)

(Continued)

- ✓ Consider a postgraduate course, either because you feel you have not yet finished with the pleasures of studying or because you know (for certain) that there is a postgraduate course that would help you in several career areas that you are contemplating as you make up your mind.

- ✓ Stay in touch with your university Careers Service. You will be offered help, both online and in person, for some time after you graduate, so you are not too late to make the most of this free service.

The only way you can fail to move forward is to stand still and wait for your career to happen to you. From now on, every professional experience you have is going to make a direct impact on your career planning and the way you see yourself. Taking any step forward, whether it is travelling, or short-term contracts, or internships and shadowing, or further training, will be maximised if you are able to add it in a systematic way to you career plan and record.

24

If you have chosen a career by your final term

The title of this guide mentions 'your perfect career' because what will one day be the perfect career for you, will not be ideal for someone else. Even if you have found the perfect career for you, it will evolve and shift as you move forward on your career path. That is a good thing, but you need to factor this into your career planning: keep an open mind about how your career might look at the start, and how it might flex.

How can I make the best move now?

Knowing where you want to be can be immensely reassuring. You can stop feeling unsettled and concentrate on one career area. This might have been the case for you throughout your time at university, or you might have made a recent decision. Your Careers Service will do its best work for you now, helping you to secure a hold in that career sector.

Where do I go first?

Although your Careers Service might be your first port of call, there is more that you can do. If you come to a decision in the last few months of your degree, you will need to go back through all of the networks you have made and see if there are any contacts there who might help you now. The study and revision groups in which you will have had regular, if brief, career discussions; the assessment groups where you know there is a contact for an area that appeals; the placement contacts that you had filed away. Work through all of this potential career material: you only need one contact to come through and help you, either with information or an introduction to a professional network, and it will have been worth the time.

Do I need a long-term plan?

Careers advice is expensive once you are in the professional world, and careers counselling organisations might not have the reach and experience of your university Careers Service, so there is a strong argument for making a long-term plan with help from a university careers advisor now. This will give you more than just one long-term goal: it will offer you a vision of where you might be in a few years' time. That vision, if you hold fast to it, will inform your thinking during that time, and will allow you to take advantage of every relevant opportunity that arises.

Top tip

A vision, and a plan of how to achieve it, can help you not just in planning: it can also save you money. If you know that you need to acquire a particular set of skills for the position you would like to hold in three years, you will be looking for opportunities to gain these skills through training courses provided by your employer, or by becoming involved in projects that develop those skills. This will save you from panic spending later, when you convince yourself that you must enrol on an expensive training course because you do not have the experience that would prove your abilities. This is no different from the way I have been advising you to approach professional development during your university course; the habits that you have developed at university will help you succeed in the years after you graduate.

25

Things to do before you graduate

Some students feel inundated with things to do before they finally leave university. This is partly a reaction to the natural anxiety about life moving on so irrevocably (however much you are looking forward to it) and partly because you want to make sure that you have left no chances behind. Rather than a lengthy list of things to do to add to the others that you (and university staff) have made for yourself, I want to focus here just on those few career-related tasks that I know my students regret most, if they fail to do them before they leave.

Checklist – things to do for your career before you leave university

✓ Is your university email forwarded to a private email, so that you can receive updates from the Careers Service, or continue conversations with potential internship providers or employers?

✓ Is the personal address to which emails are forwarded an address that looks professional and formal?

✓ For how long will this forwarding service be offered? Do you need to let any key professional contacts (perhaps from a placement) know of your personal email address?

✓ Do you need to make a 'professional network' email group? Or social media group? This would involve you asking to keep in touch with fellow students and/or members of staff for help and support in your career path (always with the understanding, of course, that you will also be helping your fellow students in the network)?

(Continued)

(Continued)

✓ Which academic will give you a reference? You will need two of these (in case one is on leave at the crucial moment) and, even though you will contact them at the point when a reference is needed, you will guarantee a speedy response if you have asked them in advance whether, in principle, they would be happy to do this. Your academic reference does not always have to be your personal/academic tutor.

✓ Can you arrange a final meeting with your personal/pastoral/academic tutor to talk through your career plans? This meeting often seems to elicit useful information, advice and, sometimes, professional contacts who will then be expecting your call.

✓ Does your degree transcript (the sheet that lists the modules you took) reflect all that you have done? If you have been involved in university life by being a student volunteer, or being part of a club or society, or taking part in a professional development scheme, can you get a certificate (or letter, or email) that confirms this crucial experience?

✓ Do you have copies of the work of which you are most proud? Given that memory sticks go missing, and online university systems will be closed to you, track down and download (to several places) or print off any work that you feel would showcase your talents to an employer or client.

26

Graduation day

We have made it together to your graduation. I hope that the patterns of working and the professional habits that we have begun together here will help you throughout your professional life.

There is one last question to ask yourself, as you prepare for graduation: how does it feel? Are you raring to go and utterly sure of your career path? Are you keen to get out into the world and know you have the tools to find your perfect career? Or are you, perhaps, feeling that this is all too quick, that you have more to do and that you are simply not ready to leave studying behind?

Source: Faustin Tuyambaze/StockSnap.io

If this sense of reluctance happens to you it can be a shock, but it is a feeling that you need not ignore. Of course, entering the professional world does not mean that study is behind you forever. You will encounter many training opportunities, especially in your early career years, and many of my students have deliberately chosen career paths that offer them this chance. Beyond this, spend at least a short while considering whether you want to leave university at all. Most postgraduates with whom I have worked only decided to go on to postgraduate study in the last few months (sometimes the last couple of weeks) of their degree. If this happens to you, know that it is commonplace enough not to confuse your tutor, or any academic with whom you have worked. We like nothing more than to hear of students who realise that they want to remain in academia.

I feel now that I have a good sense of how your university journey might have developed, and I hope that this guide will have been a productive part of that journey. I naturally wonder what will happen to you now, and where you might be in a few years' time. What I will not need to wonder, because you have worked through this entire guide with me, is whether you have the energy and determination to succeed: you clearly do.

As you approach graduation let me be one of the first to say it: Congratulations!

Glossary of terms used in higher education

Academic engagement   this usually means how regularly you attend learning events such as lectures, lab sessions and seminars.

Academic integrity/honesty   this refers to honesty in your work – not using the work of others and claiming that it is your own (plagiarism). This includes referencing your sources. It is sometimes called 'poor academic practice' if you made a mistake rather than deliberately plagiarising. Academic integrity can also include cheating in examinations.

Academic supervision   most usually, a student working with an academic on an independent project or research activity.

Academic tutor   a member of staff whose role is to support you in your studies throughout your degree.

Alumni   people who have graduated from a university.

Assessment literacy   understanding and being able to talk confidently about the feedback you have received and what it means in terms of moving forward in your studies.

Assignment   any work that you carry out for which you will receive a mark, and/or that is a requirement of your course.

Campus   your university site and the buildings on it.

Careers Service   the experts on careers at your university. They may offer you more than careers counselling: the careers centre/service may also advertise jobs, both on and off campus, and run events with employers.

Classification   the final mark you are awarded when you graduate (such as First Class or 2:1, 2:2, 3rd).

Continuing professional development (CPD)   events or courses (usually relatively short) that are undertaken to develop your professional skills. Your university may offer some of these free to its students.

Continuous assessment a system within which you are marked throughout a module or course, either based on your attendance, or participation, or a series of tests, rather than your grade relying on a final piece of work and/or examination.

Credits degrees that are made up of modules (modular degrees) allocate a number of credits to each module, and these will total up to the same number of credits for every undergraduate in the university (usually 120 a year/part at undergraduate level).

Degree the qualification awarded at the end of a course of study for most undergraduates. The most common degrees are BSc (Bachelor of Science) and BA (Bachelor of Arts).

Dissertation the final, written output from an extended piece of research, often completed in the final year of an undergraduate programme (course) or as the principal assignment in a postgraduate programme.

ELearning (also called online learning) any work carried out online and, usually, away from the classroom. A form of independent study, which might be supported by additional activity in the classroom (called 'blended learning').

Enhancement week see 'Reading week'.

Enrolment registering for your university course (sometimes called 'registration') and also for modules that you intend to take.

External examiner an academic who visits from another university to scrutinise the marking practices and outcomes at your university.

Faculty departments in universities might be grouped into faculties and/or schools, depending upon the overall structure of your university.

Flipped learning a way to teach in which an academic gives material to students in advance of a learning event such as a lecture (often in the form of an online filmed lecture or briefing) and then asks students to bring their questions to the learning event, based on the material they have seen.

Formative an assignment where the grade or mark does not count towards the final mark for a module.

Freshers first year students are sometimes called 'freshers', although this term is less common than it used to be.

Graduate attributes these are personal qualities, skills and knowledge that a student has developed by graduation; they are the attributes that the graduate can then market to potential employers.

Halls of residence these are communal houses, blocks of flats or small housing compounds, which are inhabited exclusively by students and academics from a university.

Hardship fund many universities provide funding to help students in an emergency, often through the Students' Union or the welfare office. These funds might be used if a student gets into unforeseeable financial difficulty, or needs help with a study trip or similar. Universities differ in how they manage these funds and what they call them, so it is worth investigating to see if there is funding of this sort at your university.

Internship   a period away from university in the professional world, either as an academic research project or for work experience and the development of graduate attributes. An internship may lead to you writing a report or dissertation that is counted towards your degree result. An internship is sometimes called a 'placement', a 'professional placement' or an 'academic placement'.

Joint honours degree   a degree course/programme on which you study two or more major subjects.

Lecture   a learning event at which students gather to listen to a talk from an academic. Lecture audiences can range in size from just a few students to several hundred.

Mature student   in some countries the definition of 'mature' is as low as twenty-one years, so you may not notice much difference between the mature students in your classroom and everyone else.

Mentoring   students have academic mentors in their personal/academic tutors, but they also mentor each other. First-year students might be welcomed to university by more experienced students, and students in the year above you might help you with some of your learning (this is sometimes called 'peer assisted learning').

Modular courses   modules are the building blocks of a modular degree. Each module will count for a set amount of credits towards your degree. For example, a first-year student might study six modules, each counting for twenty credits, making up the 120 credits needed to complete the year. Modules usually run over one or two terms, but this is not always the case.

Online submission/marking   this would involve you submitting your assignment through a website (your university's VLE most usually) rather than as a hard copy document. Online submission and marking is overwhelmingly popular with students, but you do need to take time to make sure you know how to find your feedback online.

Pathways   some degrees encourage students to take a selection of particular modules that add up to a 'pathway' through a degree. This allows students to develop an interest in a specialist area whilst still taking a more general degree.

Peer assisted learning   see 'Mentoring'.

Personal tutor   see 'Academic tutor'.

Placement   see 'Internship'.

Plagiarism   see 'Academic integrity'.

Portfolio   you might be required to produce assignments throughout a module, and then submit them for marking in one portfolio of work at the end of a module.

Pre-sessional   courses that are offered to students to help prepare them for a particular university course, or more generally for studying in a country other than their home country.

Reading list   a list of texts offered to students for study. These are usually associated with a particular activity or area of study, such as a course or module reading list, or an assignment reading list.

Reading week   some universities do not timetable any teaching for a week (sometimes more) of the term/semester (often around the middle of the term/semester). This gives students the chance to catch up on their studies and prepare for the next part of the term; they might also be offered additional enhancement activities during the week, linked to their study or career planning.

Research questions   if you are planning a lengthy or research-based assignment, you might not be answering a set question. Instead, you would carry out research and decide what interests you in the area; you would then form research questions that you would set out to answer in your assignment.

Semester   a period of time in the year when university teaching takes place (there are usually two semesters in an academic year). Alternatively, there would usually be three terms per academic year.

Seminar   an academic discussion group, regularly held with, often, the same academic and group of students each time it meets.

Single honours degree   a degree in which a student's focus is principally on one subject.

Sources, primary   first-hand material such as a play text, a novel, the verbatim record of an event.

Sources, secondary   mediated material such as a commentary on a play text, criticism of a novel, analysis of the verbatim record of an event.

Student card   a student identity card that allows you access to services on your campus (borrowing books, gym access, purchasing food, recording attendance and so on). Sometimes called a union card, library card, campus card or services card.

Study week   see 'Reading week'.

Summative   an assignment which has a mark or grade that counts towards the final mark of a module (that is, it gives you credit for the module).

Team-based learning   students coming together to solve a problem (problem-based learning). Team-based learning might take place over just a few minutes, or over many weeks with a lengthy project.

Term   see 'Semester'.

Transcript   a record of your university achievements, completed for you when you graduate.

Transferable skills   skills that you develop in one activity that can be transferred to another area of activity, either in your study or professional life.

Tutorial   this might be similar to a seminar, perhaps with just two or three students and an academic or study advisor, or it might be a one-to-one meeting set up to consider an assignment or other study challenge.

Virtual learning environment (VLE)   a website used by your university to support your studies, often with different areas for each module you are studying, as well as an area for more general help and support.

Word limit   assignments are usually set with word limits. Make sure that you know exactly what is to be included in your word limit for each assignment, and what penalties might be imposed if your assignment is submitted above or below the word count.

Workshop   a practical session in which students (and often academics) work together on a problem or a project so as to learn and/or develop skills.

Index

academic tutor *see* personal tutor
active learning sheets 42, 118, 181, 228
appeals against a result 188
assessment outcomes 179
assignment
  checking 183–4
  feedback 190
  feed forward 194, 198
  rubrics 179, 187–8
  submission 184–5
  titles 178–9

bibliographical software 105–6

campus card 61–2
career moments, making your own 161–2
careers service 72, 84–6, 247,
    248, 249, 250
citations 114
clubs and societies 12, 21–3
connections sheet 228
consultation hours 195
counsellor 10
CV, functional 246

doubts, moving forward 154–5

earning money 24
email forwarding 12, 251
exam
  checking 240–1
  mock 234
  nerves 225, 234–6
  opening routine 236–8
  practicalities 230–1
  timetable 231
  types 226
external examiner 192

family 14, 18, 57–8, 73, 76, 83, 192
flipped learning 139–40
formative assessment 123, 175, 187
free options and training 19, 69
friends 52, 73, 83

graduate attributes 2, 24, 71, 72–82
group
  dynamics 208–10
  skills inventory 209–10
  timeline 211–2
group work
  formative 207–8
  long-term advantages 213–4

hall warden 10
housing 64

learning preference
  aural 88–90, 232
  kinaesthetic 90–92, 232
  visual 91–2, 233
  verbal 92–3, 234
lecture recordings 43, 45
librarian 10, 59–60

mentoring 23
modules
  changing your mind 19
  choosing 17–8, 65–7

networking 83–4
notes
  for assignments 112
  from groups 110, 115–6
  from lectures 38, 39, 40,
    109–10, 113
  from seminars 110, 114

from sources 111, 115
revision 112–3
reworking 116–7, 118

office hours *see* consultation hours

personal tutor 9, 18
changing 31
checklist for meetings 31–2
placements
activity log 221–2
assessment 219–22
contingency plans 216
cost 217–8
preparing 218–9
plagiarism 114, 182
postgraduate courses 247–8, 263
presentation 49, 63, 69, 121–39
nerves 136–7
rehearsals 135–6
assessed 123–4, 125, 126
audio equipment 130–1
demonstrations 132
for seminars 122–3, 126
group 127–30
handouts 131–2
informal 124–5, 126
internet 130
interview 126
physical examples 132
videoconferencing 131, 133
problems, deceptive 151–3
procrastination
unproductive 158–9
useful 157–8

reading lists 9, 54, 59
core 97, 102
hidden 98–9
online 95–7
supplementary 97–8
reading notebook 99–102
registration 12

research plans 203–5
revision
ambush 228
stamina 229

seminar group, changing 50
social media profile 64–5, 244, 247
sources
primary 103–4
secondary 103–4
staff/student partnerships 23
student card *see* campus card
student newspaper 60
student reps 22
students' union 10, 21, 58
study
advice 10, 69
spaces 106–7
time 63–4
groups 21, 23
lecturer appointed 139–40
peer learning 141
revision 143–4
student led 141–3
virtual 144–5
summative assessment 175, 187

threshold concept 40, 51, 196
time, best use of 23, 164–6
timetable, personal 159–64
transcript of your degree 252
transferable skills 53, 72–82
Turnitin 189, 190
tutorials 29

virtual learning environment 36, 37, 54, 189–90
viva 226, 231
VLE *see* virtual learning environment
volunteering 23

wellbeing guide *see* counsellor
word count 182–3
work experience 30, 76